# The Book of Texas Days

# THE BOOK OF TEXAS DAYS

## BY RON STONE

EAKIN PRESS
Austin, Texas

1997 EDITION

Copyright © 1984 by Ron Stone
First published in 1985

Published in the United States of America
By Eakin Press
An Imprint of Sunbelt Media, Inc.
P.O. Drawer 90159  ★  Austin, TX 78709-0159

Library of Congress Cataloging-in-Publication Data

Stone, Ron, 1936–
    The book of Texas days.

    Bibliography: p.
    Includes index.
    Summary: Presents at least one event, anecdote, or item of informa-
tion for each day of the year, covering the full 150-plus-year range of
Texas history.
    1. Texas — History — Chronology.  2. Texas — History —
Anniversaries, etc.
[1. Texas — History]  I. Title.
F386.S89   1985      976.4'06'0202       85-14341
ISBN 0-9406762-30-8

*This book is dedicated to my wife, Patsy.*
*It is a fortunate man who marries*
*his best friend.*

# Introduction

I HAVE SPENT THIRTY YEARS as a journalist, albeit a television journalist. I have reported on the important and the trivial of Texas for twenty-five of those years. My love of Texas history began with a visit to the San Jacinto Battleground in 1962, shortly after we moved to the state. I walked the "Plain of St. Hyacinth," as Marquis James called the battlefield. I could not understand how it could happen. I went to the Alamo, and tried to understand why. I read the names at Goliad and wondered who these people were. The questions I was taught to ask as a reporter were the questions I asked the places where Texas was born.

Someone suggested that journalism is really a first draft of history. We report on the rise and fall of politicians, and wait for history to say whether they were significant to the state, or just bit players. We chronicle events and record them so that years later the learned historians will weigh them against the reality of time and test them against what they really meant. Paul Veyne points out that everything is raw material for history, but history is what historians have the vision to find, or what they choose to do. The historian is moved by curiosity; the rage to know for the sake of knowing.

My "knowing for the sake of knowing" took on greater proportions with a series of television programs I did on Texas, and later in my assignment on "The Eyes of Texas" program. I was struck all too often by people telling me that history was dull, and therefore they chose not to read it. How can something that is so exciting as Texas history be dull?

This book seeks to do nothing more than extend my love affair with Texas by attempting to show the varied mosaic of the state. I cannot explain the men and women who gave nerve to circumstance and changed this world. I cannot explain the almost mystic feeling people have for the land. I can only chronicle it as a journalist would, and lay out what has passed the test of time, and hope that one or two of these 365 or so people and places, events and actions will stir our readers to find excitement where dullness has been, and kindle a new love for Texas.

My son Ron Jr. was an invaluable help in doing this book. He is a history major in college, and spent his summers on the roads of Texas visiting one museum after another looking for the photos this book contains. Some day he will, I am sure, become a fine historian who will keep the flame alive. Jean Hardy edited the words with kindness and understanding. My daughter

Robin and her husband, Marc Baldo, took my scratching and made it readable. My wife, Pat, offered encouragement and love throughout the project, and shared the twenty-five years of driving around Texas to out-of-the-way places. I know there were many times she and the kids would have preferred doing something else, and had to feign excitement over Dad's finding out some obscure fact he seemed driven to know. She always thought I was worth a lot more than I did, and reminded me of that often enough to keep me going.

I have lived with this book of Texas days for many years. I hope it brings you joy.

*Ron Stone*
*April, 1985*

# The Book of Texas Days

The Battle of Galveston drove the Yankees out on New Year's Day, 1863. (Author's collection)

# JANUARY

## JANUARY 1

### 1863

The Battle of Galveston was not one of the great epic events of the Civil War, yet it proved to be a wonderful way for the South to start 1863.

The Yankees had held Galveston since October 1862, when a flotilla of Federal gunboats had entered the harbor. On Christmas Day about three hundred men had come ashore and taken over Kuhn's Wharf.

Confederate Gen. John Bankhead Magruder (see Nov. 29), a Virginian sent to exile in Texas after he botched a chance at greatness in the Seven Days' Battles, saw his chance to get back into favor, and set out to retake the island for the Stars and Bars.

Two Buffalo Bayou steamers, the *Neptune* and *Bayou City*, were outfitted with cotton bales around the decks to protect the artillery. Three hundred Confederate soldiers crowded onto the little boats on a black New Year's Eve night, and before dawn the first of January, the "cotton-clads" and two tenders steamed out into the harbor to take on the Federals.

The legend is that people from all along the coast had hurried to Galveston to watch the show. At first the events were not pleasant. The *Neptune* went down in shallow water after taking a direct hit. The *Bayou City* came on in, and sharpshooters behind the bales of cotton wiped out the U.S. steamship *Harriet Lane*. With that the *Westfield* turned to run and ran aground. The Federal gunboat that was left headed out to sea, and the Union

The New York *Herald*'s account of the Battle of Galveston. (Author's collection)

forces on the wharf surrendered. The Battle of Galveston was over. John Bankhead Magruder emerged a hero, and the Stars and Stripes would not wave over Galveston again until the end of the war.

# JANUARY 2

### 1882

Jefferson, in the northeast corner of Texas, was a teeming river-port city of thirty thousand when the most famous railroad man of his day, Jay Gould, came courting. What he offered was the chance for Jefferson to be a regional headquarters for the Texas and Pacific Railroad—if the town would give him free right-of-way. To Gould's everlasting surprise and disgust, the town said no. After all, the river traffic had built the city and showed no signs of letting up. On January 2, 1882, Jay Gould checked out of the Excelsior House Hotel and scrawled on the register, "The end of Jefferson, Texas."

He prophesied that "grass would grow in the street, and bats would roost in the houses," and that is nearly what happened. What Gould and the people of Jefferson did not realize was that the level of the river had been slowly dropping and boats had started running aground on Big Cypress Bayou leading into the port. Jay Gould was right, but it wasn't his railroad that wrote the end of Jefferson. It was the work of a young army engineer who had, years earlier, managed to clear away a huge logjam on the Red River that backed up water for miles through east Texas. With the Red River Raft gone, the Big Cypress Bayou, like all the others that fed the river, began slowly, but surely, to drain.

### 1871

George Rickard was born January 2, 1871, in Kansas City. When he was four, Rickard's family moved to Sherman, and from that time on the boy was known as "Tex."

Tex Rickard was a range rider and a deputy U.S. marshal until the gold fever hit him in 1889. In the Klondike, Tex found his calling, not as a gold miner, but as a fight promoter. He would stage boxing matches for the men who had precious little to do.

Before long he was the prime promoter in New York's Madison Square Garden. *Time* magazine said, "It was Rickard who made professional boxing into a sport more spectacular than any since the wild animal shows of the Roman Empire."

When he died of appendicitis in 1929, Rickard left an estate of three million dollars. Thirty-five thousand mourners walked by his glass-topped coffin in Madison Square Garden.

# JANUARY 3

### 1834

Stephen F. Austin had his detractors in Mexican Texas in the mid–1830s. When he went to Mexico City with a call for better protection from the Indians and a tax break for his colonists, Austin was fighting to keep his colony together and keep hotheads from starting a war with Mexico they could not win. Austin's patience was seen by some as his great strength, by others as his great weakness. But as the long summer of 1833 stretched into fall, then winter, and no action was taken on the request, Austin dashed off a letter suggesting Texas make plans to organize a separate state. Finally, the Mexican Congress called Austin in to tell him they were willing to give Texas some relief.

Stephen Austin started home to Texas, but the letter he had written turned up, and on January 3, Austin was arrested for inciting a rebellion. He was placed in a windowless cell and left there for nearly a year. He was released from prison but held in Mexico till July 1835. Austin's eighteen months in prison changed him from a man determined to see

and was an early thorn in the side of the colonists that eventually led to the revolution of 1836.

**Also on this date**, in the year 1911, the Slanton water well came in, helping to transform semiarid west Texas into a breadbasket for the nation.

Stephen F. Austin, the Father of Texas. (Houston Metropolitan Research Center, Houston Library)

his colony live in harmony with Mexico, to one who came to believe that Texas must be Americanized.

### 1823

On January 3, 1823, the Mexican Congress passed a law that would open the floodgates to immigration in Mexican Texas, at least for a while.

The law of Imperial Colonization invited immigrants of Roman Catholic faith to settle in Mexico. The law spelled out the requirements and limitation of immigration. Though it was annulled a short time after it was passed, it was the basis of other laws that followed,

# JANUARY 4

### 1948

Michael Late Benedum lived for ninety years, and for sixty-nine of those years he was more often than not drilling for oil. He looked for it in Illinois, West Virginia, Mexico, Colombia, and in the Caddo Field of Louisiana. By 1948 he had drilled a hundred wells, and seventy-five of them were dry holes.

On January 4, 1948, Benedum and his partner, Tom Slick, hit oil at 12,022 feet in Upton County—in west Texas. Dubbed the "Alford Number 1," this well looked like an opening to another oil show as big as the great East Texas Field of seventeen years earlier (see March 12).

Royalties went out of sight. Suddenly west Texas scrub land was as good as gold. The morning after Alford Number 1 hit, a one-eighth share in the oil that remained with the land-owner was going for $6,000 an acre.

In that cold winter of '48, Mike Benedum watched the oil speculators race into Midland to get into the action. "They are coming here because of the heat," he would say . . . "Alford Number 1 is the hottest damn well in the country." *Life* magazine called Benedum "The Great Wildcatter."

## JANUARY 5

### 1931

In the lean years before the Second World War, the backwoods Negro Baptist church rocked with a glorious rhythm that meant hand-clapping, foot-stomping release for an unfortunate people trapped in an awful time. You could sing, and clap, and sway; but being Baptist, you could not dance. Yet a child of that Revival-and-Baptist-Young-People's-Union upbringing was to become one of America's great dancers.

Alvin Ailey was born January 5, 1931, in the little town of Rogers, Texas, where blacks had a hard time getting along and black dancers rated even less chance of achieving.

Ailey found his way to Los Angeles, and in his early thirties was not only dancing, but choreographing. In 1958 he formed the Alvin Ailey American Dance Theatre, and his dancing and his dances have thrilled audiences around the world.

This child of the blackland Bible Belt has spoken a universal language as he reacts to the music: the United Nations recognized his contributions to the arts and to world understanding and presented him the United Nations' Peace Medal.

## JANUARY 6

### 1882

The impact that Tennesseans have had on Texas history cannot be measured—from Crockett and Houston to a twentieth century politician who became the prototypical Texan, Sam Rayburn, born January 6, 1882, in Roane County in eastern Tennessee.

When young Sam was five years old his parents moved to north Texas. Rayburn's political career began in 1906 when he ran for the state legislature. He was immensely successful and six years later was elected to Congress from the Fourth Congressional District. He had a Midas touch, a golden tongue, and a knack for playing the political game. Franklin Roosevelt called on Rayburn to sponsor much of the New Deal in Congress. With Rayburn pushing it, Roosevelt knew the legislation had a good chance to pass.

By September 1940 Rayburn was elected Speaker of the House, a job he held longer than anyone in history. (See also Nov. 16.)

## JANUARY 7

### 1899

An unlikely end came to an improbable life on January 7, 1899. W. A. A. Wallace died a natural death after having lived a long, full, and often violent, life.

History knows him as "Bigfoot" Wallace, a giant of a man who wandered into Texas in 1837 and chased Indians and Mexicans and badmen and loved to talk about it. He was a storyteller without equal.

Wallace was one of the members of the ill-fated Mier Expedition (see March 25) captured by the Mexicans, who made them draw for the black or white beans. A black bean meant death. Wallace saw the Mexican soldiers pour in white beans first, so he claims he dipped down deep to get a white one, and a new lease on life.

After a time in a Mexican prison he came home to join the famed Texas Rangers, then he drove a stagecoach from Austin to El Paso through Indian country. Part of the reason for the Wallace legend was his colorful speech and his larger-than-life stories. He once said he had been "shot at, hit, caught, broke loose, beat up, and had everything bad happen to me that could happen . . . 'cept get married."

Wallace was a young eighty-two when he quietly died at his home in Frio County. His grave marker in the State Cemetery at Austin says, "Here lies he who spent his manhood defending the homes of Texas . . ."

**Also on this date**, in the year 1905, the Humble Oil Field was discovered.

Alvin Ailey with Judith Jamison. He formed one of America's great modern dance troupes. (Alvin Ailey City Center Dance Theatre)

"Bigfoot" Wallace did not draw a black bean, and lived to be a Texas legend. (Gonzales Historical Museum)

House Speaker "Mister Sam" Rayburn with John Nance Garner. (From *Money, Marbles and Chalk*, by Jimmy Banks)

Gov. Edmund J. Davis leads a march around the Capitol for "purification," c. 1873. Painting by Bruce Marshall. (Institute of Texan Cultures)

## JANUARY 8

### 1870

In the awful days following the Civil War, Texas was ruled by martial law, until the election of 1869, when a more sinister force took over. Carpetbagger rule was to drive more hatred deep into the Texas psyche.

In the race for the governor's office that year, the radical Republicans ran Edmund J. Davis, a Florida native who had been in Texas since 1838. At the outbreak of the Civil War, Davis had remained loyal to the Union and had ended the war as a Yankee brigadier general.

Following the war he worked to disenfranchise all Confederates and tried to divide Texas into three states. In the election of 1869 he ran against a Galveston newspaper editor named Hamilton Stuart and conservative Republican Jack Hamilton. Military troops stood at every polling place, with officers serving as election judges. Men who had served in the Southern army were not allowed to vote, while Negroes were marched to vote. In some counties, where there was strong anti-Republican sentiment, the polls were closed or simply never opened. When it was over, the votes were not canvassed. Edmund Davis was declared the winner along with the entire radical ticket.

On January 8, 1870, Davis took office as governor. It took an army to get him out four years later, and it was to be one hundred years before Texas elected its second Republican Governor. (See also Jan. 17.)

## 1865

The Kickapoo Indians gave up a lot before they ever came to Texas. They moved from around the Great Lakes to central Illinois until they gave that up and moved south to Kansas and Missouri, and finally to east Texas and Indian Territory.

As a tribe, they usually found themselves on the wrong side in every fight. Their big moment in Texas history came on January 8, 1865, ironically as they were trying to avoid trouble. Chief No-Ko-Wat was moving 1,400 of his people from Indian Territory to Mexico. He swung wide across the frontier of west Texas to stay out of everyone's way, but Capt. Henry Fossett and 370 state militiamen and settlers feared the worst and gave chase. Sixteen miles south of San Angelo, on Dove Creek, the Kickapoo and the militiamen met in a furious battle. In one of the few exceptions to the rule, the Indians won. Thirty-six white men were killed and sixty others were wounded. The Indians lost eleven men, and continued to Mexico.

Walter Prescott Webb said the Kickapoo came through Texas "running like frightened game before the devastating fire of the American Frontier."

## JANUARY 9

### 1858

Failure and health problems drove many men to Texas to find their destinies. Anson Jones knew failure as well as any man, but briefly he walked in the bright, blinding light of success, and that proved to be his downfall.

Jones was in his mid-thirties when he came to Texas; he apparently picked the right time, for his medical practice at Brazoria prospered.

He fought at San Jacinto, was elected to the Second Congress, and became Sam Houston's minister to the United States from the Republic of Texas. In 1844, just eleven years after he decided to give Texas a try, Anson Jones rode on his friend Sam Houston's patronage and was elected president of the Republic. Two years later he presided at the ceremonies setting up a state government and ending the Republic (see Feb. 19).

After his brief tenure as president, Jones slipped into obscurity. He spent much of the time bitterly accusing Sam Houston of turning against him and ruining his career.

In 1857, approaching sixty, and rattling around an angry man in a failing body, Jones received his final rejection. He hoped the legislature would send him to Washington as a senator, but he did not get even a single vote. On January 9, 1858, Anson Jones checked into a room at the old Capital Hotel in Houston, the place where he had begun his government career, put a gun to his head, and killed himself.

## JANUARY 10

### 1901

The thing Curt Hamill remembered most about January 10, 1901, was that he should have been killed, but wasn't. Hamill also knew that he had had a hand in something very big that day.

Indeed he had! Curt Hamill, his brother Al, and a fellow named Peck Byrd were working on the rig at Spindletop when it blew in with a mighty rush of oil that was to change the course of history.

The oil was discovered because Patillo Higgins, a Beaumont tough guy turned Sunday School teacher, took his Baptist Church class to a picnic at some springs near the big hill they called Spindletop. The springs oozed a rainbow of colors, and you could smell whatever was in the springs long before you got to them. Higgins figured it was oil. He studied, promoted, cajoled, did everything he could to finance a well. Finally he placed an advertisement in a trade paper, and one man answered, Anthony Lucas, a naturalized Austrian, who was really looking for sulphur, not oil. (After all, oil was only good for lamp fuel and axle grease at the time!)

The two hired the Hamill brothers of Corsicana to drill the well. As the nineteenth century was turning into the twentieth, the well was started. On January 10, 1901, it was at just over a thousand feet when sand and mud started boiling up. Then the drill pipe went flying out of the hole. Curt Hamill was on the rig watching history from a catbird seat. How he got down, he never knew. It was Friday morning, and the world was never the same again.

# JANUARY 11

### 1874

On January 11, 1874, Gail Borden, Jr.'s remarkable life came to an end. He was a pioneer, a surveyor, a newspaperman, a church leader, and, finally, dairyman to a nation.

Borden came to Texas from his native New York by way of Indiana and Mississippi. Despite the fact that he had less than two years of formal education, he taught school and was a federal surveyor. Gail replaced his brother Thomas as the surveyor for Stephen F. Austin's colony in 1830. Five years later Borden began publishing one of the first newspapers in Texas, *The Telegraph and Texas Register*. Following the revolution he laid out the site of the new town of Houston, became collector at the port of Galveston, and an executive with the Galveston City Company, as well as an active temperance worker and clerk of the Baptist Church.

Gail Borden's active mind was always hatching some new scheme or invention—a wind-powered wagon that would travel by land or sea, a portable bathhouse for women—and in 1850 he was granted a patent for the meat biscuit. It was that meat biscuit that took him out of Texas and back to New York to be near the major trade centers. Try as he might, Borden never was able to market the dehydrated sandwich.

While the meat biscuit was proving to be less a boon than a bust, Gail Borden began to experiment with the invention that the world remembers. In 1853, he figured out how to process condensed milk in a vacuum. By 1856, he was issued patent No. 15,553, and his fame was assured. Five years later when the Civil War started and there was a sudden demand for condensed milk, Borden's fortune was made.

Borden spent his winters in Texas, and in 1874 died at a Colorado County town named Bordenville, in honor of the New Yorker who meant so much to early Texas.

The "wind wagon," one of Gail Borden's many inventions. (Rosenberg Museum, Galveston)

The Spindletop field ablaze. Dangerous blowouts and fires were all too frequent in the early days. (Houston Metropolitan Research Center, Houston Library)

## 1854

In February 1848 a fort was established about three and one-half miles from El Paso. The Post of El Paso protected the settlers from the Indians. On January 11, 1854, special orders came to reestablish the post, and a few months later it got a new name, "Fort Bliss." Historians disagree on whether it was named for Maj. William Wallace Smith Bliss or Col. John R. Bliss; at any rate, it has since been a significant name in military history.

In its long and colorful history, Fort Bliss has guarded the border against Mexican invaders and hostile Indians; has served the Confederacy and the Union; has trained the U.S. Cavalry; provided men to chase Geronimo and Pancho Villa; and prepared men for two World Wars. It has been destroyed, burned, and flooded; still, Fort Bliss stands proud in history and heritage guarding "the Pass."

## JANUARY 12

### 1920

Through the blood and thunder of the Civil Rights movement, no one, save Martin Luther King, Jr., stood taller than James Farmer, who was born in Marshall on January 12, 1920.

In 1942, fresh out of Howard University, Farmer and a group of friends did a radical thing—they organized the Congress of Racial Equality. CORE was dedicated to fighting segregation the way Gandhi fought the British, through nonviolence.

When the sixties came it was Farmer who pioneered the use of sit-ins to fight segregation in public places. He organized "freedom rides" to integrate bus lines.

A few years ago, James Farmer laughed at what he had been through—a bitter kind of laugh—as he recounted escaping a mob of Louisiana lawmen by hiding in a funeral hearse. He has been tear-gassed, arrested more times than he can remember, and has had food dumped on his lap during sit-ins.

James Farmer, born on the wrong side of the tracks in Marshall in deeply segregated east Texas, grew up to be one of the people who finally beat Jim Crow.

**Also on this date**, in the year 1905, singer and film actor Tex Ritter was born in Panola County.

# JANUARY 13

## 1891

If you look long enough in Beth Israel Cemetery in Austin, you will find a grave for Louis Weisberg, born January 13, 1891; died March 23, 1972.

Weisberg was a remarkable man whose career saved a generation in the First World War, and may have helped condemn the rest of us to an uncertain future. He studied chemistry at the University of Texas, and later at Massachusetts Institute of Technology. During World War I he served in the U.S. Army in France, where he was active in the French Underground, working to develop an antidote for mustard gas, the filmy poison fog that the Germans unleashed to kill thousands.

When the Second World War came, Dr. Weisberg joined the war effort one more time. He was assigned to work on the top-secret Manhattan Project, which developed the atomic bomb.

Louis Weisberg, of Waco, thought of himself not as a man of war or a man of peace, but simply as a man of science.

When others forgot, Clara Driscoll remembered the Alamo. Photo c. 1935. (San Antonio *Light* Collection)

## JANUARY 14

### 1901

On January 14, 1901, a pretty young woman just short of her twentieth birthday wrote a letter to the San Antonio *Express*. Clara Driscoll wrote that the Alamo was in gradual decline, and that "all the unsightly obstructions should be torn away from the Alamo chapel." She said, in that now-famous letter to the editor, that patriotic Texans would probably raise the money to save the shrine.

What followed was a campaign by the Daughters of the Republic of Texas to buy the property by public subscription. It did not work out that way. The money they hoped for did not materialize, nor did the state government offer any help. In the end the young woman who started the crusade to save the Alamo gave a personal check and five promissory notes to earn the title "Savior of the Alamo." She bought a thirty-day option on the public shrine and kept control of it long enough to prevent its destruction.

### 1963

On January 14, 1963, Texas got a little smaller, as the final border dispute between the U.S. and Mexico was settled. When the Rio Grande changed course in 1864, the river created a 630-acre parcel of land for the U.S. that had belonged to Mexico. For years the diplomats argued. Finally, in 1911, recommendations were made that the United States give up the land.

When John Kennedy became President he ordered the State Department to move on the old problem. Kennedy was smarting from the Bay of Pigs debacle, and was looking for anything he could find to pursue a friendly line toward Latin America.

Kennedy was dead before the official end of the border dispute. It was left to Lyndon Johnson to meet with President Gustavo Diaz Ordaz on the border to formally proclaim the settlement; 630 acres of what had been El Paso, Texas, was deeded over to Mexico in the Treaty of El Chamizal.

## JANUARY 15

### 1897

One of the darkest moments in the Texas Revolution had come at the Goliad Massacre (see March 27), when 342 of the 400 or so men taken prisoner after the battle of Coleto Creek were executed in cold blood.

James Walker Fannin thought his men would be freed by the Mexicans; instead, on Palm Sunday morning, most were marched out of the Presidio La Bahia on a trip they assumed would lead to freedom; it led, instead, to death.

When the Mexican troops suddenly began shooting into the ranks of the Texans, twenty-eight men managed to jump into the San Antonio River and swim to safety. One of those was John Duval, a twenty-year-old from Kentucky. Duval lived that day to fight again. He became a Texas Ranger, a private in the Confederate army, and a writer of some note. On January 15, 1897, John Duval, the last survivor of Fannin's Army, died peacefully in Fort Worth. His swim to safety yielded him sixty more years to reflect on that fateful day at Goliad.

## JANUARY 16

### 1934

When Clyde Barrow's buddy Raymond Hamilton was sentenced to serve 263 years in the state prisons of Texas, he said, "There is no prison that will hold me; I'll be back with Clyde before you know it."

On the morning of January 16, 1934, as a heavy fog hung over the river bottoms at the Eastham Prison Farm near Huntsville, Hamilton suddenly broke from a work crew and dived into a ditch where weapons had been hidden. Before anyone could react, Clyde Barrow and a companion rose from the ditch and sprayed the guards with small arms fire. Two guards were hit, and Barrow, his aide, and Hamilton dashed for a waiting car that carried them to freedom.

Clyde Barrow broke into a prison to free his friend. It took red-faced lawmen a long time to live that day down. But within two years, Barrow and Hamilton were both dead. (See also May 23.)

**Also on this date**, in the year 1839, the Texas Senate voted to buy the captured Mexican fleet from the French to start a new navy.

## JANUARY 17

### 1874

Edmund J. Davis, the first Republican governor of Texas, was surely the most hated man to hold the office. His Carpetbagger rule was marked with discontent, hard times, and what seemed like downright contempt for the people of Texas. It is little wonder that the first honest election held after he took office resulted in his being thoroughly beaten.

But Davis refused to accept the results of the election! The question then was how to get him out of office. Davis, naturally, said the election was crooked, and his cronies still in office agreed. But the winning Democrats took office anyway. Davis wanted to call out national troops, but President U. S. Grant did not agree, so Davis called out the local militia—the Travis Rifles. In a moment of supreme agony for Davis, the Travis Rifles surrendered and joined the other side.

On January 17, 1874, President Grant advised Davis to yield to the verdict of the people as expressed in their ballots. Two days later Davis left his office, locking the door behind him. Texans who had lived through nine years of Carpetbag rule broke the door down, and Richard Coke became the governor of a state emerging from a deep darkness. (See also Jan. 8.)

**Also on this date**, in 1821, the Mexican government gave Moses Austin permission to settle three hundred families in Texas.

## JANUARY 18

### 1971

There has been scandal in Texas government as long as there has been a government, but the size and scope of the Sharpstown scandal rates a special mention.

Sharpstown is the name of a sprawling subdivision in southwest Houston that was the brainchild of developer Frank Sharp. He made money everywhere he turned, but in the early seventies he got a lot of help from friends in high places.

Frank Sharp wanted the legislature to pass a Bank Deposit Insurance Law that could make him and his National Bankers Life Insurance Corp., and his Sharpstown State Bank, a lot of money.

Sharp loaned over $600,000 to state offi-

"Of course he wants to vote the Democratic ticket!" A Democratic "reformer" threatens: "You're as free as air, ain't you? Say you are, or I'll blow yer black head off!" Cartoon, *Harper's Weekly*, Oct. 21, 1876. (Institute of Texan Cultures)

cials to buy stock in National Bankers Life, in return for bringing up the Bank Deposit Insurance Law in a special session of the legislature. On January 18, 1971, the house of cards started falling apart as the Securities and Exchange Commission filed a lawsuit alleging stock fraud against Sharp, the attorney general, and a former state insurance commissioner.

Before it was over, charges were leveled against a couple of dozen state and former state officials. The political careers of a popular attorney general, a Speaker of the House, a governor, and lieutenant governor were shattered.

As for Sharp, the man who caused it all; he was fined $5,000, given a probated sentence, still lives in splendor in River Oaks in Houston, and passes the collection plate most Sundays at one of the city's biggest churches.

## JANUARY 19

### 1847

Before the revolution there was one religion in Mexican Texas: Roman Catholic. After 1836, it was a case of anything, or nothing, goes. There were about twenty thousand Catholics in Texas by 1847 when John Odin was named the first Bishop of Galveston. He saw an immediate need to give the youngsters a Catholic education, lest they become as wild as the majority of people who populated the new state.

On January 19, 1847, six Ursuline nuns and their mother superior, Sr. Arsene Blin, arrived from New Orleans at the Port of Galveston. Their mission was to start a series of schools. On February 8 they opened the first Catholic

Ten years after Texas won independence, the Ursulines came. These are members of the class of 1900 at the old convent in Laredo. (St. Mary's University, San Antonio)

school for girls in Texas. The school served as a hospital during the Civil War, and the nuns there have cared for victims of Galveston's string of devastating fires and hurricanes.

From the single school in Galveston the Ursulines went on to build others in San Antonio, Liberty, and Dallas, as well as Mexico.

### 1943

Janis Joplin grew up plain and undistinguished in Port Arthur. Few people remembered her, except that she was different.

She was different, all right—no white woman could sing the blues like Janis Joplin. When she was seventeen, she left her middle-class family and her life as a loner, and went away to sing. She exploded on the rock scene with an unforgettable performance at the Monterey Pop Festival in June 1967. Her style was to burst onto a stage holding a bottle of

whiskey in one hand and the mike in another, and sing her throaty blues in a voice that seemed to be strained to the limit.

Her enormous talent was eventually tempered by too much booze and too many drugs. Still she said once, "I'd rather live ten years of super hype than live to be seventy sitting in some God-damned chair watching TV."

Janis Joplin burned out ten years after she left Port Arthur, dying of a heroin overdose in Hollywood in October 1970.

She was born January 19, 1943.

## JANUARY 20

### 1925

Jim Ferguson used to say, "Never say die, say *damn!*" With that kind of spirit he got himself elected governor of Texas, and got himself impeached. When he was legally barred from holding office, he called reporters into a hotel room and announced that his wife was going to run for governor.

So it was that Miriam Amanda Ferguson became active in politics. It was the middle of the twenties, when Texas was still a rural state, and the folksy slogan of the campaign was "Me for Ma, and I ain't got a dern thing against Pa!"

It was clear that Ma would be the governor in name only, that Pa would run things, which meant fighting the Klan and the big-time education boys who wanted to do away with the Little Red Schoolhouse. Ma Ferguson was the rural people's darling. When big-city newspapers sent reporters and photographers to Texas to check out the woman candidate, Jim would make her put on her bonnet and go out in the yard to be photographed feeding the chickens.

She beat Democrat Felix D. Robertson in the primary, and swamped the Republican, Dr. George Butte, in the general election. On January 20, 1925, Miriam Ferguson took the oath of office as governor of Texas while Pa stood by smiling. Her election came ten years after the women of Texas were given the right to vote. (See also June 13, Aug. 25.)

1891

Texas has been electing governors since 1846, electing nineteen of them before getting around to choosing one who had been born in Texas.

James Stephen Hogg was born near Rusk in 1851. His father and mother died when he was very young, so Jim Hogg had to scrape to make ends meet. He tried newspaper work, the law, and law enforcement. While still a teenager, he was shot in the back by outlaws, but survived. Young Jim Hogg ran for public office in 1876 and lost. It was the last time he would lose. He became district attorney, then attorney general, and, finally, governor.

On January 20, 1891, James Stephen Hogg became the first native-born governor of Texas. He served for four years and left office as popular and respected as the day he was sworn in. The first native-born Texas governor was, in truth, one of the finest governors the state ever had.

## JANUARY 21

1861

Sam Houston, the first great Texan, knew his moments of despair as well as his times of triumph. Surely one of his worst times came January 21, 1861, when he must submit the secession resolution to the legislature. The moment Houston had worked and fought against was at hand. A special session of the legislature was meeting to decide whether Texas stayed in the Union or joined its neighboring states in secession. Four Southern states had already left the Union; and on the same day Texans met, Alabama's senators in Washington made fiery farewell speeches.

A "Ma" Ferguson campaign poster, 1925. (Barker Texas History Center)

Houston, who was governor at the time, pled with the legislature to keep Texas in the Union. There was talk of impeaching him because his feelings clearly did not match those of the majority of people in Texas. A hand-picked revolutionary convention was to meet a week later to settle the issue.

In his bitter defeat; in his failure to keep Texas in the Union; in the vitriolic hatred the hot times produced toward him; Houston was living his last, finest hours. He was to say, "I still believe that secession will bring ruin and Civil War; some of you laugh to scorn the idea of bloodshed as the result of secession, yet the North is determined to preserve this Union. They are not a fiery, impulsive people as you are, for they live in colder climates. But when they begin to move in a given direction they move with a steady momentum and perseverance of a mighty avalanche; and what I fear is, they will overwhelm the South."

Sam Houston said, "You never hear me talk of 'Southern rights' . . . for I believe all states have equal rights." (Houston Metropolitan Research Center, Houston Library)

1913

Thomas Munson just loved grapes! He loved grapes so much he moved from Illinois to Texas so he could study the vines. At Denison and throughout Texas he experimented and improved the American crop, developing some three hundred new varieties.

Munson struggled to breed grapes that resisted disease. He noted with interest that a panic had spread through Europe because a root louse called Phylloxera was ruining the great vineyards in France, Germany, and Italy. Munson bred rootstock that was resistant to the root louse and shipped the rootstock to European growers, who grafted their famous old grape varieties to the sturdier stock. The result was the saving of many of the world's finest vineyards. The French government showered him with medals and praise.

Thomas Munson died in Denison on January 21, 1913, and his family and friends planted grapevines over his grave.

Those who enjoy a really fine French Cabernet Sauvignon or a Pinot Noir should say a little prayer of thanks for the Grape Man of Denison.

## JANUARY 22

1973

George Foreman was born in Marshall in 1949. His early life was spent in the poverty and despair of Houston's teeming Fifth Ward. Deserted by his father, Foreman roamed the streets looking for fights and drifting toward a life of crime.

A sports program at a neighborhood center changed his life, and a turn with the Job Corps program turned him into a boxer. At the age of eighteen he won the A.A.U. Boxing Championship, and on October 26, 1968, stood waving a small American flag after winning the Olympic gold medal as a heavyweight boxer. His flag-waving endeared him to Americans who had been stunned by a Black Power movement that swept the Olympics that year.

By June 1969 Foreman turned pro and disposed of a string of thirty-two men who challenged him in the ring. On January 22, 1973, in Jamaica, the young man who had struggled through the ghettos climbed into the ring with Smokin' Joe Frazier, the Heavyweight Champion of the World. The kid was a 3-to-1 underdog. It was not much of a fight—it was more like an assassination. Foreman knocked the mighty Frazier down six times in the first two rounds. The last time Frazier fell, the referee stopped the fight, and George Foreman became the Heavyweight Champion of the World.

George Foreman, winner of the Olympic Gold Medal and the World Heavyweight Championship; 1974 photo. (Institute of Texan Cultures)

# JANUARY 23

### 1875

Molly Wright was born in Bell County on January 23, 1875. In a time when a woman's place was unquestionably in the home, Molly Wright was an unusual and driven woman. At the age of twenty-four, the wife of Walter D. Armstrong became Dr. Molly Armstrong, the first woman optometrist in Texas and the second in the entire country.

# JANUARY 24

### 1822

One of the three hundred original settlers in the Austin Colony was Jared Groce. Unlike most people who came here with a family and some livestock and a slave or two, the Groce immigration looked more like a migration. He was a wealthy planter in Alabama when he heard of Austin's Texas Proposition, and at the age of thirty-nine headed west.

Groce and his son Leonard led at least fifty covered wagons, a string of livestock, slaves, and family members on the trek to Texas. In late January they reached the Brazos near the present site of Hempstead and settled in.

In one of those wagons, Groce brought something that would make a significant contribution to Texas, as well as the South—cottonseed. Jared Groce introduced cotton to Texas.

*Note*: The exact date of the Groces' arrival is disputed. Records indicate they arrived late in January; the dates January 24 and 15 are mentioned. Most accounts simply say "they arrived in January of 1822."

Sam Houston in Cherokee costume. Houston lived with the Indians for years, and learned to respect them. (Barker Texas History Center)

## JANUARY 25

1819

The woman who almost became the second Mrs. Sam Houston was born January 25, 1819, in Bucks County, Pennsylvania.

Sam Houston met the teen-aged Miss Anna Raguet in Nacogdoches where he lived before the revolution. She had been educated in the best Eastern schools, and spent hours teaching Houston to speak Spanish. By 1833, Houston filed a petition to divorce his first wife, Eliza Allen of Tennessee. He actively courted the young Miss Anna, but for a long time got nowhere. By the time Houston went away to the convention at Washington-on-the-Brazos in 1836, Miss Anna had warmed to him, and clipped a lock of his hair.

From the convention to San Jacinto took just a little over a month, but a wound at the battle required a long period of recuperation. Houston wrote his Miss Anna long and syrupy love letters in which he referred to her as "the

great gem," "the fairest of fair," "the peerless Miss Anna," and "the brightest and loveliest star in Texas." More often than not he kept up with her by getting reports from a mutual friend, Dr. Robert Irion. The fact of the matter was that the more Dr. Irion talked to Miss Anna about Sam, the more Miss Anna talked to Dr. Irion about Dr. Irion. Houston reluctantly realized the Miles Standish and John Alden relationship had backfired. The lady chose the doctor and they married four years after Houston had left her side to save Texas.

**Also on this date**, in the year 1839, the Republic of Texas adopted its flag.

## JANUARY 26

1945

Audie Murphy was born in Hunt County in 1924. When the Second World War came, he was still a teenager who looked younger than he really was. A slight youngster, just 5 feet 7 inches tall, and weighing no more than 130 pounds, he looked like anything but the greatest hero the war was to produce.

Before he was through, Audie Murphy had won every combat decoration the Army offered. His greatest moment came on January 26, 1945, near Holtzwihr, France. Murphy and less than three dozen men came under attack by a company of German infantrymen backed by six tanks. As the American forces were being wiped out, Murphy began to act like a man possessed. Before the day was over he had single-handedly killed or wounded fifty Germans, and refused to go back to safety, so he could direct artillery strikes to knock out the tanks.

For these actions, Audie Murphy was awarded the Congressional Medal of Honor.

Among World War II hero Audie Murphy's many awards was the Croix de Guerre presented by Charles de Gaulle. (U.S. Dept. of the Army)

**Also on this date**, in the year 1837, the steamship *Laura* navigated up the Buffalo Bayou with a load of prospective buyers for lots in the new city of Houston. But the *Laura* steamed past the town because vegetation was so dense.

# JANUARY 27

## 1829

In 1826 Elias Wightman and David G. Burnet received permission to build a settlement at the mouth of the Colorado River. Fifty-two people floated down the Allegheny and Ohio rivers in the fall of 1828, caught a steamboat on the Mississippi, and transferred to a schooner in New Orleans.

Getting there was not half the fun. They hit a storm in the Gulf. Somehow the anchor knocked a hole in the little boat and it almost went down. Once they arrived in Matagorda Bay, stiff winds set in and they could not get close to shore. The food and water ran out,

and they resorted to shooting seagulls and turning them into stew.

Finally on January 27, 1829, the men rowed the schooner to the mouth of the Colorado and dropped anchor to begin the colony. The bad luck was not over, however. The summer brought typhoid fever, and Wightman's mother and father became the first inhabitants of the Matagorda cemetery.

# JANUARY 28

## 1960

When the National Football League decided to expand in an effort to blunt the new American Football League, Dallas was chosen as a Southern battleground. Dallas already had Lamar Hunt's "Texans," and on January 28, 1960, at the league meetings in Florida, the NFL awarded a franchise to Clint Murchison, Jr., and Bedford Wynne. They chose the name "Cowboys," and picked Tom Landry of Mission and the University of Texas to be the head coach.

The team was stocked with thirty-six re-treads and has-beens from the existing teams, but Landry traded for a midget quarterback named Eddie LeBaron, and signed a kid out of SMU, Don Meredith, to back up LeBaron.

The Cowboys were not an artistic success. In the first year in the league there were more empty seats than paying customers for the home games, but little wonder; the Cowboys lost the first ten games they played.

The Cowboys had been created because Lamar Hunt's Dallas Texans were in the American League. The two teams battled for supremacy in Dallas for three years before the Cowboys won the war for the fans, and the Texans moved to Kansas City to become the Chiefs.

By 1966 the Cowboys were winning championships, and in 971, eleven years after that rocky birth, the Dallas Cowboys won the National Conference title and went on to beat the Miami Dolphins in Super Bowl VI.

With that star on the helmet, a sphinxlike coach, the most beautiful cheerleading corps in sports, and a stadium with a hole in the top that dares Mother Nature to rain on their parade, the Cowboys are America's Team.

Murchison and Wynne paid $500,000 for the franchise in 1960. In 1984, they sold it for $80 million.

# JANUARY 29

## 1881

The stark monotony of the flatland northwest of Van Horn is broken by a dramatic series of canyons slicing through the rock. This is the place, Sierra Diablo, where fate chose the Indian and the white man to stage their last major battle in Texas.

On a frozen January morning in 1881, fifteen Rangers waited at a water hole for the day to break. In front of them lay a makeshift Apache camp with twelve warriors and eight women and children. The Rangers had tracked the Indians through the wilderness to this spot for two weeks.

As the sun broke over the multicolored rocks and the strange shapes that wind and rain had been creating for centuries, the Rangers attacked. The death and dying that followed was sudden and horrible; all twenty Indians perished. The Rangers gathered up the Indians' belongings and built a fire, and cooked breakfast. As the sun climbed higher over Sierra Diablo, the Rangers surveyed one of nature's great beauty spots, littered with bodies. The white men in that surreal setting on January 29, 1881, could not have known that this was the end; the Indian would fight no more in Texas.

# JANUARY 30

## 1890

Louis John Jordan was born January 30, 1890, on a farm near Fredericksburg; his life was a series of firsts.

At the University of Texas, he was captain of the Longhorn football team, and the first man from the South to be named to Walter Camp's All-America team.

When World War I broke out, Louis Jordan was one of the first volunteers. He was commissioned a first lieutenant, and on March 5, 1918, he became the first Texas officer killed in the First World War.

**Also on this date**, in the year 1915, Rice and Baylor met on the basketball court, the first competition of the fledgling Southwest Conference.

# JANUARY 31

1927

There are over eight hundred kinds of birds in Texas. We have a lot of room for them, and every conceivable kind of climate. So, when the state decided it had to have a state bird, the choice could have been very difficult. Our forefathers might have chosen the roadrunner, the jacana, the vermilion flycatcher, the cactus wren, the woodpecker, or the frigate bird.

But when the State Federation of Women's Clubs suggested a bird that "is a singer of distinctive type, a fighter for the protection of his home, falling if need be, in its defense, like any true Texan . . . ," the die was cast.

On January 31, 1927, the mockingbird was designated the state bird of Texas.

World War I: Barefoot boys watch as soldiers board a train in Galveston, heading "over there." (Rosenberg Library, Galveston)

# FEBRUARY

## FEBRUARY 1

### 1861

As the clock struck high noon on February 1, 1861, Sam Houston walked into the crowded House of Representatives to watch Texas legislators vote to secede from the Union. The governor had waged a losing battle to keep Texas in the Union; now he could only stand by and witness the formalities.

The presiding officer of the convention, Oran Roberts, read the Ordinance of Secession and then called for the vote. The first seventy men called voted "aye." Thomas Hughes of Williamson County was the first to vote "no." The final count was 167 for secession, 7 against. (A few weeks later the people would have the opportunity to vote on the decision of the convention [see Feb. 23]).

A group of women appeared on the floor and marched down the aisle waving a Lone Star flag, as the galleries broke into wild applause. Sam Houston, whose expression never changed throughout the proceedings, got up and quickly walked out.

### 1859

The famous old Menger Hotel in San Antonio opened for business on February 1, 1859. At one time travelers could buy the hotel's own beer, enjoy fresh turtle from the nearby San Antonio River, feast on wild game, and mix with the famous travelers. Robert E. Lee, U. S. Grant, and Philip Sheridan enjoyed the Menger, as did Teddy Roosevelt, O. Henry, and Sidney Lanier.

**Also on this date**, in the year 1845, Baylor University was founded.

## FEBRUARY 2

### 1848

The treaty that ended the Mexican War, the Treaty of Guadalupe Hidalgo, was signed February 2, 1848.

Among other provisions, it set the boundary between Mexico and the United States as the main channel of the Rio Grande River, to the southern boundary of New Mexico, then on west to the Pacific Ocean.

Early rendering of Baylor University, founded February 1, 1845. (Barker Texas History Center)

The U.S. Army stormed Chapultepec Castle in 1847 and brought Mexico to its knees. Engraving from *Album Pintoresco de la Republica Mexicana* (1848) by Julio Michaud y Thomas. (Institute of Texan Cultures)

# FEBRUARY 3

## 1959

Buddy Holly was a quiet and shy kid from west Texas who peered out at the world of the 1950s through black horn-rimmed glasses. But he changed the musical world with a drive and excitement that possessed him when he picked up a guitar.

From a radio station in Lubbock he went to Decca Records and promptly flopped. He tried again, and a little company in Clovis, New Mexico, recorded Buddy Holly and the Crickets' version of "That'll Be the Day." In 1957, the song went to number three on the charts. "Peggy Sue" went gold that same year; "Oh Boy!" was his third chart record of 1957.

When he was booked as a rock act into the Valhalla of rhythm and blues, the Apollo Theatre in New York, the management was amazed that Buddy Holly was a white man because "White men don't sing like that!" This one did, and for years to come his music was a major force in the rock music field.

After a show at the Surf Ballroom in Clear Lake, Iowa, Holly, singer Richie Valens, and J. P. Richardson, "The Big Bopper," chartered a plane to Fargo, North Dakota, the next stop on the tour. The snow was falling, there was a thirty-five-mile-an-hour wind, and the temperature was dropping to eighteen degrees as the plane took off. The Beachcraft Bonanza crashed five miles from Mason City. All aboard were killed. It was February 3, 1959 . . . the day the music died. Buddy Holly's success had lasted just eighteen months, but as Paul McCartney of the Beatles was to say, "Like rock and roll, Buddy Holly's music is timeless."

## FEBRUARY 4

### 1890

When the Civil War ended, the rumor swept Austin that Southern leaders were to be arrested and punished. The governor of Texas, from 1863 to the end of the war, was a sad South Carolina lawyer named Pendleton Murrah (see Nov. 5), who was sick with tuberculosis when he came to office and who was running out of time. On June 17, 1865, he headed for Mexico, and two months later died in Monterrey.

When Murrah ran, somebody had to take over. The job naturally fell to the lieutenant governor, Fletcher Stockdale. He became a kind of acting governor without portfolio, no doubt looking through the Capitol windows waiting for the Yankees to come and take him away.

Fletcher Stockdale, Civil War governor of Texas for thirty-four days. (Texas State Archives)

President Andrew Johnson appointed Gen. A. J. Hamilton to be the provisional governor, and he landed at Galveston on July 21. Fletcher Stockdale, who had served as Texas governor for thirty-four days, went home to Indianola. He lived for twenty-five more years and died on February 4, 1890.

## FEBRUARY 5

### 1848

Belle Starr had a face like a hatchet, but if you rode long enough and far enough, it looked better and better. She had a string of lovers, including her own son, and was apparently totally lacking in morals. It was only after her death that the dime-novel people managed to turn Belle into a Bandit Queen. In life she was an ugly scumbag who robbed people, stagecoaches, and anyone else when she got hungry.

She was born in Carthage, Missouri, on February 5, 1848. When Belle was still a child the family moved to Dallas. By the time she was twenty-three, she had two illegitimate children and was a bona fide horse thief. The first child may have been fathered by the outlaw Cole Younger, the second could have been anybody's—Belle was never sure.

She married a man named Sam Starr, and together they lived as cheap imitations of their future legend. Once they went to prison for a year, and upon release, Belle promptly ran away with another man. Sam, not being as liberated as Belle, killed the man, and Belle came back home. A year later a deputy who was a better shot than Sam, blew him away. On a cold day in 1889, as the grieving widow was returning home from a night with the boys, someone shot her in the back. She had lived almost forty-one very hard years.

## FEBRUARY 6

### 1897

Every region of the country has produced its share of badmen, but thanks to dime novels and the movies, Texas badmen seem to be the baddest of the bad. The Dalton Gang, for example, held up trains in Texas and Oklahoma Territory, even Kansas and Missouri, in the 1890s. Much of what we know about what they did came from the hand of one of the founding fathers, Emmett Dalton, who forty years after the fact wrote a best seller called *When the Daltons Rode*.

The Daltons made a huge mistake in October 1892 when they hit a bank in Coffeyville, Kansas, and everyone in the gang, except Emmett, got shot. Some hangers-on continued to use the name to create a little havoc in Texas until February 6, 1897, when Sheriff John L. Jones and a posse caught up with what was left of the gang in Menard County and shot and killed two members and captured another. The Dalton Gang ceased to exist, except in the mind of Emmett, who lived on to detail the adventures of the gang as he chose to remember them, probably not as they ever were.

## FEBRUARY 7

### 1855

Charles Siringo's life sounds like fiction. He was born on the Matagorda Peninsula on February 7, 1855, and grew up watching the Yankees and Confederates fight. The family moved east after the war. He once stowed away on a steamer and ended up in New Orleans, where he stabbed a boy and ran away again. He was a stowaway on the *Robert E. Lee* when it raced

the *Natchez*, and finally gave up his life as stowaway to work cattle in south Texas for the legendary Shanghai Pierce. He worked at several ranches and went on at least one cattle drive. He claims to have known Billy the Kid.

The wanderlust that consumed Charlie Siringo took him to Kansas in 1883, where he began to write. He produced *A Texas Cowboy*, the first authentic cowboy biography. J. Frank Dobie called him "an honest reporter." He wrote seven books in all—to, as he liked to say, "make money . . . lots of it." Charlie Siringo died in poverty, however, in 1928.

**Also on this date**, in the year 1908, Fred Gipson, author of *Old Yeller* and other popular novels, was born in Mason.

Author Charlie Siringo recounted his exploits as a cowboy. (Barker Texas History Center)

# FEBRUARY 8

### 1836

The Alamo gave Texas a little breathing room, and ironically most of the men who died there had spent their lives looking for that same kind of room.

David Crockett was a drifter, a frontiersman, a tall man quick with a quip and deadly with his rifle. After he was defeated in a try for another term in Congress, he told the voters to go to hell, and he would go to Texas.

Crockett and a dozen "Tennessee boys" set out "to fight for the right in Texas." He wrote his daughter a letter from San Augustine saying he ". . . would rather be in his present situation than to be elected to a seat in Congress for life."

T. R. Fehrenbach, who is as good a historian as Texas could want, says Crockett and his kind "rode to the scent of trouble . . . instinctive warriors, bred to arms if not formal warfare."

On February 8, 1836, Crockett and his boys arrived at the Alamo and settled in to meet their destiny. (See also Aug. 17.)

### 1895

King Vidor was born in Galveston on February 8, 1895, and by the time he was old enough to strike out on his own, a curious new industry was developing—the Movies.

Vidor was only eighteen when he broke into the infant industry as a director of a series of short subjects. In 1925, he got his big break when he was chosen to make a major silent film about the common soldier of the World War. His film, *The Big Parade*, was an enormous hit. After that classic, the Galveston boy was to spend forty years as one of Hollywood's top directors on fifty films: *Stella Dallas* with Barbara Stanwyck; *War and Peace* with Audrey Hepburn; and Gregory Peck and Jennifer Jones dying on the bloody rocks of the desert mountains in *Duel in the Sun* are just a few of his greatest efforts. Vidor was a tactician who mapped his shots as carefully as a general planned his battle strategy, and few people could match his technical skills behind a camera.

A few years before he died, Vidor said he hoped his films would be remembered as visions of yesterday that still seem fresh today.

Davy Crockett passed from legend to martyr at the Alamo. (Rosenberg Library, Galveston)

King Vidor, a native of Galveston, coaches actress Hedy Lamarr. (Barker Texas History Center)

# FEBRUARY 9

## 1914

On a night in 1942, a native son of Crisp, Texas, walked on the stage of the Grand Ole Opry and began to sing in a distinctive baritone that was to set the tone for country music for forty years.

Ernest Tubb was born in north central Texas on February 9, 1914. He got his start on a San Antonio radio station, and sang in honky-tonks and at roadhouses till he made the big time on the Opry with his first big hit, "I'm Walking the Floor Over You." He followed that with 250 songs that sold over 30 million records.

Tubb always wore a cowboy hat when he was on stage, and his band, the Texas Troubadours, always backed him. He was a member of the Country Music Hall of Fame when he died in 1984.

# FEBRUARY 10

## 1910

By 1910 the population of the High Plains was dropping and land values were near the bottom because of a prolonged drought. D. L. McDonald, a Hereford land agent, had seen one of the giant irrigation wells in New Mexico, and determined that would save his business. After all, land that could be watered by an irrigation pump would bring a very good price.

In late 1909, McDonald started digging a pit in Frio Draw south of Hereford. On February 10, he hooked a long, wide belt from a steam engine to the pump, threw the clutch into gear, and watched a steady stream of water surge out.

D. L. McDonald, a Pennsylvania native who tried pharmacy, land speculation, and car selling, became the Father of Irrigation on the Texas High Plains.

*Note*: The exact date of this event is disputed.

## 1850

The first railway in Texas, and the second west of the Mississippi, was the Buffalo Bayou, Brazos and Colorado. On February 10, 1850, Sidney Sherman obtained the charter and by 1853 the line was operating between Harrisburg and Stafford Point, a distance of twenty miles. The track became the original unit of the Southern Pacific system in Texas.

# FEBRUARY 11

## 1836

James Clinton Neill had a date with destiny, but missed it at the Alamo. In late December 1835, Lieutenant Colonel Neill was given command of a company of artillery during the Siege of the Bexar.

Early in the new year, Houston sent Jim Bowie to tell Neill to destroy all the fortifications and bring the artillery back to Gonzales to set up a new line of defense against the Mexicans. There was just one catch; the colonel had no teams to pull the artillery pieces through the mud, so he disobeyed the orders.

By February, Neill and Jim Bowie had decided not to abandon the Alamo. On the second, William B. Travis arrived and agreed it should be a key defensive position. A few days later, Davy Crockett and his Tennessee Mounted Volunteers came in.

Inside the walls it became apparent that the men were seeking out Travis and Bowie and Crockett and bypassing Colonel Neill. On the morning of February 11, 1836, Neill left the Alamo. One account says there was an illness in the family; another says the colonel took a twelve-day leave to attend to business. At any rate, he left and missed being a martyr.

Johanna Troutman, the Betsy Ross of Texas, was not a Texan and never even visited the state. (Barker Texas History Center)

Neill also missed the other great battle of the Revolution. He was wounded on April 20 and did not participate in the Battle of San Jacinto.

James Neill, the original Alamo commander, died nine years later in his bed at his home on Spring Creek in Navarro County.

**Also on this date**, in the year 1842, the crew of the *San Antonio* staged the republic's first, and only, mutiny.

## FEBRUARY 12

### 1899

You should read this one in about July or August.

On February 12, 1899, the temperature in Tulia dropped to 23 degrees below zero. Seminole tied the record thirty-four years later.

## FEBRUARY 13

### 1913

The Texas fight against Santa Anna's Mexico captured the imagination of the United States. People came from all over to join, and in many cases, to die for the cause of the Texans.

In 1835, when a battalion was being made up in Georgia, an eighteen-year-old girl was caught up in the patriotic fervor of the day. Johanna Troutman designed a standard for the Georgia boys, a white silk flag with a blue, five-pointed star. Beneath the lone star was the inscription "Liberty or Death." We know that flag flew at Velasco, and that Fannin carried it to Goliad.

On February 13, 1913, the Texas Legislature named Johanna Troutman as the Betsy

Robert E. Lee's last tour of duty for the U.S. Army brought him to Texas. (Barker Texas History Center)

Ross of Texas, the creator of the first Lone Star flag.

## FEBRUARY 14

### 1895

You don't have to live in Texas very long to realize that the weather is crazy, more often than not. The best proof of that occurred on February 14 and 15, 1895. The weather people call it an anomaly. Folks along the Gulf Coast probably had stronger, more colorful words after it started snowing and did not stop until Houston and Orange had received 20 inches, and Galveston had received 15.4 inches. There is no indication the weatherman forecast it; chances are he called for sunny and mild.

A snowy scene in Galveston, 1895. (Rosenberg Library, Galveston)

## FEBRUARY 15

### 1876

Texas has had about as many constitutions as it has had flags. Before we were a republic, there was the Constitution of 1824—the Mexican Federal Constitution that was patterned after the Spanish Constitution of 1812.

In 1827, the Constitution of Coahuila and Texas was drawn up. There was a proposed Constitution of 1833; the Constitution of the Republic in 1836; the Constitution of 1845, which provided for the government of Texas as a state, not a republic. In 1861 came the Secession Constitution; then in '66 the Reconstruction Constitution.

If you are still counting, there were two more. The 1869 Constitution, and the one we have today—the Constitution of 1876. It has been altered here and there, but still remains the fundamental law of the state. The last constitution of Texas was adopted February 15, 1876.

## FEBRUARY 16

### 1861

The war clouds that would produce the storm of the Civil War rolled into San Antonio on February 16, 1861. During the morning, Gen. David Twiggs surrendered all of the U.S. property to a committee of secessionists and the volunteers of Maj. Ben McCulloch.

Late that afternoon a wagon arrived carrying Col. Robert E. Lee, the commander of Fort Mason, one of the string of forts in Texas to help protect the frontier. It was at Fort Mason that Lee decided that if the Union was dissolved, he would return to his native Virginia. The colonel asked what all the commotion was about and was told he must resign his federal commission, then and there, and join the local volunteers, or get out of town. Lee told the rabble he owed his allegiance to Virginia and the Union, not to any revolutionary government in Texas.

That night Robert E. Lee paced the floor and the next morning left for home. Later he would be faced with turning that rabble, and the rest of the sons of the South, into an army.

**Also on this date**, in the year 1877, the people of San Antonio gathered to welcome the first train to their city.

## FEBRUARY 17

### 1889

Haroldson Lafayette Hunt, Jr., liked to say that he made his money in the oil business by listening to what people had to say. Mostly he did his listening around a poker table where he would win enough money to buy another lease. He said he would buy a lease on credit, sell it for a profit, repay the original note, then look for a poker game.

H. L. Hunt was lucky. He even decided to leave San Francisco a few days before the quake in 1906. He got lucky again in 1921 when he went broke in cotton speculation. That set of empty pockets forced him to try his hand in the Arkansas oil fields, and finally in east Texas.

It was in east Texas's heady young boom days that Hunt met Dad Joiner (see March 12, Oct. 3), a promoter who had found oil—and a string of creditors and lawsuits. Hunt offered to buy him out. Joiner took the deal and figured he had sold the big fellow a pig in a poke. That pig in a poke was a vast sea of oil that rested beneath east Texas. When he died, Hunt, the gambler, was worth several billion dollars. Only the IRS knew for sure. Before he passed away, Hunt told CBS's Mike Wallace, "We never really added it all up."

H. L. Hunt, Jr., was born February 17, 1889.

## FEBRUARY 18

### 1875

Cattle rustling was commonplace in Mason County in 1875 until Sheriff John Clark arrested nine men.

Before they could go to trial, four of the men escaped, and a lynch mob came for the other five on February 18, 1875. Of the five, two men were strung up and another was shot before the Texas Rangers showed up. A few days later the leader of the lynch mob was caught by twelve men wearing masks and black faces, a group that became known as the "Hoodoos." Another murder was committed and for over a year a blood feud roared through Mason County (see also Nov. 7). At least eighteen people died before the county shook off the war and settled down to law and order.

## FEBRUARY 19

### 1846

On December 29, 1845, President James K. Polk signed the Annexation Bill, and Texas became the twenty-eighth state in the Union. Because of certain formalities that needed attention, it was late in February before the republic officially ended.

At noon on Thursday, February 19, 1846, members of the Texas Legislature, elected officials, and citizens gathered in front of the capitol in Austin.

President Anson Jones said: "The Lone Star of Texas has followed an inscrutable destiny and has passed on to become fixed forever in that glorious constellation which all free men must revere and adore—the American Union."

The Lone Star came down, the Stars and Stripes went up the flagpole, a cannon fired, and Jones said, "The final act in this great drama is now performed. The Republic of Texas is no more."

## FEBRUARY 20

### 1807

Popular non-Texas literature frequently suggests that if the Alamo had had a back door, Texans would be speaking Spanish today. The

The railroad comes to San Antonio.

Alamo had a back door, and many of the defenders went out that door many times during the siege, and for reasons no one has adequately explained, most of them came back in to die.

James Butler Bonham, born in South Carolina on February 20, 1807, set out to become a lawyer. When the papers began to be filled with the story of the revolution in Texas, Bonham closed his law office, and by December 1835 he was in Texas. A month later he was in the Alamo.

Early in the siege Bonham was sent out that back door to find Col. James Walker Fannin and his reinforcements. Bonham found Fannin on February 29, and learned he was delaying his march to the Alamo. He hurried to Gonzales but found no more help there. On March 2, at the Guadalupe, people urged him not to go back. Young Bonham is supposed to have said, "I will report the results of my mission to Travis or die in the attempt."

At eleven o'clock in the morning of March 3, James Butler Bonham made a mad dash through the Mexican lines, weaving on his horse to dodge the bullets, so he could get back inside the Alamo with the news that they were all probably doomed.

Early on March 6 he died on a platform behind the church, killed by an eighteen-pounder that raked the walls. He was twenty-nine years old.

"The final act of this great drama is now performed." President Anson Jones lowers the flag and the Republic becomes a state, February 19, 1846. (Barker Texas History Center)

# FEBRUARY 21

## 1896

The Texas Rangers were on full alert: a special trainload of people was moving toward Langtry; Bat Masterson was on his way, too, and Judge Roy Bean had ordered a freight car load of beer. The excitement was caused by the proposed heavyweight championship fight between Bob Fitzsimmons and Irish champion Peter Maher. Originally the fight was to have been staged in El Paso, but boxing was illegal in the state, and three dozen Rangers had been sent west to make sure it did not happen.

The promoters looked around and took Roy Bean's suggestion to have the fight on an island in the Rio Grande. The fighters, the Rangers, and four hundred spectators got on the train and headed for the island. The closest they could get was Langtry, where the judge was waiting with dollar-a-bottle beer. The prices were outrageous, but after a hot train ride through the desert, the patrons paid.

Finally the two pugilists entered the makeshift ring, and the great fight was underway. The crowd sat in stunned silence as Fitzsimmons pummeled Maher for a good minute and a half, then knocked him out.

The disgusted fans went back to the Jersey Lily to drink the rest of Roy Bean's beer. The Judge remembered February 21, 1896, as the best day his bar ever had.

## 1794

Antonio López de Santa Anna was born at Jalapa, Vera Cruz, on February 21, 1794. He had at least nine lives. You have to look long and hard through history to find someone who had as many chances as Santa Anna, and who consistently blew them.

He was a war hero who was elected president of Mexico in 1833, then promptly told

Judge Roy Bean staged the Maher-Fitzsimmons fight on an island in the Rio Grande, 1896. (Western History Collections, University of Oklahoma Library)

the people they weren't ready for democracy and established a dictatorship. "The Napoleon of the West," as he liked to call himself, marched to Texas, called the Alamo battle "a small affair . . .", and was probably in his tent making love to a slave girl when Houston attacked at the battle of San Jacinto.

He got home in time to get his leg shot off in a war with France. That brought him back to the front in politics, and soon he was the dictator again. In his next war he managed to lose the battle of Buena Vista, then run back to Mexico City to lose again.

Santa Anna did not know when to quit and tried for one more shot at power, but he was caught and exiled. The old man came home to die in Mexico City at the age of eighty-two, no doubt hatching up another scheme to take over the government.

# FEBRUARY 22

## 1862

The gap between the Texas coastal islands at Aransas Pass is not only a beautiful spot, but a strategic one. The blockade runners used it to bring in guns and food, and to take out bales of precious cotton that kept the Confederate war effort alive. The islands were occupied by members of the Confederate infantry.

On February 22, 1862, the Yankees tried to take both the pass and the town on the southwest end of St. Joseph Island, but were driven back by riflemen. A year later 1,900 Federal troops overcame the 100-man Aransas garrison and burned the town to the ground.

# FEBRUARY 23

## 1836

As a handful of men were gathering in the Alamo, Santa Anna and his army leisurely moved toward San Antonio. On February 12, he was at the Rio Grande. On the twenty-first he was at Medina, eight miles away.

At the Alamo it was boring, all this waiting. There were jokes that the Mexicans weren't even coming. Daniel Cloud of Kentucky was stationed in the bell tower of the nearby San Fernando church looking out at a cold, deserted landscape. When Cloud reported that he thought he saw something, William Barret Travis sent a couple of scouts out to check. Dr. John Sutherland and John W. Smith got about a mile and a half away when they saw a line of dragoons in red coats and blue trousers carrying lances with sabres and carbines, and the cavalry smartly prancing in line in front of the artillery. There may have been as many as two thousand of them, and they looked like just what they were, the best army in the Western Hemisphere. Sutherland and Smith raced back to the Alamo where Cloud was now ringing the bell to signal the beginning of what turned out to be thirteen days of glory. It was the morning of February 23, 1836.

## 1861

The people of Texas headed for the polls on February 23, 1861, to vote on whether the state should leave the Union.

A Waco vigilance committee promised to hang every Lincoln sympathizer who voted to stay in the Union. In other places conservatives were simply told to get out of town for the election. Twenty-seven large counties' ballots were not even counted.

In the end the vote was three to one for secession. As the bells rang out from the churches, and guns were fired by happy demonstrators in the streets, Sam Houston turned to his wife and said, "Texas is lost."

# FEBRUARY 24

## 1836

Sometime on February 24, 1836, William Barret Travis sat down at a quiet spot in the Alamo and wrote one of history's most remarkable messages.

*To the People of Texas & all Americans in the world—*
*Fellow citizens & compatriots—*
*I am besieged, by a thousand or more of the Mexicans under Santa Anna— I have sustained a continual Bombardment & cannonade for 24 hours & have not lost a man— The enemy has demanded a surrender at discretion; otherwise, the garrison are to be put to the sword, if the fort is taken— I have answered the demands with a cannon shot, & our flag still waves proudly from the wall— I shall never surrender or retreat. Then, I call on you in the name of Liberty, or patriotism & of everything dear to the American character, to come to our aid, with all dispatch— The enemy is receiving reinforcements daily & will no doubt increase to three or four thousand in four or five days. If this call is neglected, I am determined to sustain myself as long*

*as possible & die like a soldier who never forgets
what is due to his own honor and that of his country—* Victory or Death

*William Barret Travis
Lt. Col. Comdt.*

## FEBRUARY 25

### 1836

Based on the available material, one is forced to conclude that history has been far too kind to James Walker Fannin, Jr. He attended West Point under an assumed name, but failed to graduate. He married and came to Texas to engage in the slave trade.

Fannin always seemed to look as if he was doing something during the critical January and February days of 1836, yet it is difficult to pin down exactly what he was doing. He was ordered once to cut a supply line, but decided not to. He recruited for the ill-fated Matamoros Expedition, but gave that up when he heard General Urrea had occupied Matamoros. He left James Grant and Francis Johnson and their elements of that expedition to be destroyed.

The first message from the Alamo calling for help reached Fannin on February 25, 1836. He started out for the Bexar on the twenty-eighth with several hundred men and some artillery. But he was only a few hundred yards away from Goliad when his wagon broke down and he decided not to go to help Travis.

Less than a month later he and his unfortunate men were martyred at Goliad. (See also March 19, 27.)

## FEBRUARY 26

### 1896

By the time he got to Texas A&M, Harry Warren "Rip" Collins was 6-feet 1-inch tall and weighed around 190 pounds. He was fast as a deer and could kick a football as far as anyone on either side of the Brazos.

In the 1915 game against Texas, he punted an incredible 23 times for a 55-yard average. He led the 1917 team with Ox Ford and Jack Mahan to an undefeated season, in which no one even scored on them in eight games.

After college, Rip Collins turned his energies to his other love, baseball. After a stint with Dallas in the Texas League, Collins went to the New York Yankees, where he spent eleven years with those great Yankee teams that included Babe Ruth and Lou Gehrig.

Collins retired in 1933 to join the Texas Rangers, and spent his later years in law enforcement.

Rip Collins was born in Weatherford, February 26, 1896.

## FEBRUARY 27

### 1917

John Connally was born in Floresville on February 27, 1917. He grew to be a tall, dashing, handsome man who had politics rushing through his every fiber. At the University of Texas he boasted he could call half the student body by their first names when he graduated. Along the way he had the good fortune to marry Idanell Brill, the University of Texas Sweetheart of 1938.

It was about 1936 that Connally met Lyndon Johnson, the National Youth Administration Director of Texas. It was the beginning of a relationship that would take them to the top of politics. Connally ran the early Johnson campaigns and laid the groundwork that would take him to the statehouse.

President John Kennedy named him secretary of the navy, but he resigned to come home to win the Democratic gubernatorial nomination in 1962. He served six years, and survived the shooting in Dallas that killed President Kennedy.

After his term as governor, Connally was back in national politics with the Nixon administration. He eventually became a Republican and ran for the presidential nomination. He spent millions, mounted a national campaign, and got just one delegate vote at the Detroit convention of 1980.

## FEBRUARY 28

### 1918

Texas, because of the image of the cowboy, has the reputation of being a wide-open, hard-drinking place. But the fact is we are not that kind of people. For a long time more of Texas was dry, under local option laws, than wet. That is to say, the people who lived like saints in certain counties had to go to other counties to buy booze. By the time Texas passed national Prohibition you could buy a drink legally in less than a dozen counties.

It was Congressman Morris Sheppard who introduced the law that was to become the Eighteenth Amendment. The state legislature

Prohibition in Texas: the feds destroying illegal liquor at Corpus Christi, 1931.
(Western History Collections, University of Oklahoma Library)

adopted it on February 28, 1918. It would be thirteen years before the country went on another binge, though old-timers will tell you that nothing really changed. As one said, the price of whiskey just went up.

## FEBRUARY 29

### 1836

History has forgotten him. He is not mentioned in the two great Alamo books, *A Time to Stand* by Walter Lord or *The Alamo* by Lon Tinkle, but the venerable old *Handbook of*

*Texas* says William Sanders Oury left the siege of the Alamo and lived to a ripe old age.

Oury came to Texas in 1833, and was in the Texas army in San Antonio in 1836. According to the *Handbook* he was sent out of the Alamo on February 29 with a message to General Houston. Oury was later given a land grant for serving in the army, and died at the age of seventy. The *Handbook* credits this story to Amelia Williams's *Critical Study of the Siege of the Alamo*.

**Also on this date**, in the year 1872, Henry Lindsley was born; he was a mayor of Dallas and the first national commander of the American Legion.

Employees at Texaco's Port Neches refinery, 1907. (Texaco)

# MARCH

## MARCH 1

### 1836

On a bitter cold March 1, 1836, an amazing thing happened. Thirty-two men, volunteers from Gonzales, fought their way into the Alamo to die.

When the call went out for help, there were not very many takers. By late in February it was apparent to almost everyone that the Alamo garrison was doomed. Still, when a courier came to the town of Gonzales, thirty-two men said good-bye to wives and children, fathers and mothers, and went to help Travis and Bowie and Crockett.

It was more than a great adventure, it was suicide. Some were teenagers. Some were wealthy. Some were poor. One had seven children and a blind wife. There was no common denominator for the thirty-two . . . except that at that time, in that place, one simply did what one had to do.

## MARCH 2

### 1836

On March 2, 1836, the Texas Declaration of Independence was signed at Washington-on-the-Brazos. One of the patriots who signed it was named Robert Potter. In his home state of North Carolina, Potter was not a model citizen. He maimed his cousin and another man in a fit of jealousy after they paid too much attention to his wife. He got two years in prison for that. Another time when he caught a man with his wife, Potter threw a rope around him, wrestled him to the ground, and castrated the man. The legend is that he then presented the man's family jewels to Mrs. Potter.

Potter got himself elected to the North Carolina House, but was expelled for cheating at cards.

He came to Texas in the summer of 1835 and plunged into the turbulent politics of the day. In March 1836 he signed the Declaration of Independence, and on March 2, 1842, exactly six years later, time ran out for Robert Potter. He was shot in the back as he jumped into Caddo Lake to escape a band of assassins. He was just forty-two years old.

**Also on this date**, in the year 1793, Sam Houston was born in Virginia.

The original building at Washington-on-the-Brazos where the Declaration of Independence was signed. (Barker Texas History Center)

## MARCH 3

### 1857

The Butterfield stage lines started in Tipton, Missouri, and Memphis, Tennessee. They joined at Fort Smith, Arkansas, and entered Texas around Sherman, then headed west to San Francisco. It took eight or nine days to cross Texas. Each coach would carry four to ten passengers with an average fare of two hundred dollars for the entire trip to the west coast. Mail went for ten cents a half-ounce. The Butterfield Mail and Stage Line was authorized by an act of Congress on March 3, 1857.

**Also on this date**, in the year 1836, Moses Rose chose to leave the Alamo rather than stay to fight to almost certain death.

## MARCH 4

### 1836

A first order of business for Texas after declaring independence was to form an army to protect that independence. On March 3 a delegate moved that a commander-in-chief be elected. Sam Houston's name was not mentioned, but he got up and made a speech anyway.

The next day the resolution was read that named Sam Houston commander-in-chief of all land forces of the Texian army, empowering him to proceed to take command and organize an army. Everybody voted for him except Robert Potter of Nacogdoches (see March 2).

A little over a month later Houston had indeed taken command and organized an army . . . and won the war!

**Also on this date**, in the year 1868, famous trailblazer Jesse Chisholm died of food poisoning in Oklahoma.

## MARCH 5

### 1836

Charles Goodnight was born in Illinois the night before the Alamo fell. When he was ten, his parents moved to Texas, and by the time he was twenty, he was a Ranger and Indian scout.

At the end of the Civil War, Goodnight and his friend Oliver Loving (see Sept. 25) established a cattle trail from Young County, Texas, to the Pecos and on to Fort Sumner, New Mexico, and into Colorado. Ten years after he blazed that famous trail, Goodnight settled down to ranching in the Panhandle. At one time he ran a hundred thousand cattle on a million acres of land.

Charles Goodnight was a tinkerer and an experimenter. Once he started breeding Polled Angus cattle to buffalo. The result was a "cattalo." Unfortunately, it combined the worst traits of the cow and the buffalo, so Goodnight turned his attention to other pursuits.

Cowboys still use one of his inventions—the chuck wagon, a traveling commissary. It was generally a large wagon that had a chuck box at the end—an upright cabinet with a hinged front that let down to make a table. The box held sugar and syrup, flour, salt, coffee, and the staple of the cowboy, dried beans.

Charles Goodnight lived a long, full life and died in Arizona when he was ninety-three.

1731

The Spanish built a string of missions across Texas to save Indian souls, and to discourage foreign adventurers. The mission brought the Word of God to the Indians and was also a school for the teaching of agriculture and primitive forms of industry. Some marvelous examples still remain in Texas.

The Mission San Francisco de la Espada was moved from east Texas to San Antonio on March 5, 1731. The chapel was one of the first of the San Antonio missions to be built of rock. It was rebuilt after the Civil War, but if you go there now you will see an image of St. Francis that has been in the chapel since the 1700s.

# MARCH 6

1836

It was between four and five in the morning of March 6, 1836, when the beginning of the end came for the Alamo defenders. With about 1,800 men, Santa Anna attacked the garrison. Manuel Fernandez Castrillón led the attack near the breach in the north wall, where Col. William B. Travis died beside a cannon. The Mexicans poured over the wall like sheep.

Martín Cós led the attack on the area that includes the chapel. Jim Bonham died there. David Crockett and his Tennessee boys were

Charles Goodnight was one of the Old West's great trailblazers. (Texana Collection, University of Texas)

Mission Concepción, San Antonio. (Houston Metropolitan Research Center, Houston Library)

assigned to defend the fence between the south wall and the chapel, and that cold, raw morning, they deflected the initial charge. When it was over, eyewitnesses say Crockett and his men lay dead with twenty-four Mexican dead around them.

Jim Bowie died in the room just to the right of the Alamo gate. He was propped up in bed, where he had been for the last few days of the siege because of illness.

Through it all Santa Anna stayed far away with the reserves and the regimental band that kept playing the Moorish battle march, the "Deguello"—the sign that no quarter was to be given.

None was, and by 6:30 on that Sunday morning in March, the Alamo had fallen. Six men were taken alive and executed before noon. Altogether, 183 Texans died and over 600 Mexican soldiers were killed or wounded. But the Alamo had bought Houston thirteen precious days to form an army.

Santa Anna, sipping a warm coffee after the battle, said to one of his captains, "It was but a small affair. . . ."

# MARCH 7

## 1862

John Bell Hood was born in Kentucky and graduated from West Point in the class of '53. For a while he served at forts in Texas under Robert E. Lee.

In April 1861, he resigned from the U.S. Army and joined the Confederate forces as commander of the Fourth Texas Infantry. A year later Hood was made a major general, and on March 7, he was placed in command of a brigade that would forever carry his name, "Hood's Texas Brigade." The brigade fought in at least twenty-four major battles of the Civil War, including Gettysburg (see July 1), Second Manassas and Antietam, Chickamauga and the Wilderness (see May 6).

When the war started there were 3,500 men in the brigade. In April 1865, when the war ended, there were only 557 officers and men left. Hood survived the war and died of yellow fever in 1879.

**Also on this date**, in the year 1901, the bluebonnet was named the state flower.

High-ranking Confederate officers from Texas. (Barker Texas History Center)

## MARCH 8

### 1912

Preston Smith was born March 8, 1912, in Corn Hill, Texas. He grew up to become the governor in 1969. In his campaign he sent 47,000 individually typed letters to people named Smith and asked, "Don't you think it is about time one of us was governor?"

## MARCH 9

### 1731

In an effort to populate Texas, the king of Spain decided to send some families from the Canary Islands.

Spain felt a permanent establishment of Spanish families would better support a claim to the land than would garrisons of soldiers. The islanders were chosen because of their pure morals, their high respect for women, and their industrious work habits; besides, there was so much poverty in the islands that most people were starving.

The governor gets ready to autograph a "sock it to me" poster. (Houston *Chronicle*)

By June 1730, twenty-five of a proposed four hundred families reached Cuba. Those twenty-five joined ten other families in Vera Cruz and started an overland march to San Antonio de Bexar to the safety of the Spanish presidio. On March 9, 1731, fifty-six people marched into the presidio. They became the first settlers of a new city in the colonies. In San Antonio today there are people who need not trace their lineage to the Old Three Hundred of Austin; they can go back to the Old Fifty-six from the Canary Islands.

## MARCH 10

### 1836

Samuel Price Carson is one of those odd characters who briefly walked across the stage of Texas history, flirted with greatness, and disappeared.

He was from North Carolina, and represented that state in Congress, but two years later moved to Arkansas. By 1836, he was in Texas, and was one of five delegates sent from Pecan Point and the Red River area to the convention at Washington-on-the-Brazos. He got there after the vote and signed the Declaration of Independence as a formality on March 10.

He must have made friends in a hurry, because a week later, on the seventeenth, he was nominated for president of the republic. The race was between David G. Burnet and Carson. Burnet won, but it was close. Carson missed becoming the president of the Republic of Texas by just six votes. He was then elected secretary of state and sent to Washington to find help for Texas. Two years later he died at the age of thirty-nine.

## MARCH 11

### 1890

During the 1930s Texans by the hundreds of thousands used to tune their radios to a Fort Worth station to hear the Light Crust Dough-boys sing and play Country and Western songs, and to hear W. Lee O'Daniel spiel out his homilies and poems that would put Edgar A. Guest to shame. "Pappy" became famous on that radio show and translated his name into a political force. He toured the state running for governor on a platform of the Ten Commandments and the Golden Rule.

Despite the fact that he had never paid poll tax, and thus could not vote for himself, a lot of other people did . . . and in 1939 W. Lee O'Daniel joined the parade of characters who have governed Texas. He was born in Ohio, March 11, 1890. (See also Aug. 4.)

Texas governor W. Lee O'Daniel in a pose reminiscent of Willie Stark. (Houston *Chronicle*)

### 1836

Nine days after the signing of the Texas Declaration of Independence, Sam Houston had gone as far as Gonzales, heading generally toward the Mexican Army.

Tradition has it that Monday, March 11, he was in the front yard of the Braches House, southeast of the town, when he got word that the Alamo had fallen. The general stood under an oak tree and sent orders out to start a retreat in the face of the advancing army of Santa Anna. The mass exodus that followed became known as the Runaway Scrape.

## MARCH 12

### 1860

Columbus Marion Joiner was born March 12, 1860, in Alabama. By the time he got to Texas he had made and lost a fortune in the land business.

At the age of seventy, he was a veteran of seventeen years of drilling dry holes. But "Dad," as folks affectionately called him, was a promoter, and he started offering ribbon clerks and farmers a chance to get rich in the dark days of the Depression. He sold pieces of the action for twenty-five dollars and up, and he sold a lot of pieces.

Eight thousand people drove out to an east Texas pasture to watch the well go down, and they danced in a shower of oil when it came in—opening the fabulous East Texas Oil Field.

Old Dad almost drowned in a shower of lawsuits from people who bought into the well. He filed for receivership, sold out to a man named H. L. Hunt (see Feb. 17) and left town.

## MARCH 13

### 1836

At midnight on March 13, 1836, Sam Houston ordered the army to start moving northeast out of Gonzales. Rear guard officers were assigned to look after the civilians of the town, who were following the army to safety. The civilians selected the few items they could take with them on the long retreat.

By morning the army was ten miles from town and behind them they could see smoke and hear explosions. It was not Santa Anna's cannon. It was whiskey barrels in the stores of the town exploding. Gonzales was burning to the ground. Santa Anna would find nothing there that he could use.

## MARCH 14

### 1845

In far-off Germany, people read the story of Texas with great interest following the fall of the Alamo and the dramatic victory at San Jacinto. Soon a floodtide of German immigrants was headed for this magic place.

On March 14, 1845, Prince Carl of Solms-Braunfels purchased a tract of land which lay fifteen miles above the town of Seguin. It contained "Las Fontanas," the beautiful Comal Springs, and five miles of the Comal Valley. The purchase price was $1,111. Soon the Prince was taking settlers there and giving them building lots and ten-acre plots of farmland. He named the place New Braunfels after his hometown.

**Also on this date**, in the year 1924, Charles Lindbergh began pilot training at Brooks Field in San Antonio.

## MARCH 15

### 1881

Many of the towns and cities of Texas exist today because the railroad came through. And many of the towns that populated the landscape died because the railroad missed them.

As the Texas & Pacific was heading across west Texas in the 1880s, the company promoted settlements. On March 15, 1881, agents for the railroad held the first auction for lots in the new townsite they hoped to come to life. One hundred seventy-eight lots were sold that day and the town of Abilene was on its way.

# ARMY ORDERS.

CONVENTION HALL, WASHINGTON, MARCH 2, 1836.

War is raging on the frontiers. Bejar is besieged by two thousand of the enemy, under the command of general Siezma Reinforcements are on their march, to unite with the besieging army. By the last report, our force in Bejar was only one hundred and fifty men strong. The citizens of Texas must rally to the aid of our army, or it will perish. Let the citizens of the East march to the combat. The enemy must be driven from our soil, or desolation will accompany their march upon us. *Independence is declared*, it must be maintained. Immediate action, united with valor, alone can achieve the great work. The services of all are forthwith required in the field.

SAM. HOUSTON,

*Commander-in-Chief of the Army.*

*P. S.* It is rumored that the enemy are on their march to Gonzales, and that they have entered the colonies. The fate of Bejar is unknown. The country must and shall be defended. The patriots of Texas are *appealed to, in behalf of their bleeding country.*                    S. H.

Sam Houston tried to bring order out of chaos during the Runaway Scrape. (Author's collection)

**Also on this date**, in the year 1912, Lightnin' Hopkins, of blues music fame, was born in Centerville.

# MARCH 16

### 1894

John Wesley Hardin was the son of a circuit-riding preacher who had named his boy after the greatest leader in the Methodist Church. Clearly, Dad had high hopes for his son.

John Wesley Hardin did become famous—as a cold-blooded killer who shot twenty-five to thirty men, mostly Mexicans and blacks or Yankees who did not say kind things about Texas. He spent sixteen of his forty-one years in prison, and the last time he was behind the walls at Huntsville, Hardin worked hard and learned the law. He was eventually pardoned from a twenty-five-year sentence for shooting a deputy. On March 16, 1894, Gov. Jim Hogg gave the state's most notorious killer a full pardon.

He stayed out of trouble for about a year and a half, till he was shot in the back of the head as he played dice in an El Paso saloon. (See also Aug. 19.)

# MARCH 17

### 1949

Frank Lloyd Wright, the grand old architect, took one look at it and decided it looked like a jukebox.

It stood there—tall, proud, but out of place, miles from the city. The Shamrock Hotel was oil wildcatter Glenn McCarthy's monument to overkill; a green roof, sixty-three shades of green inside, green ink in the desk pens, a swimming pool that was described as the world's largest, and the world's wildest opening celebration. McCarthy, who made millions drilling where the big money boys dared not go, built his hotel on the bald prairie because, as he put it, "Jesse Jones owned most of downtown anyway."

If the hotel was overdone and gauche, the opening party was the stuff Texas legends are made of. It cost $1.5 million; a sixteen-car train was rented to bring in guests; and 3,000 people were invited, including movie stars and Medal of Honor winners. The guests drank over 12,000 bottles of champagne. A live NBC radio show from the Emerald Room went off the air for a while because someone kicked the plug. It came back on in time to catch the star of the show saying a four-letter word before she realized she was back on the air.

When it was all over *Fortune* magazine said, "Texas had never seen anything like it." On the night of March 17, 1949, when the Shamrock opened, another chapter in Texas excess was written.

# MARCH 18

### 1937

The oil boom of the '30s brought thousands of people to east Texas. Little towns became bustling cities; schools strained to care for all the new students.

At New London, a brand new school building stood glistening in the sun on the morning of March 18, 1937. The school had recently changed from commercial to raw natural gas from the fields nearby. That gas started to accumulate from a leaking pipe under the building. No one knows how long it had been leaking when a spark from electrical equipment in the shop set it off, and in one mighty, ear-splitting blast, the New London school blew

When Glenn McCarthy (in pin-striped suit) opened his Shamrock Hotel on March 17, 1949, he invited Gene Autry and 174 other movie stars for a little party. (Houston Metropolitan Research Center, Houston Library)

up. The roof sailed into the air, then fell back on what was left of the building. When the rubble had finally been cleared away, workers recovered the bodies of 280 students and 14 teachers. It still ranks as the worst school disaster in the nation's history.

## MARCH 19

### 1836

In the spring of 1836, when Texas was fighting for its life, James Walker Fannin, Jr.,

missed his chance at glory because the fates were against him. His wagons broke down as he was going to help Travis at the Alamo.

On March 19, 1836, he was leading about four hundred men from Goliad to Victoria when his ammunition cart broke down in the middle of a field about two miles from Coleto Creek. The Mexican army under Gen. Jose Urrea found Fannin and surrounded his forces. The battle lasted throughout the day and into the night, but on the twentieth Fannin surrendered. The situation was hopeless. The surrender terms, according to the Mexican army, were unconditional. The Texans were

marched back to Goliad . . . and martyrdom.
(See also Feb. 25, March 27.)

1840

In an effort to sign a peace treaty with the
Comanches, a great meeting was called for the
Council House at San Antonio on March 19,
1840. Comanche tribes were asked to bring in
their white prisoners as a show of goodwill and
their intention to sign peace treaties with the
Texas government.

Many Indians came, but they brought only
one white prisoner. The angry Texans closed
up the Indians in the Council House and said
they would be held prisoner till all the whites
were released. A fight started and when it was
over, thirty-five Indians were killed, eight
were wounded, and twenty-nine others captured, including women and children. The
massacre of the Indians set off a new wave of
violence on the western frontier.

Searchers look for bodies in the wreckage of the
New London School. (San Antonio *Light* Collection, Institute of Texan Cultures)

A peace talk in San Antonio's Council House erupted into a bloody fight. From *Border Wars of Texas*
(1912), by James De Shields. (Institute of Texan Cultures)

## 1882

When Gov. William P. Hobby signed a bill in 1918 giving women the right to vote in primary elections, he presented the silver pen he used to sign the legislation to Minnie Fisher Cunningham. She had been born in New Waverly on March 19, 1882, thirty-six years before that historic day. Much of her early adult life was spent in the woman's suffrage movement. Later she was to run unsuccessfully for governor and U.S. senator. She devoted her lifetime to fighting for women's rights and crowned her achievements as the founder and first executive secretary of the League of Women Voters.

# MARCH 20

## 1687

René Robert Cavelier Sieur de La Salle was a novice priest, a farmer, a fur trader, and a bad navigator. He brought four ships and a couple of hundred colonists from France heading for the mouth of the Mississippi in 1684. On a bleak February day in '85 he arrived at Matagorda Bay—a slight miss on a chart, but a very large error in reality. Always the optimist, he set up a colony called Fort St. Louis, and began looking around the strange country.

His mistake gave France a claim to Texas territory, and alerted the Spanish that they had better pay closer attention to the land they were claiming, but largely ignoring.

After a tough time establishing a foothold, La Salle and his men left the fort and set out to find the real Mississippi River. On March 20, two years after he came to Texas, one of his own men shot him in the back at the Navasota River. The Indians got the colonists at Fort St. Louis, and only six members of the

original expedition lived to make it home to France.

## 1888

Coke Stevenson had to be a politican. He was born in a log cabin, named for a governor, started as a janitor at a bank, and ended up leaving to start his own bank. That is the stuff popular politicians are made of.

Born March 20, 1888, in Mason County, he became a millionaire lawyer-rancher-businessman-politician who was an extremely popular wartime governor of Texas.

The irony of Coke Stevenson is that he lost only one political race in his life, and that is primarily what people remember him for. He ran for the U.S. Senate in 1948 and got 494,104 votes. The problem is that Lyndon Johnson got 494,191 . . . including Box 13 in Jim Wells County that came in in "amended fashion" to give Johnson every vote but two.

Stevenson lived twenty-seven more years, a bitter man who never said much good about "Landslide" Lyndon or the Democratic party. (See also Aug. 28.)

Gov. Coke Stevenson participating in a Goodyear rubber exhibit in Houston. (Rosenberg Library, Galveston)

## MARCH 21

The "baddest" place in the Panhandle of Texas was Tascosa. You only went there if you were running from something or somebody, or if you wanted to get into trouble. Its bars and "hotels" did a land office business for a while, and the undertaker was busy, judging from the population of Boot Hill.

Popular Western movies and turn-of-the-century dime novels feature at least one good shoot-out. Old Tascosa's happened on March 21, 1886. In five minutes of smoke and bullets, four people died and were later buried in Boot Hill.

## MARCH 22

In the early days of the oil patch, the great fear was a blowout and fire. The tremendous pressure that was loosed when a vein of gas was hit could cause an explosion that would vaporize a rig.

That happened one time too many to well-driller James Abercrombie. He began to try to think up something that would prevent a blowout. The night after his third well blew up, Abercrombie did not sleep. He kept sketching out a device, a series of pipes and seals. The next morning, on March 22, 1922, he drew a sketch in the dirt floor of Harry

Equity Bar, Tascosa. (Panhandle Plains Museum)

Cameron's machine shop. They had some castings made at Howard Hughes's shop nearby, and within a short time had invented the Oil Well Blowout Preventer.

The oil field became a safer place after Jim Abercrombie's sketch that morning in Houston, and Harry Cameron's little machine shop became a million-dollar concern.

# MARCH 23

## 1893

The day Southern Methodist University opened in 1915, one of the seven hundred students who signed up for classes was Umphrey Lee. He was enormously popular and was elected the first president of the student body. After a career in preaching and teaching he came back to SMU to become its first chancellor and fourth president.

Umphrey Lee was born in Indiana on March 23, 1893.

**Also on this date**, in the year 1908, movie actress Joan Crawford was born in San Antonio.

# MARCH 24

## 1883

The real cowboys were indeed boys. Young men, mostly in their twenties, rode the horses and drove the cows. The work was ten to fourteen hours a day, every day, and few if any of the men escaped the cowboy life without a few broken bones. It was young man's work, not old, not even middle-aged men's work,

and it was probably far more romantic to read about than to do.

The pay was about a dollar a day, and all the beans you could eat. On March 24, 1883, twenty-four cowboys along the Canadian River called a strike asking for a 50-cents-a-day increase in wages. Before long, 325 cowboys from 7 Panhandle ranches had joined the strike. By April 3 some ranchers had raised wages to $1.68 a day. The strike eventually died, as the big ranchers knew it would. The men ran out of money, and had to eat—so they saddled up and went back to being a legend.

# MARCH 25

## 1843

Texans made one too many forays into Mexico on one kind of raid or another during the days of the republic. The great disaster was the Mier Expedition. It grew out of another disaster called the Somervell Expedition, which was designed to harass the Mexican army and raise hell in Mexican border towns. As the first expedition crumbled and the men started home, about three hundred stayed on and headed for the town of Mier. The day after Christmas in 1842 there was a fierce fight—over six hundred Mexicans were killed—but the Texans ran out of food and gunpowder, and surrendered.

What followed was a tortuous forced march toward a date with the executioner. In February, 170 Texans made a break from their captors, only to be caught again. This time President Santa Anna ordered them shot. However, Gov. Francisco Mexía refused to obey the order and instead said that every tenth man should die.

On March 25, 1843, an earthen jar was filled with beans—many white and seventeen black ones. The men walked up, stuck their hands into the jar and drew out beans. The seventeen who drew the black beans were blindfolded and shot. Only a handful of the men who survived that day lived to see Texas soil; most died in captivity.

# MARCH 26

## 1930

The first woman to sit on the Supreme Court of the United States, Sandra Day O'Connor, was born in El Paso on March 26,

1930. After she graduated from El Paso's Austin High School, she went away to Stanford University to become a lawyer.

After college Sandra married and settled down in Arizona for a life as a homemaker and an active politician. She was elected to the state senate in 1969, and three years later became the first woman ever elected majority leader in any state senate.

By 1974 the law had called her back and she became a superior court judge, then a member of the Arizona Court of Appeals. At one point the Republicans of Arizona wanted her to run for governor, but she declined.

She was serving on the Arizona Court of Appeals when a call came from the White House that President Ronald Reagan wanted her to fill the vacancy on the U.S. Supreme

Captives from the Mier Expedition drew for their lives. A black bean meant death. Engraving from *Journal of the Texian Expedition Against Mier* (1845), by Gen. Thomas J. Green. (Institute of Texan Cultures)

Court created by the retirement of Justice Potter Stewart. On September 26, 1981, Sandra Day O'Connor became the first woman to take the oath of office as a member of the Supreme Court of the United States.

## MARCH 27

### 1836

Col. James W. Fannin, the commander at Coleto (see March 19), had surrendered to the Mexican forces in hopes of saving his men from sure death in a fight he could not win.

Fannin's life was filled with tragic mistakes. On Palm Sunday morning, March 27, 1836, the Mexicans took the Texas prisoners captured at Coleto and started marching them away from the presidio at Goliad. One group marched toward the ford on the San Antonio River. A second group of men marched along the Victoria road, and a third column headed down the San Patricio road.

The men were in jaunty spirits; they thought they were going to be freed. Suddenly the Mexicans turned on them and started shooting at close range. One member of a group of Alabama volunteers who called themselves the "Red Rovers," realizing what was happening, said: "Let's die like men!" Then he shouted, "Hooray for Texas!" Three-hundred forty-two men were killed that day and forty-seven others were spared or managed to escape (see Jan. 15).

Less than a month later, when Gen. Sam Houston's men charged the Mexicans at San Jacinto, they shouted "Remember the Alamo. Remember Goliad."

## MARCH 28

### 1840

In popular fiction and the movies, Antonio Zapata is a dashing Mexican bandit, a Robin Hood of the Rio Grande. He was, in fact, a wealthy sheep rancher and Indian fighter until he was stripped of much of his wealth by the Mexican government. He then joined some Texans in the federalist movement in the lower Rio Grande, and at one point led a cavalry charge against the centralists.

Zapata and several Texans were captured, and on March 28, 1840, he was found guilty of treason by a military court. Mexico City decided to make him an object lesson. The next morning, Zapata's head was severed and placed on a pike in front of his house to show other would-be traitors what fate awaited them.

## MARCH 29

### 1896

There are three men named Robert Justus Kleberg who were prominent in Texas history. There was the one who fought at San Jacinto; there was his son, who took over for Richard King to run the great ranch; and there is the third, who, oddly enough, is called Robert Junior. He was a grandson of a war hero on one side of the family, and of the founder of the King Ranch on the other. He could not miss as a rancher, and he did not. Born March 29, 1896, young Robert studied agriculture and ranch management and put his knowledge to work just before the First World War. He ran the great ranch, as had his father before him, for more than fifty years.

The King Ranch covered nearly a million acres in several south Texas counties, as well as land in three states and five foreign countries. Under his direction the ranch developed a string of great racehorses, such as Assault, Middleground, and Bold Venture. Kleberg also introduced the Santa Gertrudis breed of beef cattle to the world.

In a ranch that understood breeding, Robert Justus Kleberg, Jr., certainly had breeding—and he lived up to his name. (See also Dec. 10.)

### 1899

James Allred fought the Ku Klux Klan and the big monopolies that invaded Texas, and became governor in 1935 to fight the Depression.

Allred was born March 29, 1899, in Bowie. After World War I he got into politics in north Texas and attracted attention fighting the Klan. As attorney general he campaigned against big business, and in 1934 he campaigned on a platform of no state sales tax, and was elected governor. He served from 1935 to 1939 as a Roosevelt Democrat, rubber-stamping the national recovery programs of the New Deal and putting them to work in Texas.

He left the governor's office to become a federal judge, and later got back into politics in an ill-fated try for the Senate against the hillbilly ambassador of the common man, W. Lee O'Daniel. After that, President Harry Truman appointed Allred to a federal bench. He died in 1959.

**Also on this date**, in the year 1836, the town of San Felipe was burned to the ground in order to prevent its falling into the hands of the Mexican Army. And on March 29, 1955, football player Earl Campbell was born in Tyler.

Robert Kleberg, Jr., of the King Ranch. (Barker Texas History Center)

# MARCH 30

### 1846

John Neely Bryan built a cabin in a clearing in 1841. That clearing would eventually become the Courthouse Square in Dallas.

Soon after he built the cabin, other families moved nearby. By 1844 there was a post office in the town. On March 30, 1846, the first legislature of Texas carved out parts of Nacogdoches and Robertson counties to create Dallas County. It is assumed the legislators named it for George Dallas, who was the vice-president of the United States. Some argue that Dallas was named for the Dallas brothers, James, Walter, and Alexander, who served in the army of the Republic of Texas.

### 1870

On March 30, 1870, President U. S. Grant ordered that the word "provisional" be dropped from the title of Texas officeholders. That ended military rule in Texas, and in effect meant Texas had reentered the Union following the late unpleasantness.

# MARCH 31

### 1878

Despite the bigotry and controversy that surrounded him, Jack Johnson was one of the greatest heavyweight fighters of all time. He was born in Galveston on the last day of March in 1878 and grew up to be a big, strapping hulk of a man, who built his muscles by working odd jobs at the docks and his reputation by never losing a fight.

Before long, promoters got the big black man some real boxing matches that paid him a few dollars. It was not easy for a Negro to get matches in the years after the turn of the century, but Johnson was so good he simply could not be ignored. As his reputation grew, it became impossible for the boxing establishment to ignore him, and finally on the day after Christmas 1908, Jack Johnson walked into the ring with Tommy Burns, the world's heavyweight champion. When it was over, Burns had been beaten to a pulp, and Johnson was the new champion.

He held the crown for nearly eight stormy years. He was black, and that did not set well with some folks; moreover, he was loud and flamboyant, and he liked to marry white women.

The boxing establishment made a frenzied search for someone to beat Jack Johnson—someone white. For seven years Johnson beat one Great White Hope after another, till he ran into the slashing fists of Jess Willard in 1915.

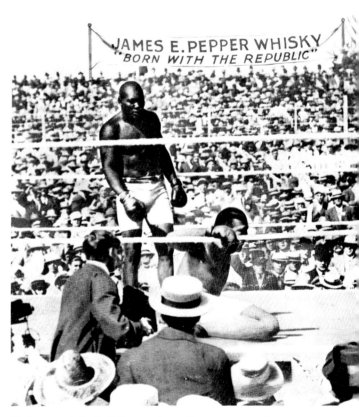

Galveston's Jack Johnson knocks out Jim Jeffries in 1910 to maintain his World Heavyweight Championship title. (William F. English/Institute of Texan Cultures)

Legal tender, the Republic of Texas, 1836–1845. (Author's collection)

# APRIL

## APRIL 1

### 1833

The inauguration of Antonio López de Santa Anna as president of Mexico was to have taken place on April 1, 1833, but Santa Anna didn't make it for the oath of office. In fact, he didn't even come within shouting distance of Mexico City for quite some time.

This seems quite an inauspicious way to launch an administration, but Santa Anna was no fool, at least not in this stage of his career. A storm of controversy had accompanied his rise to the presidency, and Santa Anna was determined to let it blow over with a minimum of damage to his prestige. He pleaded illness on April 1, and a harried vice-president carried out the duties of the chief executive while Mexico City raged with threats and counterthreats.

Sure enough, the storm died down and the president who didn't even make it to his own inauguration returned to the capital and was greeted by the cheers of a people who claimed they would die for him, and did.

## APRIL 2

### 1932

Bill Pickett was about 5 feet 9 inches tall and weighed no more than 165 pounds. But when he went flying off a horse and onto the horns of a steer, he took on the proportions of a giant who could sling a mad animal to the ground.

The black man from Liberty Hill on the south San Gabriel River did not invent bull-dogging—he simply took it to an art form. He would leap from his horse, grab the steer horns in each hand, and twist the head so he could bite the animal's tender lip and hold on till the steer fell to the ground.

The Miller Brothers' 101 Wild West Show featured Bill and his bulldogging. The crowds went wild, and Pickett was a star. No one bites a steer on the lip to bring 'im down any more, but old-time cowboys still talk about "how Pickett done it."

Bill Pickett was run down and trampled by a wild horse, and died on April 2, 1932. Forty years later he became the first Negro named to the National Cowboy Hall of Fame.

### 1957

"I ran for statewide office so many times, the voters finally elected me just to get my name off the ballot." That is what Ralph Yarborough said a few years ago at a political fish fry in Corpus Christi. "Smilin'" Ralph has been frying political fish for most of his adult life.

A respected Austin lawyer and jurist, Yarborough was bitten by the political bug before the Big War. He lost a race for attorney general and went away to fight with the Ninety-seventh Division. After the war he came home and plunged into politics again. He climbed on the back of flatbed trucks and spoke on every street corner in 1952, urging voters to throw Allan Shivers out. Yarborough lost. In

'56 he was back pressing the flesh, asking voters to elect him governor instead of Price Daniel, but again lost.

A year later he was back on the stump campaigning; this time for an even bigger prize, the U.S. Senate seat that Price Daniel had given up to become governor. On April 2, 1957, Ralph Yarborough finally won a statewide election, and served as a U.S. senator for nearly thirteen years.

Ralph Yarborough, the quintessential Texas politician. (Houston *Chronicle*)

# APRIL 3

## 1969

If you are named Maximilian Justice Hirsch, you should grow up to be a jurist or a banker, but Max Hirsch only wanted to be a jockey. He loved horses, and at the age of twelve, ran away from his native Fredericksburg in the hill country to exercise horses and later become a jockey. He rode a few winners before he became too heavy, and was forced into the profession that was to bring him fame as a trainer of horses.

Max Hirsch was without equal. He trained horses that won 1,933 races. For many years he trained thoroughbreds at the King Ranch. Three of his horses won the Kentucky Derby. The great Assault won the Triple Crown in 1946. Bold Venture won the Derby and the Preakness in '36, and Middleground won the Derby and the Belmont Stakes in 1950.

He was eighty-eight years old when he saddled Heartland at Aqueduct and watched it win going away. The next day, April 3, 1969, Max Hirsch died. The following year he was elected to the Texas Sports Hall of Fame.

## 1864

No one in Texas drove a stagecoach like Henry Skillman. He would drape himself with six-shooters and Bowie knives and roar through Indian country.

When the Civil War came, he became a Confederate scout. Skillman crossed between the Pecos and El Paso at will, carrying messages and spreading false rumors of troop movements that kept the Yankees off balance.

Finally a special force of Federal troops was commissioned to find Henry Skillman, the Great Scout. On April 3, 1864, the Yankees caught up with their prey at Spencer's Ranch in Presidio County, and shot him to death.

# APRIL 4

### 1888

There were fewer than a thousand people living in the little Hill County town of Hubbard on April 4, 1888, when Tristram Speaker was born. But if a thousand kids had been born there that year, none would have matched Speaker, because he was one in a million, a natural baseball player who was one of the best ever to play the game.

Tris began playing professional baseball with Cleburne in the old North Texas League for fifty dollars a month; he was only eighteen years old. Within a few years he was in the big leagues for a career that lasted twenty-two years. The "Gray Eagle," as the fans called him, patrolled a shallow center field and dashed back and to the left and right to display a defense seldom seen in other early baseball men. At the plate he stroked 115 home runs, stole 433 bases, and had a lifetime batting average of .344.

Speaker was named the Most Valuable Player in the American League in 1912. He led the Boston Red Sox to World Series wins in 1912 and 1915, and managed the Cleveland Indians to a series victory over the Brooklyn Dodgers in 1920.

When the Baseball Hall of Fame was opened in Cooperstown, New York, in 1936, Tristram Speaker of Hubbard, Texas, was the seventh player installed.

# APRIL 5

### 1874

Jesse Jones was born in Tennessee on April 5, 1874. As a young man he moved to Houston to get involved in the east Texas lumber

Tris Speaker was the seventh player named to the Baseball Hall of Fame. (Texas Sports Hall of Fame)

business, and before he died, he, more than anyone else, had built Houston into a great city.

For a while it seemed that every building downtown or every expensive bit of real estate was controlled by "Uncle" Jesse. He owned the afternoon newspaper, controlled the bank with the most clout, and was a political power-broker. Then FDR called him to Washington for a number of jobs before making him secretary of commerce.

Jones was a powerful man who used his power to build Houston. Thirty years after his death, people in Houston who knew him still speak of Jesse Jones with a combination of fear and respect.

From his beginnings in the lumber industry, Jesse Jones (left) rose to become a leading financier and a shaper of the New Deal. (Houston Metropolitan Research Center, Houston Library)

self the inspector general and then the commander of the Texas Army. In the Lamar administration he served as secretary of war.

His meteoric rise was given new impetus by the Mexican War, in which Johnston was cited for meritorious service. After the war he took command of the star-studded Second Cavalry, which had a myriad of future generals on its staff. As a new war loomed on the horizon, Albert Sidney Johnston found himself in California as commander of the U.S. troops there.

Johnston offered his services to the Confederacy and was given the rather staggering task of commanding all troops west of the Appalachians. In the early stages of the war, he suffered several reverses but attempted to stem the tide by savagely counterattacking at Shiloh on April 6, 1862. Although his forces won the battle, Johnston was mortally wounded. The loss suffered by the South was felt most keenly by Texans.

Johnston is buried in the State Cemetery in Austin.

**Also on this date**, in the year 1830, Mexico enacted a law to stop American immigration to Texas. It was a prime seed leading to the revolution six years later.

## APRIL 6

### 1862

The legendary status accorded Civil War generals has obscured their careers both before and after 1861–65. Albert Sidney Johnston, for example, was thought of by many of his contemporaries as the finest general in the Confederate service—but his greatest service was rendered to the Republic of Texas.

Johnston had arrived in Texas in 1836, a desolate man after the death of his wife. A West Point graduate, Johnston found him-

## APRIL 7

### 1911

The Galveston *Daily News* said in 1895 that the Grand Opera House on the island was ". . . the grandest temple of Thespis to be found in the broad confines of Texas, or the South West."

Indeed the old Opera House had that kind of reputation, built on its long list of hit plays and musicals and the talented people who came to the island to perform. Maude Adams,

Gen. Albert Sidney Johnston died at the battle of Shiloh, April 6, 1862. (Author's collection)

Lillian Russell, George M. Cohan, and Jan Paderewski thrilled theatre-goers. John Philip Sousa brought his great band to play the stirring marches. But based on all accounts, the greatest night came on April 7, 1911, when the legendary Sarah Bernhardt appeared in *Camille*. It was her farewell performance during her final tour of America.

# APRIL 8

## 1864

Throughout the War Between the States, the Union government expressed a desire to wrest Texas from the Confederacy and to re-establish Federal control. Several punitive expeditions were mounted at various points; certainly the most grandiose of these was Maj. Gen. Nathaniel Banks's Red River Campaign, which shimmied up the Red in the spring of 1864 in hopes of capturing Shreveport and then striking into east Texas.

On April 8, 1864, a hastily assembled Confederate army composed of Texans, Louisianans, Missourians, and Arkansans struck at General Banks at Mansfield, just forty miles south of Shreveport. The Confederate department commander, Edmund Kirby Smith, had ordered his field general, Richard Taylor, not to attack, but Taylor had learned his trade under Stonewall Jackson and was therefore not inclined to be cautious. Banks, with his army poorly deployed along a narrow road, never had a chance. He was so disheartened by his defeat that he gave orders to retreat and forget the whole expedition.

As twilight fell on the battlefield at Mansfield, a courier from Kirby Smith rode up to Taylor, bearing an order not to attack. Taylor read it and beamed to the courier, "Too late, sir. The battle is won." Texas had been saved.

# APRIL 9

### 1856

Robert E. Lee spent much of his military career in Texas. He first came to Texas as a young officer on his way to fight in the Mexican War. He was back with Albert Sidney Johnston's regiment and was stationed in Texas when he made his decision to go home to Virginia and fight for the Southern cause (see Feb. 16).

On April 9, 1856, Lt. Col. Robert E. Lee arrived at Camp Cooper, a desolate post in north central Texas that was to be his home for over a year. He battled the Indians, bandits, and the loneliness of a frontier fort before he was called to San Antonio in July 1857.

A few years later Lee was to become the very soul of the South; and on April 9, 1865, nine years to the day after he came to Camp Cooper, Robert E. Lee met U. S. Grant at Appomattox to end the Civil War.

### 1965

Judge Roy Hofheinz, the former boy mayor of Houston, opened his dream stadium to the world on April 9, 1965. It was officially titled the Harris County Domed Stadium, but the judge named it the Astrodome, and that is the name the world uses today.

THE LAST VISIT
TO
AMERICA

Madame Sarah Bernhardt

DIRECTION
OF
WM. F. CONNOR

Sarah Bernhardt came to Galveston on her last American tour. (Texas Collection, Baylor University)

On that April day the judge called it the "eighth wonder of the world," and the president of the United States sat in a special box to see the New York Yankees and the Houston Astros play the first game. Mickey Mantle finally settled it by hitting a towering home run in the twelfth inning to give the Yanks a 2-1 win over the Astros.

That first indoor baseball stadium became a model for sports stadiums to come.

## APRIL 10

### 1937

When a special election to fill the unexpired term of U.S. Rep. James Buchanan of the Tenth Congressional District was called, nine Texans signed up to run. One was a former high school debate coach who had given up teaching to run the National Youth Administration in Texas. Young Lyndon Baines Johnson ran on a platform that put him strongly in the corner of the New Deal programs of FDR.

Johnson won on April 10, 1937. It was the beginning of a political career that would carry him to the presidency twenty-six years later.

**Also on this date**, in the year 1962, major league baseball came to Texas with the Houston Colt .45s' 11-2 victory over the Chicago Cubs.

## APRIL 11

### 1819

Margaret Moffette Lea was born near Marion, Alabama, on April 11, 1819. She was

The skeleton of the Eighth Wonder of the World—the Harris County Domed Stadium, aka the Astrodome. (Gulf Photo)

described as having a winning manner, fair complexion, intense eyes, and brown, wavy hair that fell in long loops.

She was at the New Orleans docks in 1836 to cheer the hero of San Jacinto as the wounded and sick Sam Houston arrived. Margaret and her classmates thought the general to be a most romantic figure.

Three years later she saw him again at a party in Alabama. He was the forty-six-year-old president of the Republic of Texas; she was twenty-one. They met and fell in love, and soon Margaret was moving to Texas to be the wife of one of the most famous men in the Americas.

It was a marvelous love affair. She wrote him long, loving poems, and he composed wonderful love letters to her. After three years of the marriage the Houstons' first child, Sam junior, was born. There were to be seven others—Nannie, Nettie, Maggie and Mary, Temple Lea, Andrew Jackson, and Willie.

Houston died at the age of seventy. His last words were, ". . . Texas! Texas! Margaret!" Four years later, at the age of forty-eight, Margaret Moffette Lea Houston died of yellow fever.

# APRIL 12

## 1923

Lucille Ann Collier was born in Chirino on April 12, 1923. As a young child, she suffered from rickets and took up dancing to rehabilitate her legs. Later, after the family moved west, she tap-danced in bars and was discovered by a movie talent scout.

By the time she broke into films in 1937 the tall, talented woman had changed her name to something that looked better on the theatre marquee. The world knows her as Ann Miller.

Throughout World War II she made one low budget movie after another. At MGM she danced with Fred Astaire in *Easter Parade*, but the studio never fully utilized her talents. One major problem was that at 5 feet 6½ inches, she was a bit tall for the great male dancers of the screen. After the era of the Hollywood musicals came to an end, Ann Miller moved to Broadway where she became an even bigger star in *Mame* and *Sugar Babies*.

# APRIL 13

## 1861

At Fort Sumter in Charleston Harbor, the U.S. garrison was dead-tired, as Texas senator Louis Wigfall came to offer surrender terms.

Wigfall was a Marshall lawyer who became a firebrand Texas senator opposed to President Lincoln. He worked hard for secession, and when trouble broke out at Charleston, he rushed there from Washington to act as an aide to Gen. P. G. T. Beauregard during the bombardment.

The fury that for months had been shouted words and whispered oaths became a full-blown war with the bombardment of the fort. The vast majority of Texans welcomed the war, but before it was over it would exact a terrible toll.

Fort Sumter surrendered on April 13, 1861.

# APRIL 14

## 1958

He started to play the piano when he was three. At the age of twelve he was a piano soloist with the Houston Symphony, and when

The Dust Bowl: No place to root . . . no place to roost. (Barker Texas History Center)

Van Cliburn, winner of the first International Tchaikovsky Piano Competition in Moscow. (Texas Collection, Baylor University)

The bombardment of Fort Sumter, April 13, 186[
signaled the beginning of the War Between the States. (Author's collection)

he was twenty-four they gave him a ticker-tape parade down the streets of New York.

Van Cliburn was born in Louisiana, but at the age of six moved to Kilgore. His young life was one piano triumph after another, until he decided to go home to care for his ailing mother.

It was in Kilgore that his Juilliard teacher, Rosina Lhévinne, talked the gangling Texan into entering one more contest—the prestigious International Tchaikovsky Piano Competition in Russia.

The American in Moscow had to overcome more than the best pianists in the world: He had to beat a lingering cold war, and a distrust of Americans. Certainly an American could not win this prize of prizes. Forty-eight competitors from nineteen countries came to Moscow. After furious competition, six people were left in the finals. The American walked on stage, sat down at the piano to play Tchaikovsky's Piano Concerto No. 1, Rachmaninoff's Concerto No. 3, and a special piece by Kabalevsky. When he finished, the crowd began to chant "First prize!" even though the other competitors had not yet played.

On April 14, 1958, Van Cliburn won the first-prize gold medal. Khrushchev smothered him in a bear hug. Eisenhower invited him to the White House—and a tall, shy piano-player helped bring two worlds together with his magic talent.

### 1935

On the afternoon of April 14, 1935, the sky began to turn brown, then black, as a huge dust storm bore down on the Panhandle. Pampa seemed right in the middle of the massive cloud that roared in from eastern Colorado.

To some it seemed to be the end of the world. People rushed to church to pray; others stuffed cloth into the cracks under the door

and around the windows to keep out the choking dust. At one house in Pampa, a young folk singer, Woody Guthrie, calmly sat down, looked out the window at the swirling dust, and wrote the classic song, "So Long, It's Been Good to Know You."

## APRIL 15

### 1836

The night of April 15, 1836, Sam Houston's little army was moving up the Brazos toward the ferry at Groce's Plantation. The Runaway Scrape (see March 11) was losing its steam. The army was grumbling, itching for a fight and fearful Sam Houston was leading them on a permanent retreat. They knew that soon they would approach a fork in the road. To the left the column would march to Nacogdoches. If they turned right they would head for Harrisburg, where Santa Anna's army was believed to be.

The legend is that when the sun rose the next morning the men turned right without being told to.

## APRIL 16

### 1947

On a cool, clear spring morning in Texas City there was not a cloud in the sky—just a thin wisp of smoke that rose near the Monsanto Chemical Company plant. The word soon spread that it was not the plant that was on fire, but a ship called the *Grandcamp* docked at the nearby wharf. Soon the fire was blazing and the smoke that rose into the April sky was more orange than black or gray. By nine in the morning the firemen had pulled back because the ship's steel deck was turning red-hot. At twelve minutes after nine the *Grandcamp* blew up in a fierce explosion that shook Galveston and rattled dishes in homes forty miles away in Houston.

The anchor of the ship was thrown a mile and a half from the docks. Pieces of metal from the ship tore like hot shrapnel through other ships at the dock, and through the chemical plant next door. Within minutes of the explosion, Texas City looked like a scene out of Dante's *Inferno*. Fires were everywhere, and the dead and the dying littered the streets. As one plant after another caught fire, there were more explosions, and at 1:15 the next morning the ship the *High Flyer*, loaded with 900 tons of ammonium nitrate, blew up.

When the fires were finally out, Texas City had lost 200 businesses, over 3,000 homes, and 398 souls, with 178 people missing and never found. The Texas City Disaster of April 16, 1947, remains the worst fire and explosion in the nation's history.

## APRIL 17

1871

On April 17, 1871, the legislature of Texas voted to establish a college. Its aim was to offer white male students, at the lowest possible cost, an education. That education was

Fires rage out of control at the Texas City dock in the disaster that claimed 576 lives. (Rosenberg Library, Galveston)

to focus on agriculture and the mechanical arts. The charter spoke of classical studies as well, and of military tactics.

On October 4, 1876, Texas A&M opened its campus near Bryan. The college had a faculty of six, and a student body of nearly forty.

**Also on this date**, in the year 1929, the League of United Latin American Citizens (LULAC) was founded in Corpus Christi.

# APRIL 18

## 1847

The battle of Sierra Gorda in the Mexican War doesn't rate as much space in the history books as the more decisive Chapultepec, but it is significant for two reasons. One, it produced one of the great battle reports in history. At the end of the battle between Gen. Winfield Scott's forces and the troops of Santa Anna, one account said simply, ". . . Mexican forces 15,000: Prisoners, killed, wounded and run away, 15,000."

And it certainly changed Santa Anna's life, for the American forces captured his carriage, which contained cash, important papers, a hot meal, and the general's wooden leg.

# APRIL 19

## 1836

Sam Houston and Secretary of War Thomas Jefferson Rusk stood across the bayou from the smoking ruins of Harrisburg on April 19, 1836. Both men knew the decisive battle with the Mexican army was at hand. Each decided to draft a communiqué.

Rusk wrote:

*A few hours from now will decide the fate of our Army: and what an astonishing fact it is, that, at the very moment when the fate of your wives, your children, your homes, your country, and all that is dear to a free man are suspended upon the issue of one battle, not one-fourth of the men of Texas are in the army!*

Rusk went on to plead for volunteers to ". . . rise up and march to the field!"

While Rusk looked in vain for recruits, Houston chose to defend himself against the charge that he was beating a cowardly retreat from the Mexican army. He said,

*. . . we must act now or abandon all hope. Rally to the standard, and be no longer the scoff of mercenary tongues! . . . We must go to conquest. It is wisdom growing out of necessity to meet and fight the enemy now.*

Two days later the climactic battle came at San Jacinto.

# APRIL 20

## 1842

On April 20, 1842, something happened at Biebrich-am-Rhein in Germany that had great significance for Texas. The Adelsverein, or Society of Nobility, was founded to provide assistance for the immigration of thousands of Germans to the Republic of Texas.

In Germany at that time there was high unemployment in the midst of a terrible depression, and the political climate was less than stable. Political activists who were deemed radical were encouraged to immigrate; and farmers and craftsmen by the thousands came to set up communities in the exciting new world of Texas.

From that start in 1842 came a flood of German immigrants who settled Texas and became a distinct part of its character.

**Also on this date**, in the year 1872, an Indian battle at Howard's Well led to the government's cancellation of hunting permits for Indians.

# APRIL 21

### 1836

On April 20, 1836, Sam Houston wrote that "the enemy has occupied a piece of timber within rifle shot of the left wing of our army." When the sun came up on the twenty-first, the general and his men were camped in the timber between the Lynchburg Road and Buffalo Bayou, with the bend of the bayou and the marshes of the San Jacinto River off to the left.

Houston reported his battle strength at 783. Another report states there were 835 Texans. The Mexican force was put at "upwards of 1,500 men."

At 3:30 in the afternoon, as the Mexican army rested, the Texans charged, and the battle was won in just eighteen minutes. However, the killing continued till nightfall, with 630 enemy killed, 208 wounded, and 730 Mexicans taken prisoner.

It was one of history's most improbable and impressive battles. Against impossible odds, a gang of farmers and shopkeepers defeated a well-equipped, well-trained army, and Texas won her freedom.

# APRIL 22

### 1540

Cabeza de Vaca wandered through Texas for six years as a slave of the Indians. After his return to civilization he brought back stories of golden cities he had heard about repeatedly from the Indians. The Spanish government commissioned Francisco Vásquez de Coronado to lead an expedition to find the so-called Cities of Cibola. Coronado gathered 1,500 men, horses, mules, cattle, and sheep for a great march northward.

On April 22, 1540, the Coronado expedition set out from Culiacán, Mexico. Coronado was to wander for two years and finally return a broken man, but his journey through the Panhandle and High Plains was to give Spain a solid claim to the land that was to become Texas. (See also Sept. 22.)

### 1892

The first class to graduate from the University of Texas Medical Branch at Galveston received their diplomas on April 22, 1892. The event took place at Harmony Hall at Twenty-first and Church Street. Three men had "passed satisfactorily the course and examination." Degrees were conferred on Thomas Flavin, Houston Thomas Guinn, and Jesse P. Hendrick.

# APRIL 23

### 1862

Before the impact of the horror of the Civil War set in, it was, for those who fought it, a romantic and honorable undertaking. The letters sent home by the young men before a battle, and the attitude of the people who sent them off to war, seemed to lack reality.

On April 23, 1862, Henry Orr, an Ellis County farmer, wrote his sister this letter as he marched away with Parsons' Texas Cavalry:

*The people generally are patriots and the ladies in particular are very patriotic and everywhere seem to flock to the road to cheer us on our way with flowers.*

*We passed a splendid mansion today, in front of which was erected a beautiful floral arch with a flag upon it. Ladies said, "Three cheers for the flowers and the flag", which was responded to in a spirited manner.*

*We then marched underneath it with our beavers off by twos. . . . We silently passed away, Bugler Wilson playing a Military air. . . .*

Private Henry Orr served out the war as a cavalryman and fought at the Battle of Mansfield (see Apr. 8).

Civil War veterans, Jasper County, c. 1900. Young soldiers' hopes turned to bittersweet memories of old men. (Sam Houston Regional Library)

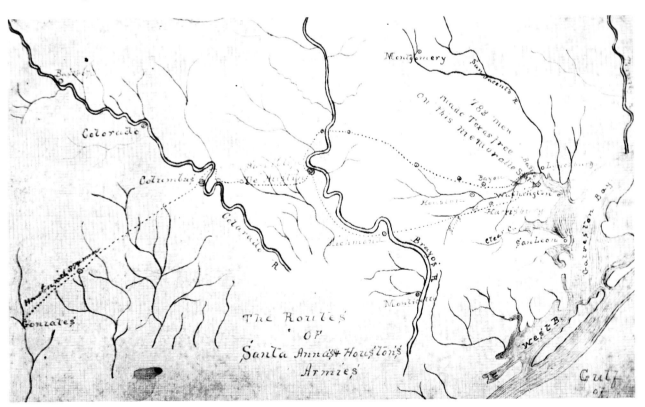

The routes of Santa Anna's and Houston's armies, spring 1836. (Author's collection)

## APRIL 24

### 1942

Texas sent nearly three-quarters of a million men to serve in the armed forces during the Second World War. The people who stayed behind kept the home front working at defense plants throughout Texas. Texans in large and small towns practiced blackouts, learned to live with rationing, and raised money for the war effort.

On April 24, 1942, with the war raging, and going badly in some spots, a war bond quota of $18,594,400 was set for Texas.

## APRIL 25

### 1846

Despite San Jacinto, Mexico refused to recognize the independence of Texas or the Treaty of Velasco that set the Rio Grande as the boundary of Texas and Mexico. There was constant dread of a Mexican invasion, and in 1842 Mexican forces crossed the river and sent a wave of fear through Texas. The problems continued until Texas gave up its independence and became a state in 1845.

With statehood, the border problem became a United States problem. Gen. Zachary Taylor was sent across the Nueces with a force of men heading toward Brownsville.

On April 25, 1846, Capt. Seth B. Thornton and sixty-two of his dragoons met a force of Mexicans, and a skirmish followed. Several Americans were killed.

In Washington, President James K. Polk was looking for a reason to declare war because Mexico had not paid its American debts and refused to recognize the border. When word of the battle of the twenty-fifth reached Washington, Polk had what he needed: "American blood has been shed on American soil," he told Congress. The lawmakers appropriated $10 million for the support of 50,000 volunteers. The Mexican War was on.

## APRIL 26

### 1837

John James Audubon, the prominent naturalist, celebrated his fifty-second birthday on April 26, 1837, in Texas, where he had come to sketch the birds of the new republic.

Audubon took a cruise along the coast of the Gulf of Mexico and spent about three weeks in Galveston, then came to Houston, where he wrote an account of his meeting with President Sam Houston. The great naturalist published his Texas bird drawings in the classic *Birds of America*.

Some Texans were so taken with Audubon that the senate discussed a bill that would have made him a citizen of the republic; however, the bill never made it out of committee.

## APRIL 27

### 1896

The greatest baseball player Texas ever produced was born in the little Runnels County town of Winters on April 27, 1896.

Young Rogers Hornsby tried to play with the Dallas team but failed and signed on with the professional team in Denison. People who saw him in his early years said he was not more than an average player. With maturity,

Zachary Taylor's army outside Corpus Christi. From here the men moved across the Nueces, precipitating the Mexican War. (Houston Metropolitan Research Center, Houston Library)

that average player became a superstar. The St. Louis Cardinals of the National League signed him for the 1915 season. He was to spend twenty-three years in the majors.

The "Magnificent Rajah," as the sportswriters called him, built a .358 lifetime batting average with 302 home runs. He led the National League seven times in batting. In 1924 he set the modern record for right-handed hitters by batting .424.

As a player-manager, Hornsby led the Cardinals to a World Series victory over Babe Ruth and the New York Yankees in 1926. In 1942, he was elected to the Baseball Hall of Fame.

# APRIL 28

## 1929

The history of the American military is closely tied to San Antonio. The air force

The "Magnificent Rajah"—Rogers Hornsby. (Texas Sports Hall of Fame)

bases and the army facilities in and around the Alamo City have trained thousands who served on the ground, in the air, and in outer space. Achievements that seem commonplace now had their beginnings on the bases and forts.

On April 28, 1929, the townspeople gathered to see what was advertised as a great event. Small planes took off from the strip at Brooks Air Force Base, and as the squadron of aircraft flew overhead, the sky was suddenly dotted with men and equipment falling, then floating beneath billowing parachutes. It was the first mass parachute drop in the history of the Army Air Force, and it proved that such a military maneuver was practical.

## APRIL 29

### 1856

The camel can survive and prosper in the deserts of northern Africa; therefore, it would seem to be the ideal animal for the great American desert. That bit of logic set into motion a strange chapter in Texas history. Jefferson Davis, the secretary of war, ordered the camels shipped in to handle transportation problems in west Texas. The Congress appropriated $30,000, and a buyer went to Africa to secure the camels.

The first mass paratroop drop was staged over Brooks Air Force Base, San Antonio. (Office of Information, Brooks AFB)

Willie Nelson's "outlaw" sounds changed country music. (KPRC TV, Houston)

On April 29, 1856, the naval ship *Supply* arrived at Pass Cavallo off Indianola carrying thirty-two camels and two calves born at sea.

It was not an idea whose time had come. For a while the camels were used to carry packs on the trail to California, and occasionally to track down Indians.

When the War Between the States broke out, the camels were scattered; some were used as baggage carriers for troops. By 1869 the novel experiment to replace the mule in the west with a camel was at an end.

## APRIL 30

### 1933

At 1:40 in the morning of April 30, 1933, a genuine Texas treasure was born in the little town of Abbott.

Willie Hugh Nelson grew up with a grandmother who told him music was anything that sounded good to the ear, and a grandfather who taught Willie chords on the guitar. By the time he was ten, he was being paid to play with a polka band.

When he was twenty-seven Willie Nelson went to the center of the country music universe, Nashville, Tennessee. He played bass for Ray Price's band and wrote a string of hits for other artists. Faron Young recorded Nelson's "Hello Walls," Patsy Cline cut "Crazy," and in November 1964 Nelson joined the "Grand Ole Opry."

But the fact is that Willie was a song *writer*, and not many people then believed he was a song *singer*. So Willie Nelson up and left Nashville, and came to Texas where he could sing his songs. He started a whole new kind of country music . . . an outlaw sound that the purists in Nashville scorned, then came to adopt.

*Music City News* called him "the best real soul country singer since Hank Williams." The *Arizona Republic* probably said it best: "Nelson is changing the face of country music. He hasn't changed all that much over the years. It's as if the rest of the country is finally catching up."

The Alamo in 1850. It was originally named the Mission San Antonio de Valero. (Houston Metropolitan Research Center, Houston Library)

# MAY

## MAY 1

### 1718

On May 1, 1718, Martín de Alarcón, the Spanish governor of Texas, founded a new mission three-quarters of a league down the creek from San Pedro Springs. It was the first of the missions established along the east bank of the San Antonio River. He called it San Antonio de Valero.

Eventually the mission became known as "The Alamo."

## MAY 2

### 1874

When Texas finally got rid of the carpet-baggers, it turned its attention to the threat from the west—the Plains Indians.

In 1874 the legislature authorized the Rangers' Frontier Battalion to handle the problem, and on May 2, John B. Jones of Corsicana was commissioned to command it. To many, Jones was a strange choice to command the Rangers. He was forty, and that was old in 1874. He did not drink or smoke, stood under six feet tall, and weighed no more than 130 pounds. Yet when he led his men against the Indians, he was a fighting machine. After the Indian threat ended, Jones turned to hunting down outlaws like Sam Bass.

He did not look like a Texas Ranger was supposed to look. He was not flamboyant or loud, and he is not generally mentioned with the Ranger legends. But John B. Jones was a great Texas Ranger. (See also May 26.)

### 1906

Henry Allen Bullock was born in North Carolina on May 2, 1906. He chose a career in education, and spent his life fighting to insure that better education was available to blacks.

Bullock taught social sciences at a number of predominately black colleges in the South. After forty years of teaching, he was asked to come to the University of Texas at Austin to teach a course called "The Negro in America." In 1970 he became a regular faculty member—the first black professor appointed to the faculty of Arts and Sciences at the university.

Dr. Bullock went on to establish the university's first ethnic studies program.

## MAY 3

### 1693

There are a thousand towns in Texas named for a thousand different people, places, and things. We don't, however, have a town named after General Gregorio de Salinas Varona.

On May 3, 1693, he left Monclova with a load of supplies for Texas missions. He was ordered to explore the region around Matagorda Bay and report on whether permanent occupation should be tried. His word was "forget

John B. Jones led the Texas Rangers' crack Frontier Battalion. (Texas Ranger Hall of Fame)

Henry Bullock, born May 2, 1906, was the first black man on the faculty of Arts and Sciences at the University of Texas, Austin. (Texas State Archives)

it." It was the view of the general that the area was simply unsuitable for settlement.

By March, 1694, the Texas frontier was abandoned—and for the next twenty-two years the Indians and a few explorers had the place to themselves.

## MAY 4

1821

Jean Lafitte was a privateer who came from New Orleans to Galveston in 1817 to live off the merchant shipping. He and his brother Pierre had cut a deal with the Spanish to keep out the revolutionaries, who used the island as a power base for forays into Mexico. The Lafittes gathered a thousand men on the island, and raided ships and smuggled along the coast until 1821.

The viceroy of Mexico never trusted the brothers, and for good reason. Finally an American naval brig, the *Enterprise*, stationed itself off the island and told Lafitte to leave. Between May 4 and 7 (the exact date is disputed), the pirates sailed away and were lost to history.

Today, Jean Lafitte is a folk hero. The fact is he was a subordinate to his brother Pierre. He was no more than a criminal who played both ends against the middle, and finally ran away when things got too hot. He most certainly was a colorful figure, but his fame largely rests on the work of modern day romantic novelists.

## MAY 5

1862

The fifth day in May, Cinco de Mayo, is to Mexicans what San Jacinto Day is to Texans;

or the Fourth of July is to Americans.

Mexico was at war with Spain. England and France joined on the side of the Spanish. Early in 1862 the English and Spanish withdrew from Puebla and left a huge French force to face the Mexicans under Ignacio Seguin Zaragoza. On May 5, 1862, the Mexican army routed the French. Upwards of a thousand French were killed while the Mexicans lost less than a hundred men. Cinco de Mayo became a national holiday, and Zaragoza became a national hero.

Interestingly enough, Zaragoza had been born at the Presidio la Bahia near present-day Goliad. With Mexico's defeat in the Texas Revolution, he moved with his parents to Matamoros. He grew up to be a soldier, and in 1857 found himself on an important military assignment the day of his marriage, so his brother married the woman for him by proxy!

# MAY 6

## 1864

In May 1864 Robert E. Lee had his first crack at fighting Ulysses S. Grant. As Grant's army was crossing a densely wooded area in Virginia known as "The Wilderness," Lee threw his outnumbered army at his new opponent. It was the worst possible place for a battle, and it accordingly became one of the most hellish battles in the War Between the States.

Like every battle Lee's army fought, the Wilderness Campaign was marked by feats of heroism on the part of the common soldier. For Hood's Texas Brigade (see March 7), it marked perhaps the most famous episode of their storied career. On a grim May 6, as the Confederate line wavered, Lee chanced to meet the brigade as they stood fast. In those

woods today stands a granite monument that bears these words:

*"Who are you, my boys," Lee cried, as he saw them gathering. "Texas boys," they yelled, their number multiplying every second. The Texans— Hood's Texans of Longstreet's corps, just at the right place and at the right moment. After the strain of the dawn, the sight of these grenadier guards of the South was too much for Lee. For once the dignity of the commanding general was shattered, for once his poise was shaken . . . "Hurrah for Texas," he shouted, waving his hat. . . . "Hurrah for Texas." The willing veterans sprang into position; he would lead them in the counter charge. He spurred Traveler on the heels of the infantrymen. "Go back, General Lee, go back," they cried. "We won't go on, unless you go back."*

*—Douglas Southall Freeman*

## 1930

Texas lies in Tornado Alley, that stretch of the midlands from Minnesota to the Gulf of Mexico. With the coming of spring, the terrible twisters form from the cold air flowing south as it collides with the warm, moist air off the Gulf.

May 6, 1930, was one of the worst days of tornadoes that Texas has ever seen. In the morning, storms hit Austin, Spur, and Abilene. After noon and before midnight, sixteen other places were hit. In the afternoon the towns of Ennis and Bynum, Irene and Frost suffered damage and loss of life. As the sun set on the awful day, Kenedy and Runge and Nordheim found themselves in harm's way, along with Bronson and San Antonio and Gonzales.

By daybreak on the morning of May 7, the damage from one day's storms would total $2.5 million, with at least eighty-two people dead because of the killer winds.

In the terrible Wilderness Campaign, the Texas boys rallied behind Robert E. Lee. (Author's collection)

A deadly Texas twister swirls down toward rooftops. (Texas State Archives)

# MAY 7

### 1860

Julius Real was born in the Texas hill country on May 7, 1860. He was a prohibitionist and the only Republican in the Texas senate in 1911, when he joined in a movement called the "Whiskey Rebellion." Despite his feelings about demon rum, the judge understood that most of the folks who sent him to Austin wanted the right to take a drink when they wanted one.

So it was that when the governor and members of the legislature plotted to make Texas dry, Judge Real led ten other state senators to the hills of Bandera County to hide until the session ended. Without their presence there was no senate quorum. Without a quorum there could be no vote. Texas stayed wet.

**Also on this date,** in the year 1915, the *Lusitania* was sunk; World War I was imminent, and Texas would send over five thousand away to die in the fighting.

Although he personally opposed drinking, Julius Real fought to keep Texas wet during the Prohibition movement. (Barker Texas History Center)

died. Thirty-six Texas men won the Congressional Medal of Honor.

Gen. Dwight Eisenhower, the Supreme Allied Commander in Europe, was born in Texas. So was Oveta Culp Hobby, the commander of the Women's Army Corps.

### 1846

The second week of May 1846 was a good one for Gen. Zachary Taylor and the American army as it battled the Mexicans in Texas. On May 8, Taylor's forces engaged in an artillery duel with a Mexican battery at Palo Alto, a few miles north of Brownsville. The Americans, with superior cannon, won handily. The next day (see May 9) was to bring even greater success.

# MAY 8

### 1945

The Second World War in Europe ended on May 7, 1945, but the official announcement wasn't made until the next day. Texas, and the rest of the free world, celebrated on May 8.

While the war raged, Texas boasted fifteen major military bases, over forty air fields, twenty-one prisoner-of-war camps, and naval installations up and down the coast. Seven hundred fifty thousand Texans served in the armed forces; twenty-two thousand of them

Infantrymen listen to V.E. Day celebrations on Heinrich Himmler's radio. The Thirty-Sixth Division had occupied the summer home of the Hitler hatchet man in Tegernsee. (Private collection)

## MAY 9

### 1846

After Gen. Zachary Taylor's successful artillery battle with the Mexicans at Palo Alto (see May 8), his infantrymen made good the claim of Texas to the territory between the Nueces and the Rio Grande with a victory at the Battle of Resaca de la Palma on May 9, 1846.

Taylor went up against a much larger Mexican army commanded by Gen. Mariano Arista. The battle was a rout, with over 500 killed, wounded, or missing, and the rest of the Mexican force running south in disarray.

Legend has it that a pay wagon was buried and never recovered. Treasure-hunters will want to know that the battle was fought on the north bank of the Resaca de la Palma in Cameron County near Brownsville.

**Also on this date,** in the year 1840, Sam Houston married Margaret Lea.

## MAY 10

### 1911

San Antonio is home of the nation's finest training facilities for military pilots. Oddly enough, one of the most famous of these facilities is named after an airman who has the unique distinction of being the first military pilot to be killed in an aircraft accident.

Lt. George E. M. Kelly crashed his plane at Fort Sam Houston on May 10, 1911. His death led to the suspension of flying activity in San Antonio for years. Kelly Air Force Base is now one of the world's largest maintenance and supply bases.

Sam Houston chose a beautiful Alabama belle, Margaret Lea, as his wife. (Sam Houston Regional Library)

## MAY 11

### 1953

There is an old Indian legend that Waco would never be hit by a tornado. On May 11, 1953, that legend was proved wrong. The weather bureau warning told the people from San Angelo to Waco to be on the alert. San Angelo was hit first; then came the monster, twisting through five miles of Waco, including two square miles of the downtown section of the city. Within seconds, 196 buildings were reduced to piles of rubble; 150 homes were blown away; 1,097 people were hurt, and 114 killed. The damage would total over $50 millions.

Lt. George E. M. Kelly in the type of airplane in which he met his death. (San Antonio *Express*)

Even the churches were not safe when the tornado came through Waco on May 11, 1953. (Texas Collection, Baylor University)

# MAY 12

### 1846

Norris Wright Cuney was born in the slave quarters of a Waller County plantation on May 12, 1846. He was to become one of the most prominent blacks in Texas history.

After schooling in Pennsylvania, he came back to Texas and plunged into Republican Party politics. He operated a wharf contracting company and a black longshoreman's association in Galveston. There he also served as an alderman and as a county school director. Cuney was later appointed to the post of customs collector for the Port of Galveston.

He loved politics, and twice ran for state office, without success. He attended national Republican gatherings and was named to the party's executive committee in 1891.

When Norris Wright Cuney died in 1898, school was dismissed and business shut down in Galveston to honor his great life. (See also Nov. 28.)

### 1903

When William L. Prather served as president of the University of Texas at Austin, he used to tell the students that the state looked to them to become leaders. He would say, "The eyes of Texas are upon you."

Those repeated reminders inspired John

Sinclair to write new lyrics to a popular song of the day, "I've Been Working on the Rail-road." On May 12, 1903, the University of Texas Glee Club performed the parody for a delighted President Prather, and the school got itself a song.

## MAY 13

### 1975

James Robert Wills was born on a farm in Kosse, Texas, in 1905. By 1913 the boy's parents had moved to the thriving community of Turkey, and it was there that Bob Wills learned to play the fiddle.

He made a scant living with that fiddle at medicine shows and on the radio until 1931 when Bob and two other players became the legendary group that played and sang on the radio for the Burrus Mills of Fort Worth—the Light Crust Doughboys.

In the middle of the dark Depression days of the 1930s Bob Wills formed his own band, the Texas Playboys. Brother Johnnie Lee, Tommy Duncan, the Whalin brothers, and Bob began to play a mixture of country and jazz that became known as "Western swing." By 1940 the band had recorded "New San Antonio Rose," with Duncan singing and Bob and the boys swinging. The record sold a million copies.

Whether the band was broadcasting at noon on KVOO in Tulsa, playing a dance somewhere, or making a movie or a record, Wills always punctuated the song with his trademark, a whining shout of "AAAH–HAAA."

Bob Wills and the Texas Playboys. (Panhandle Plains Museum)

Norris Cuney, a black man from Galveston, rose to prominence in Reconstruction Texas. (Barker Texas History Center)

When the big bands died after the war, so did the big Western swing bands. In his later life Wills was elected to the Country Music Hall of Fame, and lived to see a revival of the kind of music he pioneered. Bob Wills died on May 13, 1975.

# MAY 14

### 1836

Following the Battle of San Jacinto, Texas's traveling government settled in one of the area's oldest towns, Velasco, situated at the mouth of the Brazos. Santa Anna was taken there to await his fate after the disastrous Texas campaign.

On May 14, 1836, the president of Mexico met with Texas President David G. Burnet to sign a treaty. Santa Anna said later he felt that he would lose his life if he did not sign. The public treaty of Velasco called for the end of the war, the withdrawal of Mexican forces from Texas, a prisoner exchange, and the like.

There was also a secret treaty of Velasco. It promised Santa Anna his freedom if he would go back to Mexico and use his influence to get Texas full independence. But the government in Mexico refused to recognize anything their leader signed during his captivity, and genuine freedom from Mexican interference was not to come for twelve long years.

# MAY 15

### 1898

Col. Leonard Wood, the army surgeon who was a supreme Indian fighter, was sent to San Antonio to command the force being readied to go to Cuba to fight in the Spanish-American War. The colonel was a quietly effi-

cient army man. The recruits were on the way to San Antonio, and so was a man who was to become the colonel's second—the current assistant secretary of the navy, the former New York police commissioner, the millionaire dandy—Theodore Roosevelt.

Roosevelt was recruiting a cavalry regiment that "would see cowboys and Knickerbockers ride side by side." He had enlisted a yachting dandy, a polo great, a Harvard quarterback, the ex-captain of the Columbia crew, the best tennis player in America.

On the morning of May 15, 1898, Roosevelt arrived in San Antonio. The first thing he saw was a sign that proclaimed: "This way to the camp of Roosevelt's Rough Riders." He set off for the old fair grounds, two miles from the station. It was a trip that would take him to the White House. (See also May 30.)

### 1890

The greatest writer Texas has yet produced, Katherine Anne Porter, was born May 15, 1890, at Indian Creek in Brown County. She began her career as a journalist in Denver and later for newspapers in Chicago. In 1923 she began writing fiction and produced her first short story.

In 1931 Porter was chosen to receive a fellowship to study and work in Germany. The boat trip over led her to write her only novel, *Ship of Fools.*

In 1966 Katherine Anne Porter won the Pulitzer Prize for her *Collected Stories.*

# MAY 16

### 1942

Oveta Culp's mother named her after a character in a romantic novel, and indeed, she grew to lead an exciting and romantic life.

Her mother was a suffragette and her father was a lawyer; both supported a young candidate named Will Hobby when he ran for governor in 1918.

For six years Oveta Culp served as the parliamentarian for the Texas House of Representatives, and in 1929 ran for the legislature. She lost, and her flirtation with elective politics ended. She met Will Hobby again as both worked at the Houston *Post*—he was president, she was in the circulation department. The former governor's first wife had died in 1929, and in 1931 he married Oveta Culp.

She was a business dynamo. She revitalized the *Post*; the company radio station, KPRC; and ran other aspects of the business while continuing to work in the background in political causes.

On June 30, 1940, Oveta Culp Hobby went to Washington as the dollar-a-year head of a women's section of the War Department's public relations efforts. With the coming of the Second World War, a Congressional committee suggested a Women's Auxiliary Army Corps, and on May 16, 1942, Secretary of War Henry Stimson appointed Hobby the first director of the WAACs, with the rank of colonel.

Colonel Hobby was awarded the Distinguished Service Medal, the third highest decoration the army gives. She was the first woman to win it.

Oveta Culp, parliamentarian of the Texas House of Representatives, 1927. (Hobby Family photo)

## 1888

Ten thousand people came for the dedication. Many had watched the building rise despite delays, labor disputes, changes in the choice of stone, and constant games of politics.

Pink granite from a mountain in Burnet County replaced the originally selected limestone. Convicts from the state prison quarried the rock; others swarmed over the building. The unions boycotted the use of "slave labor." The granite cutters' union was upset because Scots were imported to do the job.

Somehow it got built and wound up 311 feet high; taller than the Capitol in Washington.

On May 16, 1888, Sen. Temple Houston gave the dedication address, and Texas finally had a Capitol building.

# MAY 17

## 1835

Archelaus Bynum Dodson was a native of the Carolinas who came to Texas with his parents in the late 1820s. He was a patriot who served as a delegate to a reform convention in 1832, and later served as a first lieutenant in a Texas defense unit.

On May 17, 1835, Dodson took time off from politics and the coming war to marry Sarah Rudolph Bradley. They were deeply in love, and she was a hopeless romantic. Once she surprised him by sewing some pieces of cloth together to fashion a flag for her husband and his company of soldiers. It was a red, white, and blue flag with a single star, and it was the banner that flew at Washington-on-the-Brazos when the Declaration of Independence was signed.

The only difference between Mrs. Dodson's flag and the one we fly today is that her stripes were vertical.

# MAY 18

## 1912

The oldest battleship in the United States is the *Texas*. It was launched on May 18, 1912. Originally a coal-burner, it was converted to oil during World War II. The *Texas* remains the only surviving battleship from the dreadnought era, when great ships with great guns were considered the country's first line of defense.

The *Texas* did not see much action during the First World War, but in the Second it fought at Normandy, and then moved to the Pacific to take part in the invasion of Okinawa and Iwo Jima.

By the end of the war, the ship was showing her age. The navy was about to scrap her, but Texans got into the act and saved the state's namesake. It is now docked by the San Jacinto Monument as the flagship of the Texas Navy. (See also June 28.)

**Also on this date,** in the year 1871, Satanta, Big Tree, and their warriors massacred seven men from a wagon train at Salt Creek.

# MAY 19

## 1836

Of all the stories of life on the frontier in Texas, none is more dramatic than the one involving the star-crossed Cynthia Ann Parker.

On May 19, 1836, when she was nine years old, Cynthia Ann Parker was captured by the Comanches during a raid on Fort Parker. For five years the white settlers and scouts searched for her, and finally found her alive and living with an Indian family. Her new family would not give her up, and she would not leave. Two years later the white world learned Cynthia Ann, now sixteen, had married Peta Nocona, a Comanche chief, and had two children. Occasionally word would filter through about a white woman at this battle or that one, until finally in 1860, at the battle of Pease River, Cynthia Ann Parker was captured along with her daughter, Prairie Flower.

To look at her photograph, with the baby girl, you would say she was an Indian, in every way. And except for her deep blue eyes and fair complexion, she looked and acted like any Comanche. She was thirty-four by the time she came back to white civilization, but she had become an Indian, and wanted to remain one. She never accepted her people, or her new surroundings, and more than once tried to escape. Four years after she was returned to the white man's world, Cynthia Ann Parker died of a broken heart.

Satanta, the Kiowa chief, who said, "I don't want to live in a house. I want to roam over the prairie where I am free." (Texas Ranger Hall of Fame)

# MAY 20

## 1927

Charles A. Lindbergh, "Lucky Lindy," has a Texas connection. As a barnstormer in the early twenties he flew into Texas. (If you were any kind of a pilot back then, you simply had to fly over a corner of Texas—it was the thing to do.)

In 1924 Lindbergh landed at Camp Wood in Real County as a stopover on his way to California. The next day he took off, but crashed his plane into the corner of Warren

Cynthia Ann Parker, shown here with her daughter Prairie Flower, died a captive in white civilization. (Texas Collection, Baylor University)

Pruett's hardware store. No one was hurt, and the damage was slight.

Also in 1924, Lindy flew to San Antonio and became a U.S. Air Service Cadet at Brooks Field. By 1925 he completed advanced training at Kelly Field. Two years later, on May 20, 1927, he took off from Roosevelt Field in Long Island and flew to Paris.

About this auspicious moment in history, F. Scott Fitzgerald wrote:

*In the spring of 1927, something bright and alien flashed across the sky. A young man who seemed to have nothing to do with his generation did a heroic thing, and for a moment people set down their glasses in country clubs and speakeasies and thought of their old best dreams. . . .*

"Lucky Lindy" received pilot training in San Antonio in 1924. (U.S. Air Force, Kelly AFB)

# MAY 21

## 1911

In 1910 and 1911 a classic Latin American people's revolution was boiling in Mexico. The rebels kept assuring the Texans the fight was an internal one to overthrow the Díaz regime, and America and Texas should not worry.

On May 21, 1911, the dictator Díaz caved in and signed the Los Tratados de Ciudad Juarez. Francisco Madero became the president and declared the civil war over. Texas breathed a sigh of relief, but then sat back to watch the bloody aftermath of another short period of calm. Two years later, Madero was murdered by the head of his army. Emiliano Zapata and Pancho Villa made their own kind of war on both sides of the border, and the Rio Grande continued to be an area of intrigue for years after Díaz stepped down.

# MAY 22

## 1953

When Texas became a state, it brought into the Union a sticky problem that was to last over a hundred years. As an independent republic, Texas claimed jurisdiction over three leagues into the sea. Three miles is traditional, and three leagues is about three times as much. That did not make much difference until oil was found offshore. Then the tidelands became very important. The question became, who had the right to the oil in the 2.5 million acres off the coastline that Texas still claimed under the old republic treaty?

There were Congressional fights and Supreme Court fights, but the tidelands issue was to be settled with the Presidential election of 1952. When the Democratic candidate, Adlai Stevenson, indicated he would oppose Texas and the tidelands, the state's rock-ribbed Democrats swung to the Republican candidate, a local boy who went away to become a war hero. Despite the fact that he rarely mentioned his Texas heritage, and chose instead to face the world as a Kansan, "Texas liked Ike."

The election of '52 spawned "Democrats for Ike," "Shivercrats" for Texas Democratic Gov. Allan Shivers, who led the state in the Eisenhower column, and cries of "Save the tidelands for our children."

The Eisenhower-Nixon ticket carried Texas, and on May 22, 1953, Ike paid a political debt: he signed the Tidelands Bill, and Texas kept the oil.

# MAY 23

## 1934

Bonnie Parker was not quite five feet tall, weighed less than a hundred pounds, and had red hair and bright blue eyes. She was the best speller at Bryan High School, and had a lively sense of humor.

Clyde Barrow was a native of Teleco, Texas, who was not handsome nor ugly, not too short, and not too tall—an average fellow who would not stand out in any crowd.

But the two of them created a legend in their two years of terror. Bonnie and Clyde shot their way into and out of a dozen gun battles that caused a dozen people to die.

U.S. Sen. Price Daniel accepts the pen Ike used to sign the Tidelands Bill. (Sam Houston Regional Library)

Their highly romanticized exploits across Texas and the Midwest in the early 1930s made them seem larger than life. In fact, Clyde was a car thief and burglar, and Bonnie was in love with him. It is probably also true that they were very mean, no-good people who robbed and killed for a living.

A roll of film the authorities confiscated in 1933 probably added to the legend more than the crimes did. The film showed the fun-loving couple snuggling in a car, and one of them showed Bonnie with a pistol at her side and a cigar in her mouth. The press had a field day.

The end came, as they both knew it would, in a hail of bullets. As the couple drove along a farm road in Louisiana on the morning of May 23, 1934, Texas Ranger Frank Hamer and five other lawmen waited in ambush. The Ranger shouted "Stick 'em up" as the car rolled to a stop, but Clyde went for his gun. The lawmen answered with automatic rifles, shotguns, and pistols. The brief, wasted lives of Bonnie and Clyde ended. (See also Jan. 16.)

**Also on this date**, in the year 1541, Coronado gave thanks for having found friendly Indians in the Palo Duro Canyon; Texas had a Thanksgiving almost eighty years before the Pilgrims.

# MAY 24

## 1690

Anxious Sisters gather around the bed of María de Agreda. She is in a deep, trancelike sleep. The Sisters know that when she wakes up, she will tell them wonderful stories of her trip across the Great Sea to visit the brown-skinned savages that she calls Ticlas, or

Techas, or Tejas. The year is 1631. María Agreda, a native of Castille, never left her native Spain except in those strange dreams. Some who heard her stories believed; others were skeptical.

Sixty years after María's death, Spanish missionaries walked into east Texas to tell the story of Jesus. The padres were amazed to find that the Indians said they knew the stories already, because a little lady dressed in blue used to appear to them to tell the stories, and urge them to keep the faith—because men of God were coming.

On May 24, 1690, the first Spanish mission in east Texas was established—San Francisco de los Tejas. "Tejas" was the Spanish rendition

Bonnie and Clyde, fun-loving killers, pose for a gag shot. (Western History Collections, University of Oklahoma Library)

of the Hasinai Indian word for friend, the word María de Agreda used sixty years before the white man came to east Texas.

# MAY 25

## 1896

During the Civil War, the women of the South set up aid societies to sew uniforms, make bandages, and raise money for the Confederacy. After the war ended, the societies continued to work in hospitals and soldiers' homes. Thirty years after the war, the aid societies of several states banned together to form the United Daughters of the Confederacy. On May 25, 1896, Katie Currie Muse organized the first Texas chapter in Victoria.

The women seek to find all eligible descendants of Confederate veterans and offer them membership; to collect and preserve the accurate story of the late "unpleasantness"; and to honor the memory of those who served.

# MAY 26

## 1900

The Frontier Battalion (see May 2) of the Texas Rangers was a colorful fighting "army" that wiped out the remaining troublesome Indians and bandits and bad men of one ilk or another. It enabled the edge of civilization to push from the Nueces to El Paso and north to the great canyon of the Panhandle.

The battalion fought a noble fight and died an ignoble death. When it was created by Gov. Richard Coke in 1874, the law read,

". . . each Officer shall have the powers of a Peace Officer. . . ." An early-day counterpart of the Civil Liberties Union seized on that phrase and asked for a court ruling. If the letter of the law were followed, only the *officers* could make arrests, not the privates in the force. Despite the fact that for over twenty-five years privates had made thousands of arrests, the attorney general ruled on May 26, 1900, that ". . . Non Commissioned Officers and Privates of the Frontier Battalion . . . referred to as 'Rangers' have no authority to make arrests."

The Frontier Battalion was destroyed.

# MAY 27

## 1909

Michael Francis Higgins was born in Red Oak on May 27, 1909. He was a gifted athlete who starred on the Texas Longhorn football team, and was captain of the championship baseball team in 1930. Higgins signed a professional contract with the Philadelphia Athletics, where he set American League records and World Series records for fielding and hitting.

As his playing days ended he became manager of the Boston team and was named the 1954 Major League Manager of the Year. He spent thirty-nine years in one baseball job or another, and was elected to the Texas Sports Hall of Fame.

To baseball fans Michael Higgins was better known by his nickname "Pinky." It was a name he first earned back in Red Oak. Seems young Michael loved to play ball so much that one day he got up out of a sickbed and pulled his clothes on over a pink nightgown. From that day on he was "Pinky" Higgins.

"Pinky" Higgins spent thirty-nine years in major league baseball. (Texas Sports Hall of Fame)

The gusher at Santa Rita filled the coffers of the University of Texas. (Institute of Texan Cultures)

## MAY 28

### 1923

When the state decided it wanted universities, it had no money, but lots of land. In a fit of generosity, the legislature gave the universities nearly two million acres of land instead of money. The fact that it was west Texas land no one else wanted seemed to be of little concern.

For a while the schools made some money from grazing leases. Finally, a Big Lake lawyer named Rupert Ricker thought there might be oil out there in those miles and miles of miles and miles. He picked a spot in Reagan County and started to drill a well he called the Santa Rita Number 1. Santa Rita is the patron saint of the impossible. It was a perfect name, be-cause everybody knew there wasn't any oil for a hundred miles around. Drilling on the dry, parched prairie was a terrible labor.

On May 28, 1923, the drillers heard a hiss, then saw the rig's bucket fly up like a shot. The Santa Rita Number 1 sat on top of one of the largest oil pools in the world. The sorry land that the legislature did not want has brought in nearly a billion dollars to the universities' permanent fund.

## MAY 29

### 1861

The stories told round the campfires and in the lodges about the tall, red-bearded white man made him almost legendary to the Indians. His bravery and derring-do caused him to be both feared and revered. Near the Llano River the Indians even painted his picture on a rock. He was Henry Robinson, and on May 29, 1861, with the man betrothed to his daughter at his side, he was headed for Camp Wood. At a place called Chalk Bluff, north of Uvalde, twenty Indians fell upon the two travelers. Both men were killed, and the Indians scalped their irksome adversary and took his beard as a trophy to prove the Great Red Beard was really dead.

## MAY 30

### 1898

Of all the legions America has sent to war, none has caught the fancy of the American public like the Rough Riders. They spent less than a month drilling and organizing in San Antonio, and their entire army service lasted barely three months. Much of their fame rested with their leader, Theodore Roosevelt, who seemed to draw the spotlight.

In the brief time they trained in San Antonio (see May 15), the press crowded in. They called the army corps by a variety of nicknames: at first they were "Teddy's Terrors," then "Teddy's Texas Tarantulas" (a name Colonel Roosevelt did not like). That gave way to "Roosevelt's Rough Riders."

Before leaving San Antonio the Rough Riders dressed in full uniform and paraded to the cheers of thousands. By six in the morning of May 30, 1898, the last of seven trains pulled out of San Antonio's station for the trip to Florida, then to San Juan Hill and destiny.

Eighty-nine of the Rough Riders suffered casualties—the highest loss suffered by any regiment in the Cavalry Division in the Spanish-

Theodore Roosevelt and one of his "Rough Riders" before the Mission Concepción. (San Antonio *Light* Collection, Institute of Texan Cultures)

American War. Three months after arriving in San Antonio for training, the surviving Rough Riders were mustered out of service.

## MAY 31

### 1881

The buffalo provided the Indians almost everything they needed to survive. The meat was good, if tough, the hide could be made into shelters or clothing, and the bone was often fashioned into weapons or utensils. Best of all, there were millions of buffalo, and they were easy to hunt and kill.

To the white man, the buffalo was a huge, thundering, dumb nuisance. As the settlers and eventually the railroad came, the animals were systematically slaughtered.

The buffalo was not easily "spooked." Hunters would find a herd and slowly shoot the animals, one at a time. A buffalo would drop dead and the others would keep on grazing, oblivious to what was happening around them. A good hunter team could kill a hundred in a morning, then spend the afternoon skinning them. The hide of a large buffalo might bring two dollars; the carcass was simply discarded.

As the white man pushed west, and the buffalo disappeared, the Indian was displaced. It's impossible to say when the hunting stopped, but it may be marked on May 31, 1881, when Fort Griffin in Shackelford County was officially abandoned by the government. The fort, and the rough-and-tumble town that grew up nearby, had been a headquarters on the frontier for the buffalo skinners.

Remains of Fort Griffin in Shackelford County, where buffalo skinners headquartered. (Panhandle Plains Museum)

The soldiers at Camp MacArthur bought WWI Liberty Bonds, then spent the day lining up for this picture. (Barker Texas History Center)

Women join the men in classrooms at Texas A&M University in 1963. (Houston *Chronicle*)

# JUNE

## JUNE 1

### 1963

The Agricultural and Mechanical College of Texas opened its doors in 1876 with a student body of about forty men. It was to remain a bastion of men for nearly a hundred years. The Fifty-eighth Legislature changed the name of the school to Texas A&M University, and proposed another change: On June 1, 1963, a Limited Coeducational Policy was initiated which allowed the enrollment of wives and daughters of faculty, staff, employees, and students. The "Maggie" was born. By 1970, A&M was fully coeducational.

## JUNE 2

### 1941

It's difficult to imagine a name more powerful than Andrew Jackson Houston. Sam Houston named his son, born in 1854, after the President, and probably expected him to carry on a mixture of Tennessee-Texas politics that both were famous for.

The younger Houston became a lawyer and ran for governor in 1892. He lost. Sam's son lost again in 1910, and again in 1912. His political career appeared to be over, but just short of his eighty-seventh birthday Houston was appointed to fill the unexpired term of Morris Sheppard in the U.S. Senate.

On June 2, 1941, Andrew Jackson Houston took the oath of office and served for twenty-four days until he died in Washington. His body was brought back to Houston and buried on the San Jacinto Battleground.

## JUNE 3

### 1965

Edward Higgins White II was born in San Antonio. He later said that the history and heritage of flying in that town made every boy want to fly.

White graduated from West Point and did master's work at Michigan in engineering. He was a brilliant engineer, but he loved to fly, and the logical progression was from air force test pilot to the elite astronaut corps. He made that move in 1962 as part of a new generation of Gemini astronauts.

Part of the experimental training of the Gemini was to see if man could venture outside the spacecraft and actually perform work as he floated around.

In the spring of 1965 Russian cosmonaut Aleksei Leonov made history's first walk in space. On June 3, 1965, White and Jim McDivitt took off in Gemini 4, and on the third revolution, White stepped out in space and became America's first space-walker. He floated on the end of a twenty-five-foot tether, moving with thrusts from a twin-barreled gas gun. For twenty-one minutes he walked, worked, and tumbled through space. Ed White, who grew up wanting to fly, was flying as only one other man ever had, and he said of it, "This is the greatest experience . . ."

The space walk of Edward White, June 16, 1965.(Office of Information, Brooks AFB)

1836

Some "Ranger smarts" helped blunt a landing of Mexican troops in Texas in the summer of 1836.

Maj. Isaac Watts Burton and thirty men on horseback were sent to the mouth of the Guadalupe near Mission Bay to make sure Mexican troops did not land. On June 3, the volunteer Rangers spotted a strange vessel in Copano Bay. Two of the Rangers sent a distress signal, and the ship hoisted a Texas flag. When the Rangers did not answer, the ship then hoisted its true colors, a Mexican flag. The Rangers answered as if they, too, were Mexicans. The captain of the ship and four sailors put a small boat over the side and came to help. Once on shore, they were seized. The Rangers piled on the boat, rowed out to the ship, came aboard without resistance, and captured it.

They worked the same ruse on two more Mexican ships within the next two weeks.

The story of how men on horses had captured three ships became popular reading around the country, and before long the heroic Rangers were known as "horse marines."

1947

On the night of June 3, 1947, Dallas's first professional theater opened in the Gulf Oil Building of the Texas State Fair.

The first play was *Farther Off From Heaven*, by William Inge, but the news of the evening was made by the genius who directed "Theatre '47," Margo Jones. A native of Livingston, Margaret Virginia Jones studied at Texas Women's University and Pasadena, California's, famous Summer School of Theatre. She had been a co-director of the original Broadway production of *The Glass Menagerie*.

Her theater was a bold departure from the norm. Not only was it Dallas's first professional theater, but it was also the first professional repertory theater in the United States to use arena, or in-the-round, staging.

A critic for the Dallas *Morning News* wrote: "The Theatre-in-the-Round will do for the summer . . . but in a year or so Theatre '47 should have the playhouse it deserves."

When Texas cavalrymen captured Mexican ships, they earned the nickname "horse marines." (Author's collection)

## JUNE 4

### 1909

On June 4, 1909, the Lone Star Gas Company filed a charter with the state to begin a gamble. The little company proposed to become the state's first major natural gas company. The charter was granted, and skeptics wondered what would happen. Lone Star began work on a pipeline from a field in Clay County to Fort Worth and Dallas.

By April 29, 1910, the pipeline reached Dallas, and by the end of the year was serving nearly 15,000 customers. The mass marketing of natural gas worked, and as time was to prove, worked very well.

## JUNE 5

### 1859

One of the strangest tales involving the Texas Indians centered around Herman Lehmann, the son of German immigrants, who was born in the Mason County community of Loyal Valley on June 5, 1859.

When Herman was eleven, he was captured by the Apaches and eventually adopted by them. As he grew to manhood he became a warrior and battled other tribes and raided isolated farms and towns on the frontier. He killed an Apache medicine man and went into exile on the Plains, where he lived alone for a year.

When he emerged from his year of solitary, he was now a Comanche named "Montechena." At Fort Sill, in Indian Territory, Montechena was recognized as a white man, and the government sent him home to his family.

The family in Loyal Valley thought Herman was long dead, and because of the way he acted at his homecoming, they may have wished he had stayed with the tribe. He refused to sleep in a bed. He often walked the streets of town dressed in body paint and feathers, and once disturbed a revival meeting by breaking into a wild Indian dance, thinking the event was a prayer for rain. Herman also had a habit of taking a neighbor's horse or cow whenever he needed one.

When the government gave lands in Oklahoma to the Indians, Herman was listed on the roles as Comanche, so he, too, got his share. He delighted in giving exhibitions of his riding and shooting skills, and even put on his headdress to pose for pictures with old-time Texas Rangers who came around to see

Herman Lehmann, a strange mixture of German, Apache, and Comanche cultures, greets an old enemy, a Texas Ranger. (Texas Ranger Hall of Fame)

the man they had once fought in pitched battles.

Herman Lehmann, the German Indian, died in 1932 and is buried in Loyal Valley.

## 1931

David Browning was born in Boston, Massachusetts, on June 5, 1931. When he was three his family moved to Texas, where David soon discovered he liked diving into swimming pools. Before his young life ended he was to become the best springboard diver the United States ever produced. Three times an All-American at the University of Texas, and three times the Southwest Conference Diving Champion, Browning was so good he made up his own dives; eventually the Amateur Athletic Union adopted them and made them part of the AAU competition.

In 1952 at Helsinki, Finland, Browning won the Olympic gold medal for diving. He came home from the Olympics to finish his degree at the University of Texas and to join the navy as a pilot. In 1956, as he was preparing for the next Olympic games, Browning was killed in the crash of a training plane in Kansas. He was just twenty-five years old.

# JUNE 6

## 1849

Gen. William Jenkins Worth was a New York soldier who had a brilliant military career cut short by a Texas cholera epidemic in May 1849. A month later, on June 6, 1849, Maj. Ripley Arnold established a fort on the Clear Fork of the Trinity River and named it Fort Worth after the general.

Six years earlier the government had negotiated a treaty with the Indians, and designated the area near the Clear Fork and the West Fork as the eastern boundary of the Indians. The fort was established to make sure the red men stayed out of east Texas and civilization. To this day Fort Worth is "where the West begins."

1944

The Allied invasion of France was inevitable. The only question for the German High Command was, where was it coming?

It came on June 6, 1944, and was aimed at the beaches of Normandy. Paratroopers from the Eighty-second Airborne and the 101st Infantrymen from the First, Fourth, and Twenty-ninth Divisions, and Rangers from the Second Battalion attacked the land. There were 73,000 Americans there that day, with thousands of men in ships offshore, and planes flying overhead. A total of 156,205 Allied troops landed on that "Longest Day," as the plan of a Texan, Dwight Eisenhower, took on the status of a crusade. Failure would have

meant one of the world's great military disasters. But it succeeded, and eleven months and a day later, the Nazis surrendered, and the war in Europe was over.

**Also on this date**, in the year 1957, Attorney General Will Wilson raided Galveston to close down gambling.

# JUNE 7

1944

On that "Longest Day" at Normandy there were no good jobs for the men who had to be there. Some tasks were just worse than others.

It can be argued that the toughest job of the day fell to a young man from Eden, Texas, named James Earl Rudder. At this moment in history, he was Lieutenant Colonel Rudder, the organizer and commander of the Second Ranger Battalion.

An early rendering of Fort Worth, "where the West begins." (Barker Texas History Center)

Supreme Allied Commander Dwight Eisenhower gives a pre-D-Day pep talk to paratroopers. (Dwight D. Eisenhower Library)

The battalion's job was to take the high ground at a place called Point du Hoc, a cliff 130 feet high that had to be climbed despite withering fire from the Germans. On top of the cliff, German guns controlled the main landing beaches called "Omaha" and "Utah." The guns had to be knocked out or they could lob artillery shells down on the Allies. Colonel Rudder's 225 Rangers put up ropes and ladders and within hours had reached the top, only to find that the guns they were after had been moved out.

By the morning of June 7, a relief column came to help the Rangers. All but seventy-five of them were dead or wounded. Rudder had been hit twice.

Twenty-one years later James Earl Rudder became the president of Texas A&M University. He served there until he died in 1970.

## JUNE 8

### 1819

When the headstrong citizens of Natchez, Mississippi, heard that the boundary of the Louisiana Purchase excluded eastern Texas, they became so angry they financed a private army to conquer Texas territory. The man they placed in charge was James Long, a surgeon who served in the War of 1812. Dr. Long promised every man who served under him free Texas land. On June 8, 1819, the Long Expedition crossed the Sabine River into Texas.

The doctor moved quickly and set up a provisional government that declared the independence of Texas. It took the Spanish officials a while, but once they began moving, Long's days were numbered. By November the Americans had been driven out of east Texas. Long escaped and continued his adventures against the Spanish for two more years before he was killed. (See also July 23, Dec. 21.)

In the summer of 1894, the city decided it needed a fresh water supply. Drillers set up a wooden derrick and cable tool rig and started looking for water. At a depth of 1,035 feet, crude oil began rising to the surface.

Some townsfolk were upset that the water well was ruined; others got in touch with a Pennsylvania oilman named Joseph Cullinan and had him come see the oil. He saw, and set up a drilling operation that was to make Corsicana a boomtown.

Cullinan's biggest day was to come less than ten years later when he hit big at Sour Lake and his "Texaco" company was born.

## JUNE 9

1894

The first commercial oil field in Texas was not at Spindletop. It was at Corsicana, just south of Dallas.

## JUNE 10

1821

Moses Austin's life had never been one crowned with success. His last idea—the idea to colonize Texas—was his best, but he never

Oil for sale: The first commercial oil field in Texas was at Corsicana, 1894. (Barker Texas History Center)

saw it through. As Austin returned home to Missouri to tell his family of success in getting a Mexican grant (see Dec. 23), he was beaten and robbed. He made it home in time to beg his son, Stephen, to carry on the colonization effort.

On June 10, 1821, Moses Austin died. The idea that had burned his brain for two years was passed on to his son, who attacked the job with a passion that Moses was never able to muster in his lifetime.

## JUNE 11

### 1832

Lucy Holcombe Pickens was born on June 11, 1832, and was one of the most prominent women of Marshall before the Civil War. In 1857 she married Francis Pickens of South Carolina, the U.S. ambassador to Russia. During her stay in Moscow, she became fast friends with Czarina Catherine II. The Russian czarina showered her with gifts, including fine jewelry.

When the war broke out, Pickens came home and was elected governor of South Carolina. Lucy was so committed to the Southern cause that she sold her fine Russian jewelry to outfit a Confederate army unit. Her greatest honor, however, came when the Confederacy started to print money, and chose her as the subject of a stylized picture engraved on Confederate money. She was "Lady Lucy, the Queen of the Confederacy."

**Also on this date,** in the year 1865, bandits tried unsuccessfully to rob the state treasury in Austin.

## JUNE 12

### 1952

Henry Cohen was born in London while the American Civil War was raging. By the time he was twenty-five he had become a rabbi and immigrated to the United States, settling in Galveston. Two years after he arrived, the Great Storm of 1900 struck the island causing tremendous damage and resulting in a horrible death toll. The young rabbi, armed with a shotgun, led the return to law and order after the storm. He seemed to be everywhere, ministering to people from all faiths, and setting up and administering relief efforts.

Henry Cohen's lasting monument is dedicated to his people, Jews from all over the world who wanted to come to America, and Jews stuck in the crowded ghettos of New York. He set up the "Galveston Plan" to find homes in the South and Midwest for immigrants. Thousands of Jewish families who are third- and fourth-generation Texans now owe that fact to Rabbi Henry Cohen, who died at a ripe old age on June 12, 1952.

## JUNE 13

### 1875

Miriam Amanda Wallace was born in Bell County on June 13, 1875. A few months before her fiftieth birthday she became Texas's only woman governor. She missed becoming the first woman governor in America by just fifteen days.

Miriam married Jim Ferguson, the free-swinging and, she said, misunderstood, governor of Texas, and stood by his side through

Rabbi Henry Cohen of Galveston with a Confirmation class in 1905. He found homes for thousands of Jewish immigrants. (Archives of Temple Bnai Israel, Galveston)

some very tough days. A grand jury indicted him, and the legislature impeached him in 1917, barring him from holding the office.

Miriam Amanda, or M. A., and finally "Ma" to the newspapers, got her dander up and seven years later ran for governor. She told the crowd she didn't know much about government and would have to ask others for advice. The crowd knew that "others" meant Jim Ferguson, or "Pa," as he was known by now.

Pa would say, "Vote for Ma and you get two governors for the price of one." When asked about women's suffrage, Pa said, "If those women want to suffer, I say, let 'em suffer!" The campaign band would play "Put on Your Old Gray Bonnet," and the crowds of people

would cheer as Ma explained that she was running to clear her husband's good name. The campaign worked; Ma won, and Pa sat beside her in the Capitol and ran the state.

Ma served as governor from 1925 to 1927, and came back to serve a second term during the Depression; but try as she might, she never cleared Pa's name. (See also Jan. 20, Aug. 25.)

1832

At Anahuac the Texas Revolution was born. It was in Anahuac that Texans first gathered and organized an army of sorts in open rebellion to Mexican rule. And it was just a few miles away, on June 13, 1832, that the colonists first drew up a written resolution of war against the Mexican government. The document, known to history as the Turtle Bayou Resolutions, deplored the actions of Juan Davis Bradburn, who was the garrison commander at Anahuac. Among other things, Bradburn had wantonly arrested William Travis and his friends, confiscated slaves, and generally acted like a tyrant.

The Turtle Bayou Resolutions spoke of constitutional violations and the breakdown of law, and included a pledge that was to be prophetic: If Mexico did not stop tromping on them, the Americans in Texas would not hesitate to fight for their liberty.

## JUNE 14

### 1875

Texas cannot claim Jefferson Davis, but it tried to. He came here first in 1847 as an officer with Zachary Taylor's force and later, while secretary of war, was responsible for bringing camels to the state in a less-than-successful experiment to provide the army with a new means of transportation.

He was wildly popular with Texans as president of the Confederacy, and during his two years of imprisonment following the war, Texans did not forget the man who had led them in those dark days.

Davis lost his U.S. citizenship and never regained it. He was living in Mississippi in poverty when people in Dallas launched a drive to purchase a home for him and move him to Texas.

On June 14, 1875, Gov. Richard Coke wrote Davis informing him that the board of the newly formed Agricultural and Mechanical College of Texas wanted him to become the school's first president. Less than a month

later, Davis declined, saying he hoped to revisit Texas some day, but he never did.

## JUNE 15

### 1937

The night Buddy Holly took off on the plane that was to fall from a snowy Iowa sky and kill him, was the luckiest night in Waylon Jennings's life (see Feb. 3). Jennings, of Littlefield in west Texas, was a bass player in Holly's group, "The Crickets." He was supposed to

Jefferson Davis was in his late sixties when he was offered the post of first president of Texas A&M. He declined. (Barker Texas History Center)

be on the plane that night, but had given up his seat.

After the death of Buddy Holly and the end of the Crickets, Waylon drifted into folk, then country music. In 1965 he moved to Nashville, and the rockabilly became a legitimate country star. After following Willie Nelson to Austin and becoming a part of the "outlaw era" of country music, Waylon Jennings's place in music was secure. He came home to his roots and is a patron saint of Texas country music.

Waylon Jennings was born on June 15, 1937.

# JUNE 16

## 1943

Throughout the history of Texas, there have been dark incidents involving a breakdown of relations between blacks and whites. There were lynchings and riots all over the state, particularly in east Texas, before the civil rights movement of the 1960s.

One of the worst riots happened on June 16, 1943, in Beaumont. The rumor spread that a Negro had assaulted a white woman. For

Beaumont race riots, 1943: A mob attempts to get at a black prisoner. (Texas State Archives)

twenty-four hours, property in the black section was sacked and burned, and sixty people were hurt before the Texas Rangers and the National Guard finally restored order.

## JUNE 17

### 1937

New Year's Day 1931 was a wild time in little Kilgore. On Christmas Day, seven hundred people lived in the little east Texas hamlet. By New Year's, there were at least ten thousand, because Malcolm Crim struck oil.

Kilgore sat atop a pool of oil, and seven years later, on June 17, 1937, the Bess Johnson-Adams & Hale Number 1 roared in. In the time before spacing, the one-acre tract it sat on became the most densely drilled spot in the world. Twenty-four wells were drilled and a forest of derricks towered over the "world's richest acre."

## JUNE 18

### 1877

Charles Goodnight set up the first ranch in the Panhandle on the Prairie Dog Town Fork of the Red River, and in June 1877 joined Englishman John G. Adair to found the "JA" Ranch. Adair put up the money, and Goodnight put up the land . . . the Palo Duro Canyon. The canyon covers about seventy-five miles and the JA took up sixty of those miles.

At one point the ranch covered over one-half million acres, and with over a hundred thousand cattle, the JA was one of the world's great ranches.

*Note*: June 18 is an approximate date.

## JUNE 19

### 1865

As the Civil War raged, and the military advantage swayed from side to side, Abraham Lincoln issued the Emancipation Proclamation declaring that the slaves in the rebellious states of the South were free. The fact that this freedom could not be enforced or guaranteed made the famous document seem hollow, and a political propaganda ploy.

But two years later, on June 19, 1865, when Yankee Maj. Gen. Gordon Granger took up his command at Galveston, he issued a series of orders. He paroled Rebel soldiers, outlawed acts of secession, and ordered all slaves freed.

The order did indeed grant freedom but suggested: "Freedmen are advised to remain at their present homes and work for wages." It further stated that ". . . they will not be supported in idleness."

There were about a quarter of a million slaves in Texas, with nothing of their own, and little or no way to make a living, but as one suggested years later, "At least from Juneteenth on we didn't have to put a bridle on a mule for anyone 'cept ourselves."

## JUNE 20

### 1899

In the last summer of the 1800s it began to rain over the Brazos, and it seemed as if it would never stop. People who lived through it talked all their lives about the great Brazos flood of 1899. The rain started on the seventeenth; by the twentieth, the river was out of its banks, and when it crested on the twenty-eighth, the old river had covered 12,000 square

Kilgore's oil boom in the 1930s produced "the world's richest acre." (Texas State Archives)

miles and killed at least 284 people. At Hearne the water flowed over the flood gauges, so no one knows how deep the water got in the great Brazos flood.

## JUNE 21

### 1917

Ross Sterling made his first money in the oil patch selling horse feed. Business was good, and he opened stores wherever the next boom was. By 1911, he had taken the feedstore profits and bought a couple of oil wells of his own. Next came a pipeline to carry crude from the Goose Creek field (see Aug. 5) to storage tanks on the wharf, where ocean-going tankers could dock.

In 1917 Sterling asked the Texas secretary of state for a charter to organize the Humble Oil and Refining Company. On June 21, 1917, the request was granted.

Sterling became president. Other officers included Robert Blaffer, who had once hocked his gold watch to pay a driller; William Farish, who had lived in a shack at the oil field and often did not have enough to eat; Walter Fondren, a driller in the Corsicana field; Henry Wiess, whose father had rented the mules to Captain Lucas at Spindletop; Charles Goodard, who had been a driller at Spindletop; and Jesse Jones, a Houston real estate man and lumber baron.

Jesse Jones did not make many bad deals in his life, but within a year he sold out shares in the company, and boasted of making a nice profit. Indeed he probably did. But had he held on, he would have been fabulously wealthy. The Humble company eventually became the largest company in the free world.

A stand of timber north of Houston became the Humble Field, and was the mother of what became America's biggest company, Exxon. (Houston Metropolitan Research Center, Houston Library)

# JUNE 22

### 1867

Yellow fever was the scourge of the Gulf Coast in the years following the Civil War. It is not easy to find much about it in the news reports of the day. News of sudden and frequent death is not the sort of thing that attracts settlers or business.

In the summer of 1867, there was death up and down the Texas coast. In June of that year, Indianola began to see an epidemic, and it was assumed the disease had been brought up from Vera Cruz where the fever was rampant. A family from Vera Cruz arrived by ship in Indianola and soon died. Everyone who came in contact with them seemed also to have been stricken.

In July a German immigrant left Indianola for Galveston and became stricken and died there. The disease was spreading. Before long, cases were reported far inland at Houston and Washington. Doctors who wrote long reports of the day assumed the disease was spread by the blankets the Mexican family slept on on the ship from Vera Cruz. It was not until much later that the means of transmission of the disease became known: the *Aedes Egypti* mosquito. Mosquitoes hatching in water storage vessels aboard ship picked up the disease from infected human passengers and spread the disease later to other humans.

*Note*: This is an approximate date. June was

the worst month of the worst year of yellow fever in Texas.

## 1876

Antonio López de Santa Anna died in obscurity on June 22, 1876. His later years were certainly not fitting for the "Napoleon of the West"; he was allowed to return to Mexico City two years before his lonely death.

In truth Santa Anna seemed constantly to exhibit a reach that far exceeded his grasp. As a general, he was a miserable failure. He lost Texas. He even lost his wooden leg in one battle against American forces. (He lost his real leg in a battle against the French.) As a leader of his people he spent about as much time in exile as he did in Mexico City trying to run the country.

Santa Anna wanted desperately to be a success. History remembers him for his monumental failures.

# JUNE 23

## 1931

Wiley Post was born in Grand Saline, Texas, four years before the Wright brothers flew the first plane. He was fourteen years old when he saw an airplane for the first time—at a county fair. It was love at first sight.

Before Post was twenty-five, he was flying planes at fairs and giving exhibitions of stunt flying and parachute jumping. By 1930, he was a test pilot, a racer, and a cross-country flier.

On June 23, 1931, Post took off in his plane, the *Winnie Mae*, on a trip around the world. He completed the eastward circle of the globe in eight days, fifteen hours, fifty-one minutes. Two years later he made the trip again and cut a day off his record time.

Wiley Post of Grand Saline flew around the world in the *Winnie Mae*, and later died in a crash with Will Rogers. (Western History Collections, University of Oklahoma Library)

Wiley Post loved to fly, and that led to a friendship with the great writer and comic Will Rogers. Together they set out in the *Winnie Mae* on a trip to Siberia. In August 1935, as they tried to take off from a small Alaskan village, the engines failed, and both men were killed in the crash.

# JUNE 24

## 1840

Henry Wax Karnes was a short, stocky man with a shock of red hair. He was one of the bravest of the men who fought in the Texas

Revolution. Later, as he turned to fighting the Indians, they called him *muy wapo*, which means "very brave."

Joseph Nance, in his book *After San Jacinto*, writes about the time Comanches captured Karnes, and squaws almost drowned him trying to wash the red out of his hair. When they discovered it would not come out, they started pulling out locks as souvenirs.

When President Mirabeau B. Lamar decided to move against the Indians west of San Antonio, as well as Mexican marauders, he chose Karnes to lead a regiment of volunteers to put down the problems.

On June 24, 1840, Karnes issued a call for volunteers. They were to furnish their own horses, guns, and equipment for six months. By the middle of July he had five hundred men pledged from Washington County and another two hundred from Fayette. As Karnes was preparing to take his force to the frontier, a mosquito did what Indians and the wars could not. Karnes contracted yellow fever and died before summer's end.

**Also on this date,** in the year 1716, to celebrate the feast of St. John, soldiers of the Ramón Expedition staged the first horse race in Texas.

# JUNE 25

## 1864

John Salmon Ford fought with the Texas army, and gained a nickname. As he sent out death notices, he would write, "Rest in Peace." Later the notation became "R.I.P." John Ford became "Rip" Ford, and as the War Between the States broke out, Rip Ford was named to command the cavalry of the west in the Rio Grande district.

The problem Ford found toughest was that the war was always being fought somewhere east of him, and he and his army were largely forgotten. Supplies were practically nonexistent, and news of the war in the east traveled very slowly.

In June 1864, suffering from a bad fever, Rip Ford ran into the Yankees at Las Rucias in Cameron County. On June 25, in a driving rainstorm, the cavalry of the west destroyed the Federal forces. Only eight Yankees managed to escape that day.

The victory at Las Rucias doesn't rate much space in most history books, but it was a big one for Ford's men, for they came up with magnificent spoils: Yankee horses, saddles, guns, wagons, and food.

The cavalry that the South forgot continued its thankless mission. On May 13, 1865, it ran into Lt. Col. David Branson and a force of Yankees at Palmito Ranch. The Confederates attacked with piercing Rebel yells, and routed the Federal forces. As the stragglers were rounded up and taken prisoner, they explained that the attack had been a surprise, because the war had already ended! Lee had surrendered and the Confederacy had collapsed.

Rip Ford and his cavalry of the west always got the news last, so it was fitting they should win the last battle of the Civil War, even though the war was over!

# JUNE 26

## 1928

In the hot summer of 1928 Houston was bustling. Jesse Jones had lured the Democrats to town for their first national political convention in the South since the Civil War.

Houston had built a convention hall for the 25,000 delegates and the 1,000 newsmen.

On June 26, 1928, the convention was gaveled to order. Franklin D. Roosevelt placed into nomination the name of New York Gov. Al Smith, the "Happy Warrior." Texas nominated Jesse Jones as a favorite son. The convention debated whether a Roman Catholic like Smith could win, but finally agreed on his nomination, with Joseph Robinson of Arkansas as his running mate.

As the summer turned into fall and then winter, the voters grew cold to the "Happy Warrior," and Herbert Hoover swamped him to win the Presidency.

1832

A preliminary bout for the main event of the Texas Revolution came at Velasco on June 26, 1832. The trouble spot in those days was at Anahuac, where the military commander declared martial law and arrested some citizens, including William Barret Travis. The Anglos were incensed, and sent some men down the coast to Velasco to pick up one of several cannons that they knew of.

The Mexicans in the Velasco garrison thought that was a bad idea, so they set out to stop the brash Texans. There may have been 100 to 150 Texans, and 100 to 200 Mexicans.

Official welcoming banner, 1928 Democratic National Convention. (Author's collection)

They shot at each other till the Mexicans ran out of bullets. Five Mexicans died, and twenty-one Texans were killed. It was the first case of bloodshed between Texas and Mexico.

# JUNE 27

## 1874

Adobe Walls was the name of a buffalo hunters' trading post on the South Canadian River in Hutchinson County. It is famous because of two important Indian battles that took place there in a ten-year span. The second of these occurred on June 27, 1874, with Quanah Parker and Lone Wolf leading seven hundred Cheyenne, Comanche, and Kiowa against twenty-eight hide-hunters and one woman gathered in a saloon and a couple of stores.

Two white men died in the initial charge. The great Chief Quanah Parker's horse was shot out from under him, and to survive he had to hide in a decaying buffalo carcass.

The Indians had been urged to fight by a medicine man named Isatai, who painted his horse with magic which would deflect bullets. After the initial repulsion, Isatai called for a siege; so the Indians surrounded Adobe Walls and waited, and that was a fatal mistake. The buffalo hunters, who made their living shooting things, were armed with fifty Sharps long rifles. One day one of the hide-hunters shot Isatai's magic horse right out from under him. Although he survived, he lived out his life in disgrace and was known no longer as Isatai, for the other braves renamed him "Coyote Droppings."

The shot that won the battle came later as Billy Dixon aimed his Sharps at the Indians high on the bluff and squeezed off a shot. An incredible 1,538 yards away (the buffalo hunt-

ers claimed it was a mile), an Indian tumbled from his horse, shot between the eyes. The Indians backed off, and soon left, as a rescue party arrived to save the day. (See also Nov. 26.)

Quanah Parker, the last great war chief of the Comanches. (Panhandle Plains Museum)

# JUNE 28

### 1892

After Congress passed a bill providing for a couple of new armored ships in 1886, a fierce competition developed over the design. An English company won, and designed a ship with two 12-inch guns and a 12-inch-thick belt of steel armor. The ship would carry 30 officers and 362 men. The proud ship would also carry a proud name—the *Texas*.

The first battleship *Texas* was launched on June 28, 1892. The *Texas* did well at the Battle of Santiago during the Spanish-American War, but superstitious seamen called her a "hoodoo ship" because of a succession of minor accidents, and the *Texas* never overcame the bad rap.

By February 1911 she had been renamed the *San Marcos*, and was ingloriously sunk as a target during gunnery practice. (See also May 18.)

**Also on this date,** in the year 1860, Southern Democrats nominated John C. Breckinridge of Kentucky for President.

The first battleship *Texas*, depicted here as it looked during the Spanish-American War, was thought to be a "hoodoo" ship. From *History of Our War With Spain*, by James R. Young. (Institute of Texan Cultures)

## JUNE 29

### 1907

The fine marble statues of Sam Houston and Stephen F. Austin in the capitol at Austin and in Statuary Hall in Washington, D.C., are the work of an eccentric, beautiful German woman who titillated and scandalized Texans.

Elisabet Ney was a liberated woman born a hundred years too soon. She dressed, acted, and lived differently, and therefore was forever strange to the people who lived in Texas in the late 1800s. Elisabet and her husband came to Texas from Europe, where she had made a reputation as a sculptress of the great and near-great. A German nobleman suggested to Elisabet and her husband, Edmund Montgomery, that they join him in a commune in America, and they did, settling in Thomasville, Georgia, in 1870. After the nobleman died, the doctor and his wife moved to Texas and bought a plantation house outside Hempstead.

Elisabet fell in love with the place, known as Liendo Plantation, and lived out her life there and in Austin. It was in the Hempstead house that Ney's most scandalous episode occurred. Her small son, Arthur, died of diphtheria. She made a plaster death mask, then threw the body on the logs in the east room fireplace.

As she grew older, her work improved, and her eccentricity developed to its fullest. She continued to call herself "Miss Ney" and lived apart from her husband much of the time. In her later years she cajoled the legislature into appropriating money for the arts, and her dinner parties became the center of cultural gatherings in Texas. Her last great work, a statue of Lady MacBeth, is now in the National Gallery of Art in Washington.

On the night of June 29, 1907, the independent life of Elisabet Ney came to an end. She was buried on the plantation grounds with the death mask of her son Arthur.

## JUNE 30

### 1835

The Mexican garrison at Fort Anahuac had been a source of early trouble to the Texans as well as the Mexicans (see June 26). In June 1835 one of the Mexican soldiers shot an Anahuac citizen, and a few days later Andrew Briscoe and DeWitt C. Harris were jailed without reason.

When news of this reached San Felipe, citizens resolved to send a force of men to disarm the garrison. The man chosen to head the force was William Barret Travis, who had lived in Anahuac and knew the fort inside and out. He took his men to Morgan's Point and boarded the sloop *Ohio* for a trip across the bay to the fort. As the craft neared its destination, Travis fired off a five-pound cannon to let the Mexicans know he meant business. The first marine assault was then launched as the men rowed ashore.

On the morning of June 30, 1835, the Mexican troops capitulated and agreed to leave Texas immediately. It had been a blatant attack, and it was one move toward a war that would surely come.

The state's premier sculptress, Elisabet Ney. (Texas Collection, Baylor University)

The charge of Pickett's Brigade. Texans fought and died at Gettysburg. (Author's collection)

# JULY

## JULY 1

### 1863

In June 1863 the Army of Northern Virginia, under the command of Gen. Robert E. Lee, was heading into Pennsylvania and eventually to the big prizes of Baltimore, Philadelphia, and New York.

Gen. George Meade's Army of the Potomac was sent to check Lee's advance. On July 1, 1863, at 5:30 in the morning, the armies ran into each other outside a town called Gettysburg. John Bell Hood, now commanding a division that included his old Texas Brigade (see March 7, May 6), moved his men out from Chambersburg and headed for Gettysburg.

His division stopped at a place called Seminary Ridge, then moved to a rocky hill called Round Top, where a fierce battle ensued. Jerome B. Robertson, the ex-Texas state senator who now led the Texas Brigade, fell wounded during the battle.

The Battle of Gettysburg was to last until July 3. Union troops suffered 23,000 casualties, and about 20,000 Confederates fell at that place that was the turning point in the war; never again was there a serious Confederate attempt to invade the North.

## JULY 2

### 1888

On July 2, 1888, the Young Men's Democratic Club of Fort Bend County was formed.

That set up one of the bitterest feuds in Texas history. The Democrats split into two segments. The "Woodpeckers" were officials and ex-officials who held office as a result of the Negro-dominated Republican government that had been in place since Reconstruction, and the other Democrats, the "Jaybirds," were active in trying to get rid of it.

A month after the organization of the club, a Jaybird leader was shot and killed. It was the beginning of a series of shootings that culminated in a shoot-out in Richmond and the calling out of the Houston Light Guard to establish martial law. Finally the Jaybirds won and the black-dominated Woodpecker government was thrown out of office.

### 1716

Soldiers and priests of the Ramón Expedition decided to place a presidio at the edge of a lake west of the Neches River in Cherokee County. The priests ministered to the friendly Indians, and the tribe set to work to build a house for the Spanish. A grass-roofed house was completed on July 2, 1716, an event that marked the beginning of continuous settlement in the province of Texas.

## JULY 3

### 1897

America's first country blues singer to gain wide acceptance was a black man who was born blind on a farm near Wortham on July 3, 1897.

Blind Lemon Jefferson sang the blues in the 1920s, and his influence is still felt. (Barker Texas History Center)

As a teenager the blind boy sang on street corners and in churches and built up a loyal following of people who told him he had the gift. He took that gift to the dives and whorehouses of Dallas and eventually to tent shows and legitimate audiences in far-off Chicago.

When he sang the blues, whatever the audience, they listened. His recordings are prized today, and many a rock star traces his writing or singing style back to one of those records made in the 1920s by Blind Lemon Jefferson.

Jefferson started recording when he was twenty-eight years old. By the time he was thirty-two he had frozen to death in a Chicago snow bank.

## JULY 4

1883

The folks in Pecos in Reeves County claim the first rodeo held anywhere in the world happened there on July 4, 1883.

Cowboys from nearby ranches constantly argued about who was the fastest steer roper, so Pecos decided to settle the issue. Men from the "Lazy Y," the "NA," and the "W" ranch entered. Settlers came to town for the annual Fourth of July picnic, and to see the roping. The prize was a blue ribbon cut from a young girl's dress. The man who won the blue ribbon was Morg Livingston of the "NA" Ranch.

Thirty-four years later, on July 4, 1917, the first Indian indoor rodeo was held in Fort Worth.

## JULY 5

### 1901

John Henry Kirby came out of Tyler County as a lawyer, but he was to make his fortune as a lumberman. Kirby built his first sawmill in 1896 at Silsbee, and on July 5, 1901, chartered his Kirby Lumber Company. At one time the company owned 368,000 acres of timberland in east Texas and Louisiana, and over 16,000 people worked for him.

The story is told that a stranger asked a black porter in a Beaumont barbershop who that distinguished gentleman was who had just gotten a shave. The porter answered, "That is Mister John Henry Kirby, and when he crows, it's daylight in east Texas."

## JULY 6

### 1893

Kearie Lee Berry was born in Denton on July 6, 1893. He was a tough kid, some say because he had to fight often about his funny name. At the University of Texas he was the Southwest Conference Heavyweight Wrestling Champion in 1915 and 1916. He was a four-year letterman on the Longhorn football team, and lettered in track.

His tough nature was to serve him well when World War II broke out. He was in the Philippines when the Japanese overran the island and took the U.S. troops from Bataan on the infamous "Death March." Berry survived

that and nearly four years in a Japanese prison camp. He came out of the war a general with a chest full of medals.

## JULY 7

### 1911

That day on the plain at San Jacinto (see April 21), only thirty-four Texans were wounded and nine were killed in the brief, historic battle. One of the wounded was a young man from Kentucky, Alphonso Steele. He recalled charging, firing, reloading, and being struck down just as he was about to fire again. Steele survived his wounds, and lived seventy-five more years. On July 7, 1911, Alphonso Steele died; he was the last survivor of the Battle of San Jacinto.

Kearie Lee Berry, the Texas football star who became a hero of the Bataan Death March. (Texas State Archives)

## JULY 8

### 1907

C. W. Post and his famous "Toasties" make an interesting chapter in Texas history. Post was born in Illinois, and worked as a clerk there for years until a nervous disorder sidelined him. Young Post moved to Fort Worth to convalesce. The bad stomach and the nerves persisted, so he went to a sanitarium in Michigan.

Before long he had developed a cereal drink called "Postum." Then came "Toasties" and "Bran" and other breakfast foods that made Post rich. Apparently the money helped his nerves, because in 1906 he came back to Texas and moved out by the Cap Rock to start his own town, which he called "Post City." He fenced off great areas, built houses, and soon attracted over a thousand families.

Trying to bring rain to dry west Texas, C. W. Post ordered a series of rain-making experiments. Fifteen stations were set up on the Cap Rock, and whenever a cloud floated over, each of them fired off dynamite blasts until it rained or the explosives ran out.

A few years after he returned to Texas, Post's health failed and he died. His city remained, and on July 8, 1907, became the county seat of Garza County.

**Also on this date**, in the year 1833, Stephen F. Austin reached Mexico City with a proposal to establish a separate state government for Texas.

## JULY 9

### 1857

The stagecoach is as much a part of the folklore of the West as the six-gun or the rope. Until you actually ride in one, stagecoaches seem like an ideal way to travel. In 1857 they turned out to be an excellent way to deliver the mail.

James Birch made a contract with the government to open a mail run between San Antonio and San Diego, California. He used four-horse Concord stages and charged passengers $200 for the one-way fare. The distance was 1,476 wild miles, and it took an average of twenty-seven days to make the trip, at an average speed of about three miles an hour. That allowed plenty of time to enjoy the scenery, and the Indians.

The San Antonio–San Diego Mail Route's first stage rolled out of San Antonio on July 9, 1857.

## JULY 10

### 1824

Richard King was born in New York on July 10, 1824. When he was about eleven he stowed away on a ship headed for the Gulf of Mexico. By the time he reached manhood, King had been a cabin boy, a steamboat pilot, and a soldier in the war against the Seminole Indians. Later, in the Mexican War, he transported troops and supplies for Zachary Taylor's army. In 1850 Captain King joined Mifflin Kenedy in a boat business on the Rio Grande.

In 1852 the two men decided to leave the river and look for something on land that would make them a good living. They chose to buy a 75,000-acre Spanish land grant called "Santa Gertrudis" and turn it into a ranch. The world knows it today as the King Ranch. (See also Dec. 10.)

## JULY 11

### 1949

George Taylor Jester went away to fight under John Bell Hood and came back to serve in the legislature and later as lieutenant governor. It seemed natural that his son Beauford should follow in his footsteps. In World War I, the Corsicana native served as a captain in the Ninetieth Division. When Beauford Jester came home he settled into the law and backroom politics, but seemed to have little interest in an elected office until he was fifty and became a member of the railroad commission. In 1946 Beauford Jester was elected governor and in 1948 won a second term.

On July 11, 1949, as he was riding a train from Austin to Houston, Jester died—the first Texas governor to die in office.

**Also on this date**, in the year 1881, William Buckley was born at Washington-on-the-Brazos. His son James became a U.S. senator from New York, and his son William Jr. is famous as a writer, magazine editor, and television talk show host.

## JULY 12

### 1870

When you look into the number of Indian raids and savage battles that were fought in Texas, you have to marvel at the indomitable spirit of the pioneer men and women. Nothing was safe on the frontier.

In early July 1870 Indians attacked a mail stage, and Capt. C. B. McLelland was sent out of Fort Richardson with men from the Sixth Cavalry to find the war party. On July 12, he found Kicking Bird and 250 Kiowas near the Little Wichita in Archer County. For two days they fought. Thirteen medals were awarded McLelland's men for heroism. For the troopers it was literally just another day's work, and no sooner were they shaved and fed than they knew they would go out again and again to fight the nameless battles that were slowly but surely wearing down the Indian.

## JULY 13

### 1859

Juan N. Cortina was a natural leader of men, despite the fact that he was uneducated and illiterate. Because of his boldness and bravery, Cortina became an idol along the Rio Grande.

He may have been a common killer and a thief before he came to the attention of people on the north side of the river, but after July 13, 1859, he became a force to be reckoned with. On that July day the city marshal of Brownsville arrested one of Cortina's men, and that started the Cortina Wars, which were to last for over a year and which would require Robert E. Lee and the army to stop.

Cortina would dash across the river with a band of men, shoot up a town and empty the jails of Mexican prisoners. In late October the Brownsville town guard, replete with cannon, went looking for Cortina. The fight that resulted was a debacle for the Americans and the apex of the prestige of Juan Cortina. He even captured the Brownsville cannon!

By then there was talk that Cortina could drive the Anglo-Americans back across the Nueces—a fear that brought in the army. Two days after Christmas, at Rio Grande City, the U.S. Army soundly whipped the Mexican outlaws. Cortina later made a comeback, trying to capture a steamboat and conducting other minor raids.

When Col. Robert E. Lee took command of the Eighth Military District, he demanded that Mexico break up Cortina's little army. His orders said if Mexico refused, Lee could take his army into Mexico to pursue the marauders. Lee advanced to the Valley, and Cortina's wars were over. As for Juan Cortina, he stayed on the south side of the river, plunging into politics and remaining a powerful man.

# JULY 14

## 1943

Jules Bledsoe was born in Waco in 1898. As he grew, so did his magnificent baritone voice. He sang in the choir at the Baptist church, belting out the spirituals of his people.

Bledsoe left Waco for Columbia University, then Chicago's Musical College, and finally studied overseas. In 1924 he made his New York concert debut.

The crown jewel of his career came four years later when he was chosen to sing the wonderful "Ol' Man River" in the Broadway production of *Show Boat*. He later played the lead in Eugene O'Neill's *Emperor Jones* in Europe and America.

Jules Bledsoe died at the age of forty-five on July 14, 1943. One of the greatest voices Texas ever produced was stilled.

# JULY 15

## 1839

Sam Houston understood the Indians, and spent a good deal of time living with them. In 1837 Houston went to see Chief Bowles of the Cherokee tribe and asked his help to pacify the wild Indians in west Texas. Later Houston struck a treaty giving Bowles and his tribe land along the Angelina River. But the Texas Legislature rejected the deal, and President Mirabeau B. Lamar order the tribe out of east Texas.

Bowles mobilized his warriors, and on July 15 and 16, 1839, with 800 braves, met 500 troops from the Republic of Texas at the Neches River a few miles west of Tyler. On the field of battle that day was David G. Burnet, the vice-president of the republic, and Albert Sidney Johnston, the secretary of war. In the Battle of the Neches, the Texans had overwhelmed the Indians, and Indian trouble in east Texas was virtually over.

# JULY 16

## 1839

Chief Bowles was the last to try to leave the Neches battlefield on the sixteenth (see July 15).

The betrayed chief of the Cherokees entered the battle wearing a sword and sash, a silk vest, and a military hat. He was very old, and had been wounded in the thigh. The old chief climbed down from his horse and started to walk away. A man named Henry Conner shot him in the back. The chief fell, rose to a sitting position, and waited for the Texans to come toward him. He made no attempt to surrender. He asked no quarter. A soldier named Robert Smith, whose father-in-law had been scalped by the Cherokees, drew his pistol and shot Chief Bowles in the head.

The sword that had been given the chief by his friend Sam Houston was removed, but his body was left on the battlefield that marked the last major fight between the Cherokees and the white man in Texas.

Juan Cortina terrorized the Texas border in the late 1850s. (Western History Collections, University of Oklahoma Library)

Jules Bledsoe in the role of Eugene O'Neill's *Emperor Jones*. (Texas Collection, Baylor University)

## JULY 17

### 1797

Philip Nolan was a superb horse thief who stole horses from Spanish Texas in the late 1700s, when it was a capital offense even to be there without a special license from the king of Spain. But in going in to steal wild horses, Nolan also led the first American expedition into Texas, and was the first Anglo-American to map this land.

Nolan was an Irishman working for James Wilkinson, a supreme schemer who wanted to be king of the southwest for starters, and the devil take the hindmost. At one time Wilkinson was paid by the Spanish while he was governor of the Louisiana Territory and commander-in-chief of the U.S. Army, and "was a traitor to every cause he ever embraced," according to *The Oxford History of the American People.*

Wilkinson somehow got his friend Nolan into Spanish Texas legally. On July 17, 1797, Nolan received a passport. It was to be the start of a series of forays into and out of Texas that ended with Spain fearing Nolan was gathering Indians and Americans to build a force to expel the Spanish. In 1801 he was murdered.

## JULY 18

### 1917

National Guard troops of Texas were organized into the "Lone Star" Thirty-sixth Division on July 18, 1917, and began furious training to get ready to fight the Hun.

Less than a year later the first elements of the Thirty-sixth arrived in France. By October 1918 the division went into combat. For twenty-three days it served in the Champagne sector during the Meuse-Argonne offensive. In those terrible twenty-three days the Texans suffered 2,600 casualties, but managed to free Reims from the Germans.

The division was demobilized at Camp Bowie in June 1919. Twenty-one years later it was brought back to life and sent out to gain even greater glory. (See also Aug. 14, Sept. 9.)

Twenty-nine hours and thirteen minutes later, on July 18, 1938, he landed in Dublin, Ireland. Corrigan said he had become confused and simply flew the "wrong way."

On July 19, an embarrassed commerce department suspended the certificate for Corrigan's plane so he could not fly home. It was too late; Douglas Corrigan was a hero.

Not many people believed the accident, but "Wrong Way" Corrigan became the darling of the American public. His ticker-tape parade in New York was the biggest since Lucky Lindy eleven years before (see May 20). It was, after all, quite an accomplishment: A 3,100-mile flight in an old plane without a wireless, weather reports, or adequate instruments.

The Houston *Chronicle* wrote, "Corrigan was the type to feel at home anywhere, even sailing alone at night, over the Atlantic in a nine-year-old airplane, with his Irish eyes twinkling at the stars."

## JULY 19

### 1938

Clyde Corrigan was born on a cold January day in Galveston. He changed his name to Douglas, however, because he so admired the actor Douglas Fairbanks.

The Corrigans moved to San Antonio, then to California, where Douglas fell in love with flying. In July 1938 he flew nonstop from California to New York. He wanted to fly the Atlantic, but authorities refused to give him clearance for the trip.

A disappointed Douglas Corrigan got into his plane and took off, supposedly on the return trip to California. But once he cleared Floyd Bennett Field, he turned the Curtiss-Wright monoplane east instead of west.

## JULY 20

### 1969

One of the most extraordinary events of the twentieth century occurred on Sunday, July 20, 1969.

Apollo 11 had left Cape Kennedy at 8:30 (CDT) in the morning of July 16, heading for the moon. American spacecraft had orbited the moon, but this time we were going to land on it.

Three brave men were aboard, Michael Collins, Edwin "Buzz" Aldrin, and Neil Armstrong. All had come to Houston to train for the flight at the facility that would direct it, once it left the ground in Florida. The flight was flawless. They flew 238,000 miles to do what no one had ever done. Collins stayed aboard the command module *Columbia* as Aldrin and Armstrong climbed into the lunar module. On July 20, the landing craft separated and moved into a descent orbit. At 3:17 P.M. a blue contact light came on in the lunar module, the *Eagle*, and Armstrong said, "Houston, Tranquility Base here. The *Eagle* has landed!" There was a tremendous emotional response around the world. The impossible had happened.

At 9:56:20 on that Sunday night, millions watched on TV as a shadowy figure in a silver-white suit gingerly climbed down the ladder of the *Eagle*. Armstrong, a twenty-eight-year-old American, was now standing on the surface of the moon.

There had been great conjecture on what the first words from the moon might be. The world remembers Armstrong's "That's one small step for man, one giant leap for mankind!" But in fact the first word ever uttered from the moon was "Houston." Sam would have been proud.

Apollo 11, the mission that put a man on the moon. (Author's collection)

Douglas Corrigan flies home to Galveston a hero. (Rosenberg Library, Galveston)

# JULY 21

## 1878

Sam Bass robbed from the rich, and kept it. He cowboyed around Denton for a while, then went north to the Black Hills of the Dakota Territory looking for gold. In Deadwood, Sam lost most of his money playing poker, and went out to find easier gold in stagecoaches and trains.

He came back to Texas telling friends he had struck it rich. Soon his men were holding up stagecoaches and trains around Dallas.

At Round Rock, Sam spotted a bank that looked like easy pickings, but Maj. John B. Jones and his Rangers were waiting, and in a furious gun battle Sam Bass was seriously wounded. One of his men, Frank Jackson, helped him to his saddle and the two made it to a live oak thicket several miles from town, but Bass was to die two days later.

A reporter from the Galveston *News* had once asked Bass who his gang members were, and Sam said, "If a man knows anything, he ought to die with it in him." He died on July 21, 1878. It was his twenty-seventh birthday.

# JULY 22

## 1933

If you had been in Freeport on July 22, 1933, it would have been a week before you saw the sun. The problem was not the dust that was beginning to blow through the Panhandle—it was rain. A huge storm, a cloudburst some said, sat over Freeport and dropped an average of twelve and one-half inches of rain over a 25,000-square-mile area. Floods caused property damage of well over a million dollars.

Sam Bass (far left) looks more like a frightened schoolboy than a cold-blooded killer. (Western History Collections, University of Oklahoma Library)

# JULY 23

## 1798

Jane Long's life was a sad but spectacular adventure. She was the first woman of English descent that we know of to enter Texas territory. She gave birth to the first Anglo child in Texas (see Dec. 21).

Jane Herbert Wilkinson was born on July 23, 1798, and married Dr. James Long, the star-crossed adventurer, when she was still a teenager. She followed him to Texas in 1819. Once, she spent a winter virtually alone in a frozen Galveston, of all places, fighting Indians and wild animals. Her husband was killed and she was forced to leave Texas. But Jane Long came back as one of Stephen F. Austin's Old Three Hundred colonists, and was linked romantically with at least two famous names in Texas history, Ben Milam and Mirabeau B. Lamar. She operated a boarding house at Brazoria and a hotel in Richmond, where she lived to a ripe old age.

## JULY 24

### 1958

Of all the Texans who have changed our lives in one way or the other, Jack Kilby has probably affected us the most. Kilby came up with an idea that eventually led to the computer-based society in which we now live.

While working for Texas Instruments in Dallas, Kilby conceived the idea for a monolithic integrated circuit. On July 24, 1958, he drew out on paper the central idea to put capacitors and resistors on a chip of silicon. The idea revolutionized electronics and opened a new era in the field. On September 12, Kilby demonstrated the first test of the integrated circuit.

## JULY 25

### 1974

On February 21, 1936, a black preacher in Houston's dirt-poor Fifth Ward prayed for a better life for his newborn daughter. The girl, Barbara Jordan, was to become one of Texas's greatest contributions to America, and bring a better life to many.

She became the first black member of the Texas Senate since Reconstruction. In 1972, she was elected to Congress, and was placed on the House Judiciary Committee against her will. She had wanted the Armed Services Committee, but Lyndon Johnson urged her to go for the Judiciary Committee, saying, "Some day when you get the hell beat out of you, you can become a judge."

She was a member of that second-choice committee when the question of impeaching President Richard Nixon came before it. On the night of July 25, 1974, the poor black woman from Houston got her chance to speak: "'We, the people,' is an eloquent beginning, but when the Constitution of the United States was completed . . . I was not included in 'We, the people.'" She said she felt for years she was left out by mistake, "but through the process of amendment, interpretation and court decision, I have finally been included in 'We, the people.'" She went on in that beautiful, deep voice of hers to deliver a civics lesson on the Constitution and impeachment, and ended by suggesting that if the eighteenth century Constitution did not reach Mr. Nixon, perhaps we should abandon it to a twentieth-century paper-shredder.

The *Texas Observer* said that after that speech, Barbara Jordan became a myth, an institution, a legend, a folk hero. For awhile there was talk she might be a vice-presidential candidate, or a Supreme Court justice, or an

Barbara Jordan, first black member of the Texas Senate since Reconstruction, U.S. Congresswoman, teacher. (Houston *Chronicle*)

attorney general. Instead, she served out her term and "retired" to the University of Texas as a teacher.

1882

On July 25, 1882, Roy Bean sent a postal card to the San Antonio *Express* announcing the opening of his first saloon west of the Pecos. The card said:

> . . . *My saloon is at the meeting point of the Great Southern Pacific and western extension of the Sunset Railway. No other saloon within a mile and a half from my place, and visitors will always find a quiet, orderly place, where they can get a good drink.*

The town was called Eagle's Nest Springs then. Later it became Langtry, and Roy became the justice of the peace dispensing the law west of the Pecos.

# JULY 26

1863

Sam Houston's final years on earth were probably not happy ones. His decision to try to keep Texas in the Union turned the hero into a villain for many Texans. Near the end his popularity began to return, but it was too late. He sat in his house in Huntsville and thought about old days of glory.

Early in July he went to Sour Lake to bathe his old battle wounds. When the general came home he had a bad cold that turned to pneumonia. On July 25, he fell into a druglike sleep and the family took up a death watch. In the morning he stirred, reached for his wife's hand and said, "Texas, Texas! Margaret . . ." Then he died.

A Union prisoner of war made his coffin.

The Jersey Lilly Saloon of Judge Roy Bean, Langtry. (St. Mary's University, San Antonio)

They buried him during a driving rainstorm in the little cemetery near his home. They marked his grave with a plain slab bearing his name. Later a shaft of Texas granite twenty-five feet high was placed over the grave. It bears the epitaph Andrew Jackson spoke: "The world will take care of Houston's fame."

## JULY 27

### 1931

One of the great brouhahas in Texas history happened in the July heat of 1931. It was much ado about nothing, but for that month it was news all over the world.

When a new bridge was opened across the Red River between Denison and Durant, Oklahoma, the company that owned the old toll bridge between the two states went to court to close the new one, claiming the state of Texas had failed to keep its agreement to buy the old bridge.

A judge ordered a temporary closing of the new bridge. The governor of Oklahoma screamed long and loud. He was "Alfalfa Bill" Murray (see Nov. 21), an eccentric, expatriate Texan. He called out the National Guard to break down the barricade. Texas put it back up with the Rangers. Murray came to the "war zone" armed with an old pistol, and directed his guardsmen to stand fast.

On July 27, 1931, Governor Murray extended martial law to the south end of the bridge and stationed guardsmen on Texas territory. Newspapers sent reporters to cover the "invasion." A week went by without anybody shooting at anybody, and the courts finally settled the matter; the free bridge was opened. Murray withdrew his guardsmen and sent them back to enforce martial law in the oil fields.

Gov. "Alfalfa" Bill Murray of Oklahoma exhorts his constituents during the Red River Bridge controversy. (Western History Collections, University of Oklahoma Library)

## JULY 28

### 1933

The Spanish were growing some cotton in Texas as early as 1745. When Jared Groce came to Texas in 1821 he brought cottonseeds and reintroduced cotton farming. With slaves to do the field work, cotton became king in Texas as well as the rest of the South.

It stayed that way for a hundred years. Then came the dust storms of the 1930s, and the Depression. You could not eat cotton, and the mills did not want it any more because people did not have money to buy clothes.

Roosevelt's New Deal offered something for everyone, and on July 28, 1933, William E. Morris of Nueces County received the first payment from the federal government for plowing under his forty-seven acres of cotton. It was an unpleasant thought, to be paid for doing nothing, but the times dictated the necessity. To many Texas farmers the cotton acreage reduction payment was the difference between surviving and starving.

## JULY 29

### 1961

In its long and colorful history, Texas has produced some great songwriters and performers. Think of a country song and it probably has a Texas theme, or a Texas performer or writer connected with it.

The first Texas songwriter to become nationally famous was a hill country native named Oscar Fox. He was a prolific songwriter who wrote pure cowboy songs that sold like hot cakes. Fox lived for eighty-two years and died July 29, 1961.

Oscar Fox composing a song at the piano.

## JULY 30

### 1923

Before noon on July 30, 1923, a crowd estimated at between five and ten thousand people gathered around a scaffold in Waco. Roy Mitchell was to die for murder. He had confessed to killing eight people. A noose was placed around his neck and the trap was sprung. It was the last public hanging in Texas.

Roy Mitchell, the last person to be legally hanged in Texas. (Western History Collections, University of Oklahoma Library)

# JULY 31

## 1964

Jim Reeves grew up in Carthage in east Texas. He was one of the best baseball players in town. He was also one of the best singers.

After pitching for the University of Texas and a couple of minor league teams, he worked as a disc jockey for a Henderson radio station and later used his wonderful voice to sing and record country songs. Before long the mellow voice of Jim Reeves was heard on the "Louisiana Hayride" and later "The Grand Ole Opry" in Nashville.

He recorded one hit record after another—such as "Four Walls" and "He'll Have to Go"—and was at the height of his popularity at age forty-one when he was killed in a plane crash on July 31, 1964.

An oil field at West Columbia, 1919. (Texaco)

# AUGUST

## AUGUST 1

### 1966

Around noon on the hot, clear, first day of August 1966, Charles Whitman started firing from the observation deck of the University of Texas tower. It was a day of absolute horror on the campus.

Whitman killed his mother and his wife early in the morning, then went to the University tower with a footlocker filled with guns. He killed three people on the tower, then started shooting at students walking across the campus. Ten people were killed on the ground and thirty-one were wounded. Finally police reached the observation deck and shot and killed Whitman.

Seventeen people died that day. No one ever knew why.

## AUGUST 2

### 1973

The Chicken Ranch was America's oldest continuously operating whorehouse. It was run by a madam named Edna Milton, who used an iron hand to make sure the big old white house in the woods near La Grange was as good a house as a house could be good. It can be argued that everyone knew it was there. It can be argued that countless young men who grew to be leaders of Texas visited the

place. It can be argued that Sheriff Jim Flournoy was negligent in not closing it. But the Chicken Ranch was an institution of sorts, beyond the law.

In the summer of '73 a Houston television news reporter, Marvin Zindler, began to report on the whorehouse, and asked the governor and the attorney general why they did not close the place. Gov. Dolph Briscoe reacted with great indignity upon learning from Zindler that Texas actually had a whorehouse in it, and if he had to, he would have the Rangers close it—after all, they had done everything else.

The pressure built, and on August 2, 1973, Sheriff Jim closed the house. He later said, "It's been there all my life and all my Daddy's life and never caused anybody any trouble. Every large city in Texas has things one thousand times worse."

## AUGUST 3

### 1974

As the one o'clock whistle sounded at the walls in Huntsville, the daily tedium of prison routine was shattered by another sound—gunshots. Inmates Fred Carrasco, Rudolfo Dominguez, and Ignacio Cuevas took over the prison library and turned it into a fortress. It was the beginning of the Huntsville siege that brought the world press to the walls and ended the only way it could: in death.

At the takeover, the inmates grabbed fourteen hostages, ten of whom were prison employees. Demands were made; deadlines passed; one hostage suffered a heart attack; and Fred Carrasco, a San Antonio killer, vowed to make good his escape.

The siege began on July 24, and it was not to end until Saturday night, August 3, 1974, an incredible eleven days later. As the ordeal progressed, prison officials gave Carrasco most of what he wanted, and on Saturday the third he ordered escape vehicles to wait outside. He started out of the library in a "piñata" built from large blackboards, books, and desks from the library. Inside with the prisoners were hostages Yvonne Beseda, Julia Standley, Novella Pollard, and a priest, Father Joseph O'Brien. Five employees and three inmates were handcuffed to the outside of the piñata to form a human shield. But Texas Rangers and corrections officers were waiting. They hit the escape shield with high-pressure water, and cut the handcuffs from the human shield outside, as gunfire came from inside. A gun battle raged. Within minutes it was over—Carrasco killed himself.

Rudolfo Dominguez and hostages Yvonne Beseda and Julia Standley died of gunshot wounds. Father O'Brien was critically wounded. The third member of the Carrasco group, Ignacio Cuevas, was captured. The eleven awful days of the Huntsville siege were over.

### 1861

In the early stages of the Civil War, the Federal blockade of Galveston harbor caused great financial problems in the Island City. Many local firms closed their doors, and about 40 percent of the population moved away.

In that first summer of the conflict, the U.S.S. *South Carolina* was off Galveston enforcing the blockade. On August 3, 1861, the Yankee schooner *Dart* came in close to scout Galveston and was fired upon by the south defense battery. That brought in the *South Carolina*.

As a crowd gathered on the sand hills to watch the excitement, the Yankee ship opened fire to answer a volley from the beach battery. A battle continued for a few minutes until an incoming shell landed on the beach, killing one of the spectators and injuring three others. The crowd scattered, and the word of the incident sent fear through Galveston's already tense population.

**Also on this date**, in the year 1859, the Comanches were expelled from Texas and relocated in Indian Territory.

---

# AUGUST 4

### 1941

W. Lee O'Daniel enjoyed being governor (see March 11), although by all accounts he wasn't a very good one. He won a second term, but in the middle of it, after Andrew Jackson Houston died shortly after being appointed a U.S. senator, O'Daniel decided to take his good-ole-boy manner and Golden Rule to Washington.

He entered a crowded field in the special election that contained such well-known names as Congressman Martin Dies and young Lyndon Johnson, as well as twenty-three other lesser-known men. He won, and on August 4, 1941, resigned the governor's office. Coke Stevenson, the lieutenant governor, moved into the mansion, and "Pappy" O'Daniel went to Washington. A political foe later was to say that no single proposal Pappy made in the Senate got more than two or three votes.

## AUGUST 5

### 1917

Goose Creek cuts through Harris County for only twelve miles before it empties into Galveston Bay. But the little creek has given its name to one of the state's great oil fields.

The creek had produced a muddy kind of rainbow-laden water that attracted prospectors after Spindletop. Those rainbows came from a pool of oil that was found in a variety of sands. In August 1916 a gusher roared in that brought up 8,000 barrels. In the years to come, deeper sands produced more oil and on August 5, 1917, the Simms-Sinclair Number 11 Sweet came in with an amazing 35,000 barrels a day.

All over nearby Tabb's Bay, you could see submerged wells, the first in Texas, bringing up the oil under Goose Creek.

## AUGUST 6

### 1889

The invention of barbed wire spelled the end of free grass in the Western plains. Not only could a fence keep cows in a pasture, it could keep cows out of a farm. A farm on that sea of grass was an abomination to many a cowman.

By the 1880s fences were going up all over the West. And they often were being cut down as well, to drive cows through, or to steal the ones inside. A notice of August 6, 1889, by W. G. Hughes of Boerne was typical: "I will pay a hundred dollars reward for information that will lead to the conviction of the felon who maliciously cut the Hamilton pasture on the Bandera road last night."

Fence-cutting reached epidemic proportions and the Rangers were called to form fence-cutting squads. The legislature went into special session to pass laws about fences and cutting them.

For nearly ten years there was a fence in north Texas that ran from the northeast corner of the Panhandle, southwest to Dumas, and then west to New Mexico. It took sixty-five carloads of wire to build it. After the Second World War, someone measured the fence row on the famous King Ranch and claimed it ran for 15,000 miles. The great historian of the plains, J. Evetts Haley, wrote: "The first spool of barbed wire . . . spelled change, radical change, and finally system for the new cow country of the West." The fence war was really a struggle as old as time itself, a struggle against change.

### 1945

Early in the morning of August 6, 1945, after a forty-three-second fall from the B-29 called *Enola Gay*, an atomic bomb exploded over Hiroshima, Japan.

There had been other possible targets that morning, and three weather reconnaissance planes went out looking for them. One of them, *Straight Flush*, was flown by a young Texan named Claude Eatherly. He flew over Hiroshima while others checked Kokura and Nagasaki. An hour ahead of the *Enola Gay*, Eatherly flew through clouds, then into a clear patch with the city below him. He radioed, "Cloud cover less than three-tenths at all altitudes. Advice: Bomb primary."

Eatherly's advice was taken, and aboard his plane the men debated whether to wait to see what the secret bomb might do or go home to the base at Tinian Island. Eatherly listened to the debate, then told his men, "Listen, if we don't get back to Tinian by two o'clock, we won't be able to get into the afternoon poker

While one well runs wild, workers in the Goose Creek field tend a slush pit. (Houston Metropolitan Research Center, Houston Library)

game." In the debate over poker vs. a secret bomb, poker won, and the *Straight Flush* left and missed the most important event of the Second World War.

## AUGUST 7

### 1907

When Johnson Blair Cherry came out of Texas Christian University, he took a job as the football coach at Ranger. After several winning seasons there, he moved to Fort Worth, and in 1930 began a spectacular career as the head coach of the Amarillo High School "Golden Sandies." In seven years Cherry and the Sandies won four state championships while losing just five games.

D. X. Bible, the head coach of the Texas Longhorns, brought Cherry to Austin as his assistant. For ten years he helped Bible mold Longhorn teams, and after the '46 season, Cherry became head coach. He was to stay on four years. With a new kind of formation called the "T", and a Dallas youngster, Bobby Layne, as the quarterback, Blair Cherry's team kept on winning. His Texas record included one Southwest Conference championship and three bowl games, a number two national ranking, and the first undefeated Longhorn team in the conference.

Blair Cherry was born in Kerens on August 7, 1907. Shortly before he died in 1966, he was elected to the Texas Sports Hall of Fame.

# AUGUST 8

## 1865

One of the most famous and certainly among the most flamboyant of cavalry generals, George Armstrong Custer spent about a year in Texas to support the Reconstruction government.

Custer was a general three years after he graduated from West Point, and still under thirty when he got the call to come to Texas. On August 8, 1865, Custer and his troops left Alexandria, Louisiana, for Texas. Later that month they arrived in Hempstead, where Custer remained until the fall, when he went to the state capital to help the Carpetbag government maintain law and order.

Gen. U. S. Grant had earlier said that he suspected a large force of cavalry would be required in Texas and he wanted someone like Custer to be in command.

Eleven years after Custer's stay in Texas, the legislature passed a resolution of condolence: ". . . in relation to the massacre of General George Armstrong Custer and his men at Little Big Horn."

# AUGUST 9

## 1809

William Barret Travis was born in Saluda County, South Carolina. So was young James Butler Bonham, and ten men who became state governors, and two Civil War generals. From the crowded ground of greatness, Travis, by legend and deed, stands very tall. He was born on August 9, 1809, according to the family Bible, though the date is questioned by several historians.

His biographer, Archie McDonald, suggests any schoolboy knows Travis died at the Alamo, but we don't know much more. It is, says McDonald, as if Travis was a tropical hurricane that rose unseen and unknown until it became a full-blown storm that quickly blew away, leaving a vivid memory of its brief moment of glory.

We know he taught school, studied the law, married, had a son, and suddenly left wife and child and came to Texas. He spent no more than five years in Texas. He plunged into the politics of the day, and was an adventurer, a firebrand, a lady's man (see Dec. 28), and, finally, a martyr at the Alamo.

He did all that in less than twenty-seven years, and if he always seems larger than life, it is because he was. For the purposes of history, the Alamo was the right place at the right time. For purposes of the kind of life Travis pursued with great vigor, it was in the wrong place, at the wrong time.

# AUGUST 10

## 1862

Near Comfort in Kendall County stands a monument with the words, "Treue Der

Union." It stands there to keep alive the memory of nearly seventy men, mostly German, who graphically demonstrated "loyalty to the Union." The men were trying to make it to Mexico where they hoped somehow to join up with Federal forces.

On the morning of August 10, 1862, as the Union sympathizers were camped on the bank of the Nueces River, Confederate soldiers caught up with them and attacked. Some died then; others escaped to be killed in a second attack on the eighteenth. Of the seventy Germans, thirty-two were killed and some others were taken prisoner and later shot.

When the war finally ended, a group of Germans gathered the bones of the men and buried them in a common grave.

# AUGUST 11

## 1849

The closer a family lived to the frontier in the years before the Civil War, the closer that family was to tasting the wrath of the Indian. When the army could not keep the peace in south Texas, a call went out for help. On August 11, 1849, Gen. George Brooke asked Gov. George Wood for three companies of Rangers. They would be stationed in Corpus Christi and cover the area from Goliad to the Rio Grande.

General Brooke reported that thirty-six people had been murdered by Indians and

Company F of the Texas Rangers' Frontier Battalion, early 1880s. (Texas Ranger Hall of Fame)

1,300 head of livestock had been stolen in Nueces and San Patricio counties alone. Men like Bigfoot Wallace, John S. Ford, Henry McCulloch, and J. B. McGowen commanded the Indian fighters, and until the fall of 1851 the Rangers and the Federal troops made a potent force.

## AUGUST 12

### 1840

The Comanche was a superior guerrilla fighter. He could hit and run with the best of them, but in August 1840, Comanches attacked the town of Victoria and killed and looted. They stole over two thousand horses in the raid, and in subsequent attacks stole everything that was not nailed down.

As the Indians headed west, an army of soldiers and settlers gave chase. On August 12, 1840, near Lockhart at a place called Plum Creek, the white man caught up.

The battle of Plum Creek was a slaughter for the Texans. Over eighty Indians died that day, and just one Texan. Although the horses were scattered, the stolen goods were recovered. Never again did the Indians raid a major Texas town.

### 1936

It was Gen. Philip Sheridan who said, "If I owned hell and Texas, I would sell Texas and live in hell." Indeed it sometimes does seem hot enough in Texas to make the switch. The U.S. Weather Bureau says the hottest day ever recorded in Texas was August 12, 1936, when the mercury hit 120 degrees at Seymour.

**Also on this date**, in the year 1860, Temple Houston was born in Austin, the first child born in the Governor's Mansion.

## AUGUST 13

### 1912

One of America's great golfers was born in Dublin, Texas, on August 13, 1912.

He charged around the world's golf courses like a Banty rooster, and sportswriters gave the slight young man the name "Bantam" Ben Hogan. Hogan was a perfectionist on the golf course and was a ruthless competitor who won sixty-three tournaments, including all four of the world's major titles.

Ben Hogan's career almost ended in 1949 in a tragic automobile accident. After months of recuperation, he entered the Los Angeles Open to see if he could withstand the stress and pain of playing seventy-two holes of golf. Ben Hogan tied for first.

"Bantam" Ben Hogan was one of the greatest golfers of all time. (Texas Sports Hall of Fame)

# AUGUST 14

### 1945

On Sunday, December 7, 1941, as a convoy of U.S. ships steamed seven days out of Hawaii heading for the Philippines, the Japanese bombed Pearl Harbor. The convoy of ships looked for safe harbor. Aboard one of the ships were men of the Second Battalion, 131st Field Artillery Regiment, Thirty-sixth Infantry Division, mobilized from the Texas National Guard. The convoy tried the Fiji Islands, then Australia, and finally Java.

The men reached Java just in time to run into a Japanese invasion force, and by early March, the entire battalion, along with Dutch, British, and Australian forces, had become prisoners of war.

For forty-two months the men worked in the jungles of Singapore and Manchuria. They were forced to build ships and roads, and one group of the Texans was sent to help the British build the famous bridge over the River Kwai for the Burma-Thailand Railroad.

All this time, there was not one word for the folks back home concerning the whereabouts of the Second Battalion. The war department censored any word about them. For the duration of the war they were spoken of only as the "Lost Battalion."

Liberation for the men came on August 14, 1945, shortly after the atomic bomb fell on Hiroshima, and for the first time mothers, fathers, and wives learned the fates of their loved ones in the Lost Battalion. (See also Sept. 9.)

### 1952

The age of the super highway dawned following the Second World War. Elevated ribbons of concrete began to stretch from every city, as more and more automobiles crowded in and looked for room.

On August 14, 1952, the Gulf Freeway linking Houston and Galveston was dedicated amidst much fanfare and celebration. To the three and one-half million people who use it in the 1980s, an oft-repeated joke is that it is either the state's longest parking lot, or that it will be a hell of a road if they ever finish it.

# AUGUST 15

### 1844

For five years, from 1839 to 1844, the ground in Shelby County ran red with blood because of a classic Texas feud called the Regulator-Moderator War.

The thousands of people who lived in deep east Texas had been in a no-man's-land. The Spanish and later Mexican governments refused to claim them, and the United States had no jurisdiction over them through most of the early and middle 1800s. With the birth of the republic, the east Texans continued to dish out their own brand of law and order, which usually included summary judgment. In 1840 a district judge was appointed by the republic, but the measure didn't help.

Charles Jackson, a rather shady fellow who came to Texas running from the law, charged counterfeiting of land rights was rampant in Shelby County. He killed a man over the issue, and was brought to trial. After he was acquitted of murder, Jackson decided to take the law into his own hands by forming a group of vigilantes that gained the name "Regulators." They "regulated" justice by burning homes and barns of people they did not like, and making arrests and holding trials. The armies grew to about 150 on each side, and Shelby, Panola, and Harrison counties were not safe.

Ceremonies on August 14, 1952, launch the opening of the Gulf Freeway connecting Houston and Galveston. (Houston *Chronicle*)

On August 15, 1844, President Sam Houston issued a proclamation calling on both sides to lay down their arms. He sent a militia force to arrest the leaders, then sat down as a mediator with the men and worked out a peace. The militia stayed on to keep down trouble, and despite some deep and lasting family hatreds, the Regulator-Moderator War was over.

# AUGUST 16

### 1798

Consider the rise of Mirabeau Buonaparte Lamar. He was a private before the Battle of San Jacinto started. He was a colonel when it ended. Ten days later he was secretary of war. A month later he was commander-in-chief of the army. In five more months he was the vice-president, and within less than two years he was elected president of the republic.

Lamar was born in Georgia on August 16, 1798, and was clearly a slow starter. He made several runs for public office in his home state that left him bitter and ill. When he was thirty-seven he drifted into Texas in time to become a war hero and begin his meteoric rise to greatness. In later years he was a senator, a lieutenant colonel with Zachary Taylor's army at Matamoros, and ambassador to Nicaragua and Costa Rica.

Through it all he wrote fairly decent poetry, courted the widow Jane Long (see July 23, Dec. 21), and remained one of the almost legendary giants who walked at the right time on Texas soil.

## AUGUST 17

### 1786

If you think of a pure American man of the frontier you don't have to search your mind long to come up with Davy Crockett. He was born in Tennessee on August 17, 1786.

Though he had little formal schooling, he was far from an uneducated, ignorant back-woodsman. He wrote poetry and made intelligent speeches in his terms in the U.S. Congress. He was also a skilled woodsman, an excellent shot, and terribly brave. He came to Texas after he lost a campaign for reelection to Congress. When he heard of the problems at the Alamo, Crockett and some of his Tennessee friends marched in to help. He died there.

During his lifetime, he added as often as he could to the romantic legend that was growing up around him, and long after his death he became the subject of a Broadway play. Books have been written trying to explain why he did what he did. His credo explained it best: "Make sure you're right, then go ahead." Even if he had not been martyred at the Alamo, David Crockett would have been a singular American.

## AUGUST 18

### 1983

At 3:15 on the morning of August 18, 1983, Hurricane Alicia found the land at San Luis Pass on Galveston Island. As it swept the west end of Galveston Island, the storm headed toward the most populous area of the state, aiming its fury at downtown Houston.

Storm tides at Baytown ran ten feet, with five-foot waves in front of the surge. The wind gusted to 103 miles per hour. Twenty tornadoes were spawned from the giant storm cloud. Boats were scattered at Seabrook; beach homes disappeared; billboards and trees snapped in Houston; and flying debris smashed the windows in the skyscrapers. Twenty-one people died, and the damage added up to an astounding $1.2 billion.

It was not the most violent, nor deadliest hurricane to strike the coast, but it was Texas's first billion-dollar hurricane.

## AUGUST 19

### 1895

Everybody in El Paso knew who he was. The slight man with the blue eyes and sandy moustache was John Wesley Hardin, reformed killer (see March 16). Hardin had come west after being given a pardon from the Huntsville prison. He was not a model of the city, but he did manage to lead a respectable life for a while.

Hardin's brush with being a nice guy came to an abrupt halt on August 19, 1895, after an argument with one John Selman. Selman walked into the Acme Saloon and calmly shot John Wesley Hardin dead. He had lived forty-one years and had killed about thirty men. They buried him in Potter's Field after a brief service totally devoid of any mourners.

## AUGUST 20

### 1905

When Jack Teagarden was seven years old, he picked up a trombone, and that was the beginning of one of the great careers in jazz.

Teagarden was born in Vernon, August 20, 1905. He was influenced by the songs he heard both from the black families who lived along the Red River and his Indian ancestors. The love for black music led to his becoming the first white man to make a record with a black artist.

In the early 1920s Teagarden played with a number of jazz groups and dance bands around Houston and New Orleans. Strangely enough, white audiences thought that only black musicians could play jazz, so jobs were hard to find, and young Jack headed east.

He played with Tommy and Jimmy Dorsey and their famous bands; with Paul Whiteman; and later formed his own band. His career was to last over forty years, and he recorded hundreds of tunes. To many, Jack Teagarden was the greatest jazz trombonist who ever lived.

It was said that John Wesley Hardin was so mean he once shot a man for snoring. (Western History Collections, University of Oklahoma Library)

## AUGUST 21

### 1906

The most famous story you hear about the Texas Rangers is the one about a town calling for a company of Rangers to quell a mob. When the train pulled into town and a single Ranger got off, the local citizens protested that the Ranger could not do the job alone. The Ranger looked around, expectorated a stream of tobacco juice, and calmly said, "Well, you ain't got but one mob, have you?"

That Ranger was supposed to have been Captain W. J. (Bill) McDonald. In the quiet, aw-shucks tradition of the Rangers, Bill was something of a hot dog. But he was very good at what he did. When a riot broke out involving black soldiers at Brownsville, the Rangers were called. On August 21, 1906, Captain McDonald arrived and went to Fort Brown where the Negroes were holed up. Despite warnings that he would be killed, Ranger McDonald walked up to two heavily armed black soldiers and said, "I'm down here to investigate a foul murder you scoundrels have committed." Then he barked out, "Put up them guns." They did, and the riot was over. Maj. C. W. Penrose of the U.S. Army, who witnessed the incident, said, "Bill McDonald would charge hell with a bucket of water."

## AUGUST 22

### 1938

Sam Robertson should have died on more than one occasion. In 1916, as a scout for Gen. John J. Pershing's army in Mexico on the hunt for Pancho Villa, he was captured, dragged behind a horse, beaten, and left for

The flamboyant Capt. Bill McDonald (far right) with his Texas Rangers, 1897. (Western History Collections, University of Oklahoma Library)

dead. Robertson survived, and as the First World War started, he joined the army and organized the Sixteenth Engineers.

In 1918, he was given one of the worst jobs of the war. Robertson, now commanding the Twenty-second Engineers, was asked to build a small rail line to the front of the trenches. The line was built even though the men were constantly under fire. For that feat, Col. Samuel Robertson won the Distinguished Service Medal and the Congressional Medal of Honor.

On August 22, 1938, the man who had cheated death so often died in bed at Brownsville. He was seventy-one years old.

On August 23, 1917, Houston police roughed up a black soldier and a woman and then arrested a black military policeman who came to the soldier's aid. What followed was a series of rumors that the black soldiers were marching into town, and the police were marching out to Camp Logan. Finally about 150 troops clashed with the police, and when it was over seventeen people on both sides were killed, sixteen people were wounded, and in a subsequent court martial, thirteen soldiers involved in the so-called Camp Logan riots received the death penalty; forty-one got life imprisonment.

## AUGUST 23

### 1917

Camp Logan was a National Guard camp in what is now Houston's Memorial Park. It became an emergency training center in World War I.

About one out of every four men called up in Texas in the First World War was a black man, but most were relegated to labor battalions, segregated on the base, and restricted in their movements in cities.

## AUGUST 24

### 1949

History was made on August 24, 1949, when the University of Texas announced that Herman Barnett, a twenty-three-year-old Negro from Lockhart, would be admitted to the U.T. Medical Branch. He would actually register at the Texas State University for Negroes at Houston, but would be a student in Galveston at the medical school. Barnett would become the first black admitted for study alongside whites in the university.

Polls of the day indicated that 76 percent of all Texans opposed college integration, so while Barnett went to class, the legislature passed a quick appropriation bill to fund a separate black medical school in Houston. However, the impact of subsequent segregation rulings by the U.S. Supreme Court prevented construction of the school.

# AUGUST 25

## 1917

Gov. Jim Ferguson carried on a running feud with the University of Texas. He tried to abolish fraternities, tried to get rid of some members of the board of regents, and referred to professors as "butterfly chasers." In June 1917 Governor Ferguson vetoed a $1.5 million appropriation for the university.

The governor's foes, and he had many, began to mass. Late in July he was called to testify before a Travis County grand jury. A few days later he was indicted on nine charges, including misapplication of public funds. He was also accused of contempt for refusing to say where he got $150,000 (he later admitted it had been a campaign gift from the state brewing industry), and charges were brought for what amounted to bad treatment of the University of Texas.

The legislature began an investigation and drew up twenty-one articles of impeachment. The senate considered the charges for three weeks and convicted the governor. On August 25, 1917, Ferguson resigned, and Lt. Gov. William P. Hobby became governor of Texas.

Jim and Miriam Ferguson got into their Packard automobile and drove out of Austin. Seven years later the old Packard pulled into the driveway of the governor's mansion again.

This time Miriam was governor. (See also Jan. 20, June 13.)

# AUGUST 26

## 1836

August 26, 1836, as the smoke was clearing from the Texas Revolution, a couple of New York brothers, John and Augustus Allen, bought the John Austin half-league of land that lay along Buffalo Bayou not far from Harrisburg. They laid out a town and named it after the hero of the Battle of San Jacinto.

The brothers aggressively promoted the new town. One of their newspaper ads proclaimed:

*There is no place in Texas more healthy, having an abundance of excellent spring water, and enjoying the sea breeze in all its freshness.*

Houston has been a town for promoters ever since.

# AUGUST 27

## 1908

Lyndon Baines Johnson was born near Stonewall on August 27, 1908. He went on to become a congressman, a senator (see Aug. 28), the senate majority leader, the Vice-President, and the thirty-sixth President of the United States.

Once, as Johnson completed an inspection at a military base in the South, a young officer saluted and said, "Your helicopter is over here, Mr. President." LBJ looked out across the military base and said, "Son, them's *all* my helicopters."

This inaccurate artist's rendering of the new city of Houston was widely circulated in the Eastern press and helped to sell Houston to settlers. (Barker Texas History Center)

Pa and Ma Ferguson at the polls, 1917. (Barker Texas History Center)

(Author's collection)

Lyndon Johnson in Houston. (Gulf Photo)

# AUGUST 28

### 1948

To a great many old-time Texans, Lyndon Johnson was "Landslide Lyndon." On August 28, 1948, Johnson met Coke Stevenson in the runoff for the U.S. Senate (see March 20). Stevenson had won the primary by 72,000 votes. Johnson worked hard, and as the votes were counted, the lead seesawed. Six and one-half hours after the polls closed, Stevenson was leading Johnson by 54 votes, when Duval County, the bastion of political boss George Parr, reported Johnson had gotten 4,600 votes to Stevenson's 40.

The lead changed hands again and again and finally, on September 1, all the votes were in and Coke Stevenson had won by 114 votes out of a million cast. Two days later, George Parr was heard from again. Jim Wells County, the neighbor to Duval County, announced amended returns. Among the "amended" returns was Box 13 in Alice, which had not been counted for some reason. It gave LBJ 202 votes and only 1 for Stevenson. "Landslide Lyndon" won the Senate race by 87 votes.

# AUGUST 29

### 1839

When Sam Colt's new handgun arrived in Texas around 1837, it attracted widespread attention, though few sales were recorded. It

was too light, and to reload it required breaking the pistol down into three pieces.

To a cowboy on a horse, that kind of gun was of little use. Texas Ranger Sam Walker went north to New York to suggest a few changes to Sam Colt. Colt and Walker spent several days at the gun factory, drawing out ideas, trying this option and that. After a month, Colt had a new revolver—"The Walker"—named for the Ranger. It was heavier, stronger, with a simpler spring system, and the revolutionary feature—a lever rammer that seated the bullets without having to take the gun apart.

Colt applied for and received a new patent on August 29, 1839. After that, things were never quite the same on the frontier.

## AUGUST 30

### 1874

In the mid-1870s it became apparent that Cheyennes, Comanches, and Kiowas that were supposed to be on reservations in Indian Territory were actually hiding in the Texas Panhandle.

Gen. George Miles and 750 soldiers were sent from Fort Dodge, Kansas, to start moving them out. Miles found the Indians at Palo Duro Canyon on August 30, 1874. The five-hour fight that followed was the first of fourteen battles in the Red River War, battles that broke the Indian power in the Panhandle.

## AUGUST 31

### 1871

James E. "Pa" Ferguson was born in Salado on August 31, 1871. His father was a Methodist preacher who announced to his church's conference meeting that "We have named him Jim. He weighs thirteen pounds, and some day he will be governor of Texas."

Young Jim inherited the gift of gab from his father. He was a great and prolific storyteller who finally passed the bar and was elected city attorney of Belton. He got into banking in Belton and Temple, but longed for more, and decided to run for governor.

He told farmers he was a farmer, and businessmen he was a banker, and he made great long speeches that spellbound the listeners. In January 1915, he became the governor. Two and one-half years later he became the only Texas governor to be impeached (see also Jan. 20, Aug. 25).

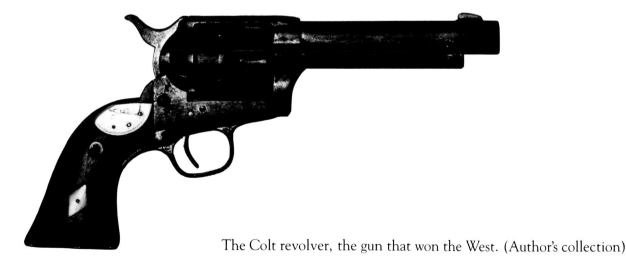

The Colt revolver, the gun that won the West. (Author's collection)

# SEPTEMBER

## SEPTEMBER 1

### 1972

In the late sixties the Mexican-American began to establish himself as a potent political force in Texas. A political organization called La Raza Unida had elected officials to local offices in twenty-two counties by 1970. By 1972 some Hispanics wanted a statewide office and a nationwide voice. They wanted bilingual education in all schools, free legal service to all Mexican-Americans, and restoration of Spanish and Mexican land-grant rights.

On September 1, 1972, the founding national convention of La Raza Unida was held in El Paso. Delegates voted not to endorse either George McGovern or Richard Nixon, and told the Democrats and Republicans they would have to earn Hispanic votes by words and deeds.

## SEPTEMBER 2

### 1945

The greatest admiral of the Second World War was born in landlocked Fredericksburg, Texas, in 1885. Chester W. Nimitz graduated from Kerrville's Tivy High School and the U.S. Naval Academy. He was a great navy man with tremendous talent for letting people around him have their room to think and act. He said he learned from the German stock farmers in the hill country that the team with the slack plowed the deepest and the easiest.

When the Japanese bombed Pearl Harbor he was made admiral and became commander-in-chief of the Pacific Fleet. Nimitz surrounded himself with capable officers and gave them room to work. The turning point of the war came when Nimitz and his men decided

An early photograph of Chester Nimitz, who directed naval operations in the Pacific in World War II. (Houston Metropolitan Research Center, Houston Library)

that Japan's Admiral Yamamoto was aiming his navy at Midway Island. Yamamoto had 162 warships; Nimitz had less than half that many, and three aircraft carriers with about 230 planes. The staff worked out what they expected the Japanese to do, and Nimitz trusted them enough to order an attack. The Americans won, the Japanese navy was decimated, and MacArthur's island-hopping could continue to Tokyo. Nimitz called Midway the greatest sea battle since Jutland. Throughout the war the taciturn Nimitz shunned the press, quietly and efficiently doing his job, while occasionally chafing at the publicity MacArthur reveled in.

On September 2, 1945 (it was September 1 in the United States), the Allies and the Japanese representatives gathered on the deck of Adm. Bill Halsey's *Missouri*, while overhead fluttered the American flag that Commodore Perry flew when he entered Tokyo Harbor in 1853.

A chaplain gave the invocation, the band played the national anthem, and MacArthur spoke and invited the representatives of Japan to sign the instrument that would end the war. The general then signed, and invited Adm. Chester Nimitz to come forward and sign for the United States of America.

## SEPTEMBER 3

### 1844

Henri Castro, a Frenchman, secured a contract from Texas to settle a colony in southwest Texas around the Medina River. He brought in 485 families and 457 single men between 1844 and 1847.

On September 3, 1844, Castro and his first thirty-five colonists started building houses twenty-five miles west of San Antonio in the

place that became Castroville. Most of the early houses were built to resemble the Alsatian dwellings the pioneers remembered from their homes in France. Nine days after they arrived, the settlers started building a church, St. Louis, the first Catholic church between San Antonio and the Rio Grande.

The colony battled Indians, disease, and the unpredictable weather, but survived.

## SEPTEMBER 4

### 1766

To live on the Gulf Coast of Texas is to live in the way of a hurricane. For five months each summer Texas is in harm's way. A hurricane that gets into the Gulf has to hit land somewhere, and the path of many storms leads them into the long, curving Texas coastline. The Spanish records indicate the first known storm happened on September 4, 1766. It raged through Galveston Bay and destroyed a mission.

Typical early Alsatian architecture of Castroville. (Barker Texas History Center)

## SEPTEMBER 5

### 1898

One of the strangest tales of the Civil War involves Sara Emma Edmonds, who was born in Canada in 1814. She ran away to America, and when the war broke out disguised herself as a man and joined the Union army as a male nurse.

After Bull Run the small, frail "male" nurse was singled out by a commanding officer who was looking for spies. He suggested the young nurse dress up like a woman and spy on the Southerners. So it was that Emma Edmonds, pretending to be a man, started pretending to be a woman. After two years of service she left the army in 1863.

After marrying Linus Seelye, Emma moved to LaPorte. She had written a sensational book of her war experiences called *The Nurse and the Spy* that became a best-seller. In her later years Emma received a twelve-dollar-a-month pension for services to the Union army.

On September 5, 1898, Emma died in LaPorte.

## SEPTEMBER 6

### 1890

When Claire Lee Chennault was born on September 6, 1890, in Commerce, Texas, he could trace his family tree to the likes of Sam Houston and Robert E. Lee.

Chennault taught school for a while. When the First World War broke out he became a pilot and a flight instructor. His career appeared to be over when illness forced him to be grounded at the age of forty-six. That un-

fortunate situation led to his greatest fame: Chennault became an adviser to the Chinese air force of Chiang Kai-Shek.

With the coming of the war with Japan, Chennault organized the American volunteer group in China, "The Flying Tigers." That famous group became the Fourteenth Air Force in 1943, and Chennault was promoted to major general.

He died in 1958 and was buried in Arlington National Cemetery.

## SEPTEMBER 7

### 1863

The hero of the most spectacular Civil War battle in Texas was an Irish barkeep named Dick Dowling, who disobeyed his orders. Dowling ran a Houston saloon called the Bank of Bacchus. He volunteered for the Confederate army and was in charge of a Texas artillery battery. His general, John Magruder, ordered Dowling to spike the guns guarding Sabine Pass. Instead, Dowling and his men strengthened the fort and engaged in target practice out in the river.

In September 1863, twenty ships, carrying 5,000 troops, left New Orleans to invade Texas. On the night of September 7, the fleet arrived off the Sabine bar, and three gunboats, the *Clifton*, the *Arizona*, and the *Sachem*, went in to silence the guns at the fort. The next afternoon, as two of the ships got within firing distance of the fort, Dowling opened fire and hit them both. One went aground, the other surrendered, and the Union ships off the bar turned around and headed back to New Orleans.

There was never another serious attempt to invade Texas by way of Sabine Pass as long as Dick Dowling and his men were waiting.

Capt. Claire Lee Chennault (right) and other officers review an aerial display by flying students at Brooks Field, 1929. (San Antonio *Light* Collection, Institute of Texan Cultures)

# SEPTEMBER 8

## 1900

The greatest natural disaster in American history occurred at Galveston on September 8, 1900. Ships reported the progress of a giant storm across Cuba and into the Gulf of Mexico. As it neared Galveston, the city lay unprotected. There was no seawall, and the city was teeming with people who were attracted to the island's good life and growing economy.

On the seventh, people crowded the beach front for a while to watch the waves break.

But soon it became apparent the storm's fury would be aimed directly at Galveston. By the morning of September 8, 1900, the wind was screaming and the water was sweeping over the island. By eight that night the wind was blowing about 120 miles per hour and a tidal wave broke over the city. Buildings were shattered; others floated on wild, careening rides down what had been streets. It was a horrible night, and when the day broke, Galveston was in ruins. Half the city had been destroyed and between six and eight thousand people killed. There were so many dead there was not time to bury everyone, so bodies were stacked on barges and taken out to sea to be dumped.

The Galveston Storm of 1900 remains the worst natural disaster in American history. (Rosenberg Library, Galveston)

A few days later many of them floated back to the beach. (See also Oct. 27.)

Thomas Edison brought his new motion picture camera to the island and recorded one of history's first newsreel films of the devastation. The disaster spawned a popular song: "Wasn't that a mighty day? Wasn't that a mighty day? When the sea wave hit the town."

**Also on this date**, in the year 1907, the world-famous Neiman-Marcus store opened in Dallas.

## SEPTEMBER 9

### 1943

Late in November 1940 the Texas National Guard was inducted into the Federal service as the Thirty-sixth Infantry Division. The division was made up of citizen-soldiers who trained at hometown armories, and some officers who had been around since the First World War (see July 18).

Less than three years after the call-up, the Thirty-sixth was chosen to lead the landing at to the heartland of Hitler's Germany. In fact, some men from the Thirty-sixth overran Heinrich Himmler's summer home at Tegernsee and listened to V-E Day celebrations on the Nazi hatchet-man's own radio!

In nineteen months of combat the Thirty-sixth had the third highest casualty list of any American division. The dead numbered 4,000, with another 4,000 listed as missing, and 19,000 wounded.

Much of what we knew about the Thirty-sixth division came back to Texas in reports from a young war correspondent who wrote for the Dallas *Morning News*, and who became a world champion chili-maker in peacetime—Wick Fowler.

1861

One of the most famous fighting forces in the Civil War was Terry's Texas Rangers. On

This Catholic church was not exempt from the storm's wrath. (Rosenberg Library, Galveston)

Salerno in Italy. It was one of the bloodiest operations of the war, and on the morning of September 9, 1943, the Texas division became the first American force to invade the European mainland to test Hitler's Fortress Europe.

Before the division ever got off the beach, Pvt. James Logan of Luling won the Congressional Medal of Honor. There would be fourteen others, along with ten Presidential Unit Citations.

Before the men of the Thirty-sixth stopped, they had engaged in five major campaigns that took them from Camp Bowie to Rome, and on

Men of the fighting Thirty-Sixth with a sign in Italy pointing the way home. (Private collection)

September 9, 1861, Benjamin F. Terry and Thomas Lubbock mustered in the volunteers who said they were willing to fight for the Confederacy in the state of Virginia. It was a unique group by today's standards. Each man agreed to sign on for the duration of the war. Each man furnished his own rifle, side-arm, saddle and horse. Ten companies of a hundred men each became the Eighth Texas Cavalry of the Confederate States of America.

The Rangers left Texas on September 11 and went out to fight at Woodsonville and Shiloh, Bardstown and Perryville, and Murfreesboro and Chickamauga. Benjamin Franklin Terry was killed leading a charge against Union troops only three months after he organized the famous Rangers that bear his name. (See also Dec. 17.)

## SEPTEMBER 10

### 1961

From the time she formed to the time she died, Carla was a killer. Carla was the name given to the third tropical storm of 1961, and she may have been the largest hurricane of modern times.

The storm developed on the third of September, reached the coast on the tenth, and finally blew herself out somewhere in the midwestern United States on the fifteenth. She boiled and looped in the Gulf of Mexico as she grew to monster proportions. She approached Texas very slowly, seeming to toy with the coastline. Her wind gusts were esti-

Hurricane Carla's winds and waves dealt a deadly blow to the upper coast. (Houston *Chronicle*)

mated at 175 miles an hour at Port Lavaca. Killer tornadoes followed her into Galveston.

## SEPTEMBER 11

### 1862

William Sydney Porter, known to the world as "O. Henry," was born in North Carolina on September 11, 1862. He came to Texas when he was twenty, hoping the climate here would be more conducive to better health.

Porter was a draftsman with the General Land Office and later a teller at an Austin bank. Critics say that is where he learned to write fiction. He resigned from the bank, edited a humor magazine, and then began to write columns for the Houston *Daily Post*. But his career was interrupted by a charge that he allegedly had embezzled funds from that Austin bank when he worked there. Porter ran to New Orleans, then to Central America, only to be arrested and sent to prison in March 1898.

While he was in jail, O. Henry polished his writing skills, and after his release in 1902 went to New York, where he wrote a series of popular short stories, including "The Last Leaf" and "The Gift of the Magi." He died in New York in 1910.

## SEPTEMBER 12

### 1874

Twenty-two miles southeast of Canadian in Hemphill County is a historical marker that says, "Stand silent! Heroes here have been who cleared the way for other men." The battle that occurred on that spot holds no

Before achieving fame as a short story writer, O. Henry was a Texas newspaperman. (Barker Texas History Center)

great historical significance; but it is another example of the tremendous courage exhibited during the Indian Wars.

On September 12, 1874, scouts Billy Dixon and Amos Chapman set out with four soldiers to deliver dispatches to Fort Supply. The half-dozen men were attacked by a band of Kiowa and Comanche warriors.

Four of the men were wounded, but Dixon gathered them into a little hole in the ground where buffalo came to roll in the sand and mud—a buffalo wallow. As the Indians rode in circles around them, a fire-fight continued all day. That night a band of soldiers appeared, but their officer refused to join the fight, saying he would tell the people at the fort, and they could send help if they wanted.

Two days later, the cavalry appeared and chased away the Indians. For three days, a half-dozen wounded men had held off over a hundred warriors. One of the white men died of his wounds. The five survivors were awarded the Congressional Medal of Honor.

1818

1880

The king of the Gulf Coast for a while in the early 1800s was French pirate Jean Lafitte. He and his brother had worked the Gulf from New Orleans since about 1804. By 1817 they made Galveston their home base, and it became the center for smuggling and privateering.

On September 12, 1818, the pirate's little fleet was caught in port when a huge hurricane came in and inflicted heavy damage. Four ships were lost, and water flowing four feet deep through the island destroyed all but six buildings.

By 1821 the pirate and his men were gone from Galveston. (See also May 4.)

Of all the people who have walked through Texas history, few have touched as many varied areas as Carlysle Raht. After schooling at the old Fort Worth University and the University of Texas, he worked for the railroad and was a cowboy, a miner, and a newspaperman. His greatest adventure came when he served as a scout for the Eighth Cavalry under Gen. John Pershing and spent some time fighting Pancho Villa.

Raht settled down to write books of history, and then the Second World War broke out.

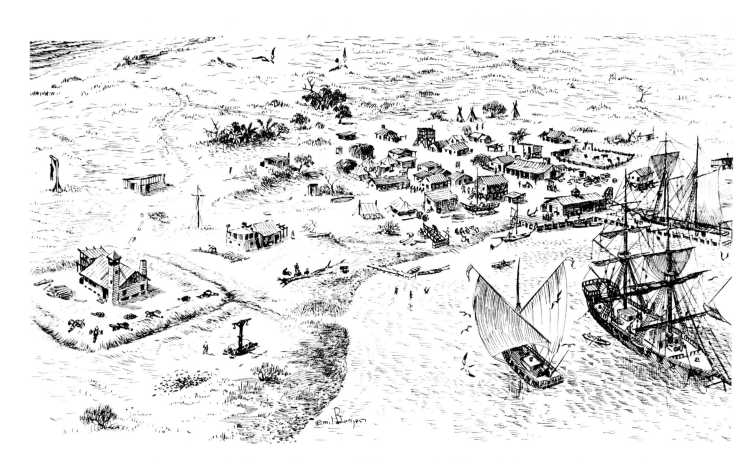

Early drawing of pirate Jean Lafitte's settlement in Galveston, which he called Campeachy. (Rosenberg Library, Galveston)

Carlysle Raht was sixty, but he volunteered to do something and was assigned to a scientific research and development project of the Atomic Energy Commission. The project led to the development of the atomic bomb!

Carlysle Graham Raht, the man who hunted Pancho Villa and helped develop the atom bomb, was born September 13, 1880, in Cooke County, Texas.

A versatile and patriotic Texan, Carlysle Raht. (Texas State Archives)

## SEPTEMBER 14

### 1874

This story might sound like a movie script, but it really happened near Canadian in the Texas Panhandle.

As Capt. Wyllys Lyman was leading a wagon train filled with supplies, marauding Indians attacked on the ninth. There were 95 soldiers against about 400 Indians. A scout slipped away and went for help.

As a fall rainstorm raked the Panhandle, Company K of the Sixth Cavalry made a wild dash to save the wagon train. On September 14, 1874, they arrived just in the nick of time.

After five awful days, the Indians broke off the longest fight in the Indian Wars of the Panhandle, and ran; the day was saved.

## SEPTEMBER 15

### 1896

Throughout history, from the chariot races in the Colosseum, to a tractor pull in the Astrodome, people have been attracted to strange spectacles.

The champion of them all took place on September 15, 1896, on a field between Waco and West. William George Crush proposed to aim two steam engines at each other, let them build up a good head of steam and slam into each other—a head-on train wreck!

Fifty thousand paying customers came to see it. The two MK&T locomotives aimed at each other. They built up a speed of ninety miles an hour and hit head-on. The two boilers exploded, killing two spectators and injuring several others. Survivors said they

The trains are readied for the spectacle. . .

. . . and the crash at Crush becomes history. (Texas Collection, Baylor University)

thought the crash had been worth the ticket price.

**Also on this date**, in the year 1883, the organizational session of the University of Texas was attended by 221 students.

# SEPTEMBER 16

### 1875

Big hurricanes had hit the Texas coast in 1818 and 1837, but on September 16, 1875, a major hurricane slammed into a populated area, the city of Indianola on Matagorda Bay, and blew it away. So devastating was the storm that before it hit, Indianola was a major city in Texas, and twelve years after it hit, the post office closed and the town died forever.

As the storm neared and the water rose, escape from the town was cut off. The docks began to break up, and a schooner tore loose from its anchorage and smashed the telegraph office. The wind gauge blew away as it registered eighty-eight miles per hour. Later weather bureau officials guess the wind hit 150 miles per hour before it quit. Small buildings were swept away. People who survived said that around midnight they noticed the horrible noise of the wind going away. It got deathly still as the eye of the storm was directly over Matagorda Peninsula.

As suddenly as the still came, the wind came back, and the tide began to rush out to sea. Buildings that had withstood the earlier pounding now collapsed, and more people died. The initial reports to the outside world indicated nine-tenths of the houses gone, a tenth of the population dead or missing, and bodies as far as twenty miles inland.

After that powerful storm there was nothing as far as the eye could see but ruin and devastation, with men poring over immense piles that used to be houses in a grim search for the dead.

A hurricane in 1875 turned the port of Indianola into a ghost town. (Houston Metropolitan Research Center, Houston Library)

In August 1886 a second storm hit what was left of the town, and Indianola ceased to exist.

**Also on this date**, in the year 1873, R. L. More was born in Decatur; he amassed the world's largest private collection of bird eggs.

## SEPTEMBER 17

### 1869

In the popular imagination a Texas Ranger is often viewed as an uneducated, paid gunfighter who did nothing but chase Indians and badmen. But this is an inaccurate image, especially in the case of Roy Aldrich, who served longer than any early-day Ranger, and shattered some stereotypes.

He was born in Illinois on September 17, 1869. Aldrich never found time to get married because he used up his youth in adventures like the Spanish-American War, the Philippine Insurrection, and the Boer War in South Africa, and then as a sheriff in Indian Territory.

When he was thirty-six, Roy Aldrich threw off his life as an adventurer and went into business in Corpus Christi. He sold real estate for eight years, and, at the age of forty-six, when most men were thinking about a rocking chair on a front porch, he joined the Texas Rangers. He stayed in that job for thirty-two years, longer than any other Ranger.

Through all this adventure, Aldrich managed to collect a ten-thousand-book library. He had a significant collection of fruit flies, and his collection of flowers became an important source of study for the botanists at the University of Texas. Aldrich died in 1955 when he was eighty-five years old, having lived a very full life.

## SEPTEMBER 18

### 1842

In September 1842, the French soldier of fortune Adrian Woll led a force of Mexican soldiers to capture San Antonio; it was the second Mexican invasion of Texas in that fateful year.

Two hundred Texas volunteers gathered at Salado Creek, east of San Antonio, as Jack Hays and a company of men went into the city on September 18, 1842, in an attempt to make the Mexican cavalry chase them. The ruse worked, and the Hays men raced to Salado Creek with the Mexicans in hot pursuit. Caught in an ambush, the Mexicans lost sixty men.

A mile away from the battle, as Nicholas Dawson and a group of reinforcements hurried to join the action, they ran into the Mexican army. In the battle that followed, Dawson and thirty-five of his men were killed; fifteen were captured and marched off to prison in Mexico.

What began as a Texas victory ended in tragedy because of the Dawson Massacre. However, the events of September 18 at Salado Creek forced President Sam Houston to adopt a strong stand against Mexico's incursions into his republic.

## SEPTEMBER 19

### 1905

Leon Jaworski was the son of a minister. He was named Leonidas after a great warrior, but became a gentle man of peace.

He was admitted to the Texas bar while still a teenager. He defended a black man accused of murder in a famous trial, when he was ex-

pected to put up a cursory defense and let the
"nigger" go to jail. Jaworski risked his reputation to give the prisoner a stinging defense.

After the Second World War he was a prosecutor at the War Crimes Trials of the leaders
of Nazi Germany. Jaworski came home to head
up one of the nation's most prestigious law
firms, and was elected president of the American Bar Association. On at least two occa-
sions President Lyndon Johnson offered him
cabinet positions, but he turned them down.

During the Watergate scandal, Leon Jaworski was called to Washington as the special
prosecutor. He served with diligence and dignity in the time of one of the country's deepest Constitutional crises. When Jaworski went
to court for the last time in the Watergate case,
he never went back; he died a few years later
chopping wood at his ranch near Wimberley.

Leon Jaworski was born in Waco on September 19, 1905.

# SEPTEMBER 20

## 1967

When folks in the lower Rio Grande Valley
talk about hurricanes they usually mention the
one that became known as "The Storm"—
Hurricane Beulah.

The storm was born west of Martinique in
the first week of September 1967. She lum-
bered slowly across the Caribbean and almost
died in Jamaica. But on the afternoon of the
seventeenth, she moved into the Gulf of Mexico and began to boil. Beulah headed for the
mouth of the Rio Grande, then veered to the
west as if to go into Mexico. The folks along
the Texas coast went to bed that night breathing a sigh of relief, only to awaken to find the
storm had circled and was coming at them.
On September 20, 1967, Beulah came ashore.

Leon Jaworski (right) shakes hands with President Lyndon Johnson, who is relaxing in the White House
swimming pool. Texas Atty. Gen. Waggoner Carr looks on. (Jaworski Family photo)

The aftermath of Hurricane Beulah. (Houston *Chronicle*)

With her came rains of ten to twenty inches and nearly a hundred tornadoes, with hurricane-force winds from the mouth of the Rio Grande to Corpus Christi. Thirteen people died, thirty-seven were hurt and there was $1.5 million in damages.

# SEPTEMBER 21

## 1846

Gen. Zachary Taylor once called the Texas Rangers a "lawless set of licentious vandals," but the fact is he may have had more problems winning the Mexican War if it had not been for the Rangers. When Taylor led American troops into the disputed strip between the Nueces and the Rio Grande, he asked for Ranger regiments to help with scouting.

Throughout the campaign they did much more than scout. By September 21, 1846, the army was in Monterrey and fierce battles took place all over the city. The most dramatic came when Ranger Capt. Robert Gillespie led his men up the hill to attack the Bishop's Palace. Gillespie had been in Texas since 1837, and was a veteran fighter who had survived wounds at Walkers Creek, the troubled Somervell Expedition, and the War of the Rio Grande.

His luck ran out on that September morning as a Mexican bullet cut him down. The Rangers helped the army take the palace, and the battle of Monterrey was over. By the end of the week the Rangers' enlistment expired, and they rode north to Texas.

## SEPTEMBER 22

### 1554

Francisco Vásquez de Coronado could have stayed in Spain or later in Mexico and been a rich and forgotten citizen. But he is remembered three hundred years after his death because he left the relative comfort of Mexico City to lead the famous expedition that searched for the golden cities that never existed.

Coronado's wanderings established Spain's claim to the New World. He returned to Mexico and settled back into the life of a minor politician. He died quietly in Mexico on September 22, 1554, at the age of forty-four, totally unaware that his failure of an expedition would change the world. (See also Apr. 22.)

## SEPTEMBER 23

### 1867

John A. Lomax was born on September 23, 1867. When he was two, his family loaded into a covered wagon and headed from Mississippi to Texas. John grew up with the cowboys and wrote down the words of the trail songs they sang. When he went away to the University of Texas he tried to convince people that these songs were really literature. Finally, at Harvard, of all places, he found an audience and the support to publish his collection of cowboy songs. The year was 1910, and suddenly the songs the cowboy sang to the cows and to his horse became an art form.

Lomax, who became a professor at the University of Texas, spent his life with common men, white and black, recording their songs of

life in Texas and on the frontier. (See also Dec. 6.)

**Also on this date**, in the same year, William Marsh Rice was murdered in New York. His will set up Rice University in Houston.

## SEPTEMBER 24

### 1913

In 1900, when the two campus newspapers at the University of Texas merged, both existing names were rejected for the new paper. The *Calendar* did not seem right, and the *Ranger* sounded like the guys with the guns, not the school, so they settled on *Texan*.

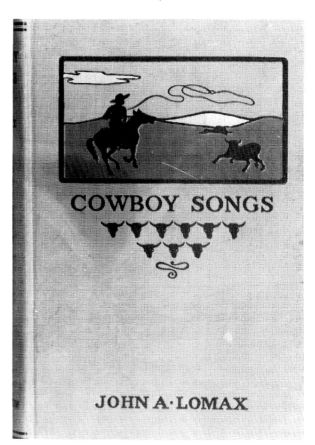

John A. Lomax collected a folk heritage preserved in song. (Barker Texas History Center)

An early staff of the *Daily Texan*, the first college daily in the South. (Barker Texas History Center)

Within a few years the student body decided there was enough news being made on the forty acres to fill up a daily newspaper. September 24, 1913, the first issue of the *Daily Texan* rolled off the presses. It was the first daily college newspaper in the South. Today it is the largest daily college newspaper in the nation.

## SEPTEMBER 25

### 1867

Oliver Loving was a Kentucky-born farmer turned Texas cowman. What Loving did was altogether foolish and very daring. In 1858 he drove a herd of cattle from Texas all the way to Chicago. In 1860 he headed west across unknown territory with a herd of cattle bound for Denver.

With Charles Goodnight (see March 5), Loving blazed the trail from Young County, Texas, to the Pecos River, and up the Pecos into New Mexico, and then north and west to Denver.

A cattle drive was a long and desperate trip, but the economy added up to make it a worthwhile journey. A range cow worth three dollars a head in Texas would bring ten times that much at the northern markets.

In 1867, out on the trail, Indians attacked and Loving was fatally wounded. He was taken to Fort Sumner, New Mexico, but died of gangrene on September 25, 1867. Loving's last request was that he be buried in Texas, so they preserved his body in charcoal and the following year brought him back to Weatherford for burial.

## SEPTEMBER 26

J. Frank Dobie was born on September 26, 1888, in Live Oak County. He studied the law, worked for newspapers, and taught school before he joined the faculty of the University of Texas and became its most famous teacher. Dobie studied the people of the state and spent his lifetime writing and talking about Texas. His book *Coronado's Children* (1931) made him a national literary figure.

His books and lectures show him to be a loving historian who understood the land and the people. His newspaper articles and interviews show him to be a salty maverick who was liberal to the core, and who dealt in common sense and delightful homilies.

J. Frank Dobie was awarded the Presidential Medal of Freedom just before he died in 1964.

J. Frank Dobie (right) and Walter Prescott Webb, two of Texas's greatest men of letters. (Barker Texas History Center)

## SEPTEMBER 27

1956

When the Associated Press chose the greatest woman athlete of the half century 1900–1950, it was no contest. The winner was Mildred Ella Didrikson, who was born in Port Arthur in 1911.

At the 1932 Olympics in Los Angeles, there were five sports women could compete in, and one person could enter no more than three events. She won gold medals for the javelin throw and eighty-meter hurdles, and a silver for the high jump.

She had been a star amateur basketball

Babe Didrikson Zaharias of Beaumont, America's greatest woman athlete. (Texas Sports Hall of Fame)

player, and a barnstorming baseball player with a men's team, but golf was her game. With her husband, George Zaharias, as her manager, she plunged into the world of professional golf and left the sports world agog. She won over eighty tournaments. Some of those victories came after the woman they called "Babe" learned she had cancer. She battled the disease the way she approached athletics, but on September 27, 1956, she died.

When the Associated Press picks the greatest woman athlete of the century, Babe may win that award too.

**Also on this date**, in the year 1876, former Civil War Gen. Braxton Bragg dropped dead as he crossed a street in Galveston.

## SEPTEMBER 28

### 1874

Gen. Ranald Mackenzie finally ended the Indian problem in Texas—not by killing Indians, but by killing their horses. The general, with five hundred men, discovered a camp in the Palo Duro Canyon that included Cheyenne, Kiowa, and a large force of Comanche. The Indians thought they were safe at the bottom of the canyon, but Mackenzie and his men managed to snake down the canyon wall before they were spotted. The Indians fled in panic, leaving horses and supplies behind.

On the report of the battle, only four Indians were listed as killed, and one trooper was wounded. But more than a thousand horses left behind were shot. The Indian, afoot in the canyon, his food and lodging gone, had no choice but to head to the reservation.

September 28, 1874, is the date of one of the last major Indian battles in the Panhandle.

## SEPTEMBER 29

### 1907

Gene Autry was born on September 29, 1907, in the little Texas town of Tioga. After he graduated from high school he got a job as the telegraph operator for the railroad in Oklahoma. To keep himself busy on the night shift, Gene played the guitar and sang.

One night a man came in to send a telegram and heard young Autry singing. He was impressed and suggested Gene quit the railroad and get a job singing on the radio. The man's name was Will Rogers.

Autry took the famed entertainer's advice and landed a job on Tulsa station KVOO. A few years later he cut a record of a song he had written called "That Silver-Haired Daddy of Mine." It sold five million copies. That led to more radio broadcasts on network hookups, and then a role in a Western movie. The Republic Studios signed him to a contract to make the first singing Western, *Tumbling Tumble Weeds*.

Autry starred in over a hundred films; his network radio program from "Melody Ranch" was a family favorite; and his recordings of "Frosty the Snowman" and "Rudolph, the Red-Nosed Reindeer" remain seasonal favorites.

## SEPTEMBER 30

### 1830

Jim Bowie was born in Tennessee, and when he was thirty-five came to Texas. His reputation had preceded him because of the famous knife that bears his name.

On September 30, 1830, Bowie was granted citizenship by the Congress of Coahuila. Citizenship was necessary because Bowie was going into business, and a foreigner was not allowed to engage in a trade unless he became a citizen.

Bowie spent less than ten years in Texas, and by all standards they were not good times. He wasted time looking for a nonexistent gold mine. His wife, children, and father-in-law died in a cholera epidemic. And he was martyred at the Alamo.

Gene Autry with his horse, Champion. (National Cowboy Hall of Fame Collections)

# OCTOBER

## OCTOBER 1

### 1849

The first prisoner of record at the state prison in Huntsville was a cattle thief named William Sansom. He was sentenced to three years. On October 1, 1849, he began serving the sentence. Less than a year later he was pardoned.

## OCTOBER 2

### 1835

The Alamo has been called the "Cradle of Texas Liberty." Anahuac calls itself the "Birthplace of the Texas Revolution." Velasco claims the first bloodshed in the Revolution, and Gonzales calls itself the "Lexington of Texas."

The sleepy little town on the Guadalupe became a battleground because of a cannon. The Mexicans had given it to the village to keep out the Indians. Mexico City wanted it back, for fear it would be used to keep out Mexicans. The eighteen men in Gonzales who could be rounded up buried the cannon and blocked the river by hiding the ferryboat.

On October 1 a Mexican force arrived. There were shouts and taunts, but little more. During the night, John Moore was elected colonel of the Texans. He ordered the cannon dug up. Someone made a flag, which surely must rank as the least misunderstood flag of any war. It was a white sheet with a cannon painted on it, and emblazoned across it were the words, "Come and Take It."

At dawn the Texans fired the cannon at the Mexican forces. It was a foggy October 2, 1835. The first shot missed. After a parley both sides formed a line and shot at each other again. The Mexicans withdrew.

The first shot at Texas's "Lexington" may have missed its mark, but there was no turning back from here.

## OCTOBER 3

### 1930

The two men who found the giant East Texas Oil Field were not oilmen—they were promoters. Columbus Joiner, who had studied law, been a farmer, and looked for oil, was an old man when he came to Texas. His partner and geologist was Doc A. D. Lloyd. He was not a doctor, nor was he a geologist, and his named wasn't Lloyd. He was a druggist from Ohio who had a habit of marrying and forgetting to get a divorce before the next marriage, and therefore he needed to adopt a new name.

In east Texas "Dad" Joiner and "Doc" Lloyd leased some land and started a promotion. "Dad" took a map, drew a line from Spindletop to Pennsylvania, and to the fields he knew of to the north and east and west. The lines crossed at a point that "Doc" said was the apex of oil in the world.

The apex was on the farm of a widow named Daisy Bradford. In 1927 they talked Mrs. Bradford into letting them drill, and for three years they spread stories of the drilling and how close they were, and sold innumerable shares in the eventual outcome. Some months they only drilled on Sunday when investors drove out to check on progress. As the word spread that Doc and Dad were ready to bring in the well, an amazing thing happened. Five thousand people flocked to the Bradford farm to watch. Cars were parked for miles on both sides of the road. Kids sold hot dogs and soda pop. On October 3, 1930, the Daisy Bradford well blew in. No one was more surprised than Dad and Doc.

As for Doc—well, he got his smiling picture in the paper after the great find, and a spurned wife or two began to get off trains leading a string of kids. The great geologist beat it out of town and died in Chicago in 1941. Dad had sold so many pieces of the well that there were lawsuits and threats, so he

quickly sold out to a gambler named H. L. Hunt. (See also Feb. 17, March 12.)

## OCTOBER 4

### 1876

The Agricultural and Mechanical College of Texas opened its doors on October 4, 1876. The campus had two buildings and five homes for faculty members. There were six in the original faculty, so someone did not get a house. Forty men enrolled for the first class. The school was created to offer white male students a liberal and practical education related to agriculture and the mechanical arts. The first board of directors set the total cost of a nine-month session at $250.

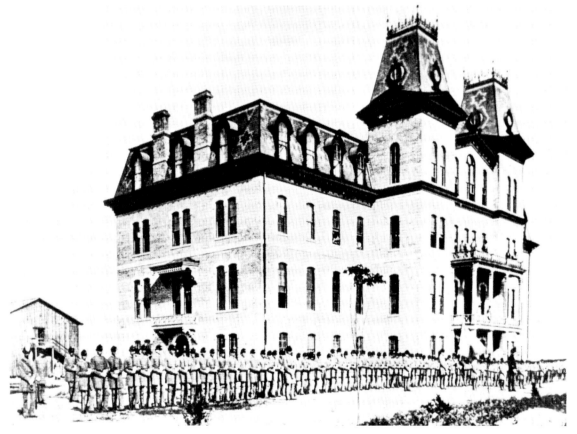

A corps of cadets in front of Texas A&M's Old Main in the late 1870s.

## OCTOBER 5

1908

Joshua Logan, one of Broadway's greatest producers, was born in Texarkana on October 5, 1908. He was educated at Culver Military Academy and Princeton University. After several seasons of acting in summer stock, Logan moved to New York where he quickly established himself as a successful Broadway director. Some of his greatest achievements there included *Mister Roberts*, *South Pacific*, which he co-authored and produced; and *Picnic*. He eventually became a Hollywood director and producer and was responsible for the modern classics *Picnic*, *Bus Stop*, *South Pacific*, and *Camelot*.

In 1950 Joshua Logan won the coveted Pulitzer Prize for drama.

**Also on this date**, in the year 1899, Ned Green drove the first car in Texas, making the trip from Dallas to Terrell at an average speed of 6 miles per hour.

Texarkana's Joshua Logan became a Pulitzer Prize winner. (Houston *Chronicle*)

## OCTOBER 6

1968

To celebrate the 250th anniversary of the founding of San Antonio, the city staged a world's-fair-like exposition called "HemisFair." It was the first international exposition ever held in the South.

To build the fair, the city transformed a blighted area of nearly one hundred acres near downtown into a beautiful plaza. Over six million people came to the fair, and San Antonio benefited in many ways. The HemisFair closed on October 6, 1968.

## OCTOBER 7

1835

Greenberry Logan was born a slave in Kentucky in 1799, but was a freeman by the time he came to Texas in 1831. He settled on Chocolate Bayou and leased a blacksmith shop in Brazoria County. In June 1832, he joined other settlers in the skirmish at Velasco (see June 26). As war clouds became darker Logan joined the Texas army on October 7, 1835, and fought with Fannin at Concepción.

In December at the siege of the Bexar he was wounded and crippled for life.

As a freeman, Logan could go where he wanted, but as a black man he was not always allowed to stay where he wanted, so, after the revolution a group of prominent Texans signed a petition requesting that Logan be allowed to stay in Texas as a freeman.

Greenberry Logan stayed in Texas till he died, but told his white friends the constitution he had fought for and was crippled for "deprived him of every privilege dear to a freeman . . . no vote or say in any way."

## OCTOBER 8

### 1838

Near Dawson, in Navarro County, there is a common grave that contains the remains of eighteen men who lost their lives at the fight of Battle Creek. On October 8, 1838, twenty-five surveyors ran into about three hundred Kickapoo Indians who were on a buffalo hunt. The Indians told the surveyors to leave the country. The white men refused to go. The Indians rode away, then came back in a fierce attack. The battle lasted an entire day. Only seven white men lived through it.

## OCTOBER 9

### 1835

Just as there is dispute over the beginning of the Texas war for independence—whether it was at Velasco or Anahuac—so is there dispute over the first man wounded in the war. The honor probably should go to a free Negro named Samuel McCullough. He was born in

South Carolina and arrived in Texas in May 1835. Five months later he was a soldier with Collinsworth's company at the attack on Goliad. Late in the evening of October 9, 1835, McCullough was seriously wounded. He was the only soldier wounded that night, and he petitioned the Texas Congress later to recognize that he was "the first whose blood was shed in the war for independence."

## OCTOBER 10

### 1837

Some of the first known white men to venture into what is now Wise County died there. On October 10, 1837, eighteen men of the Republic of Texas Army went hunting stolen horses. At a place northwest of the modern-day town of Decatur they ran into 150 Indians. In the battle that followed, the so-called battle of the Knobs, ten of the Texans died. One was Lt. A. H. Miles, who had fought at San Jacinto and was one of the men who found and captured Santa Anna.

**Also on this date**, in the year 1835, Gail Borden, Jr., began publishing the *Telegraph and Texas Register*.

## OCTOBER 11

### 1878

Bill Longley was no good. There is absolutely nothing laudatory in his short and violent life to include in an obituary notice or a eulogy. He stole cattle and money and killed thirty-two men that we know of.

A native of Austin County, William Preston Longley had a career in crime that might have been cut short, had it not been for a faulty hanging. Some vigilantes caught Bill and a buddy stealing cattle and strung them up to a tree. As they were hanging, the vigilantes shot them. But the bullet hit Longley's belt buckle and ricocheted up and cut the rope nearly in half.

He killed blacks and Yankees, but was finally caught. On October 11, 1878, he was strung up in Giddings. They did not take any chances this time. They let him dangle on the rope for eleven minutes. He was just twenty-seven. Before they hung him he said, "I see a lot of enemies out there and mighty few friends."

Copy of a faded photograph of William P. Longley, made just before his execution at Giddings. (Western History Collections, University of Oklahoma Library)

## OCTOBER 12

### 1974

The Big Thicket of east Texas remains one of the most primitive forest areas in the United States. At one time it covered over three million acres. It contained magnificent flowers, birds of every possible type, and wild animals, and in some places the trees and vines were so dense the sun could never penetrate, so there was no grass, just a carpet of pine needles.

Indians, outlaws, and Yankee sympathizers have used the thicket as a refuge, and timber men have gotten rich off its spoils.

In the late 1920s people started trying to get the thicket set aside as a national park. The idea ran into great resistance. Finally the U.S. Senate approved making a portion of the thicket a national preserve, and on October 12, 1974, President Gerald Ford signed the bill.

## OCTOBER 13

### 1821

The Wright brothers flew the first controlled powered airplane in December 1903. But back in Gillespie County, Texas, old Jacob Brodbeck kept saying, "I told you so."

Brodbeck was born in Germany on October 13, 1821, and immigrated to Texas when he was twenty-five. All his life Brodbeck was a tinkerer. He tried to build a clock that never needed winding, and fooled around with a flying machine. When the Civil War ended, he set up a company to build a plane with wings and a propeller driven by a coiled spring. He figured the wings should be movable so you could take advantage of the wind. He built as much as he could, but ran out of money and investors. He went all over the country speaking about his plane, but in the years after the Civil War there was not much money around for investment in crazy inventions.

In 1870 Brodbeck bought a farm near Luckenbach and was living there when the newspaper came from San Antonio one day announcing that a couple of Ohio brothers had actually flown a plane with a motor on it. Jacob Brodbeck died a few years later still believing his plane could have flown.

## OCTOBER 14

### 1890

The thirty-fourth President of the United States, Dwight David Eisenhower, was born in Denison, Texas, on October 14, 1890. The family moved away when "Ike" was still a baby, and he always considered himself as being from Abilene, Kansas.

He came back to Texas after he graduated from West Point and served as a young lieutenant at Fort Sam Houston. His rise through the ranks in the army led him to the job of Supreme Allied Commander in the Second World War. On May 7, 1945, he received the surrender of the Germans. (Thus Texans accepted the surrender of both the Germans [Eisenhower] and the Japanese [Nimitz].) (See Sept. 2.)

He served as president of Columbia University, and then went to Europe to organize the North Atlantic Treaty Organization.

Oilman Sid Richardson flew to Paris early in 1952 to try to talk Eisenhower into running for President, and reportedly pledged to kick $3 million into Ike's campaign. In July of '52 he resigned from the army and ran for President. He beat Adlai Stevenson and was inaugurated the thirty-fourth President in 1953.

A political billboard in the 1952 presidential campaign. (Author's collection)

## OCTOBER 15

### 1929

In the fall of 1929 a couple of nurserymen in Hidalgo County made a strange discovery. They found grapefruit growing in their orchards that had red fruit. The men, A. E. Henninger of Mission and Dr. J. R. Webb of Donna, flipped a coin to see who would get the patent. Henninger won and named his grapefruit the "Ruby Red."

"Thompson Pink" wood budded on "Sour Orange" rootstock and planted in the saline-alkaline soil of the Rio Grande Valley produces the rose-colored meat in this delicious fruit.

*Note*: The exact date of this event is disputed.

## OCTOBER 16

### 1902

Carry Nation is one of those people who seem to catch the imagination of a country simply because of the degree of audacity of their deeds.

She was born in Kentucky but came to Texas at an early age. When Carry was still a teenager she married a man who turned out to be an alcoholic. He died, and she married a preacher and tried to farm with him in the San Bernard River bottoms of Brazoria County. Carry was running a boarding house in Richmond when the Jaybird-Woodpecker feud broke out (see July 2). Her husband said the wrong thing about a Jaybird and got himself severely beaten. The Nations moved out of Texas. By this time Carry Nation decided God wanted her personally to cure the world's ills.

Demon rum was the root cause of all ills, she believed, so she went to the source, attacking liquor stores and bars with bricks and a little hatchet. She would be put in jail for destroying property, and some crusading preacher or woman's group or another would spring her so she could smash another saloon.

On October 16, 1902, she came back to Texas. Some clever students had contacted her saying some of the law school professors were drunks needing to be dealt with. She came to Austin, wrecked a few saloons, and then marched on the campus of the University of Texas, seeking out the drunken law school profs. In 1904 other pranksters brought her back to attack an engineering school dean who was in reality a Sunday school teacher. Despite her reform efforts, at last report people still drank at the university.

**Also on this date**, in the year 1869, A. D. Topperwein was born in Boerne. He is in the Texas Sports Hall of Fame as the greatest trick shooter of his day.

## OCTOBER 17

### 1835

In the territory that became Texas, there were Indians in the west, Mexicans in the south, and Anglos in the east. When the west and south threatened the east, Stephen F. Austin called for some force to help keep the peace. On October 17, 1835, a resolution was offered to create a corps of Texas Rangers. Twenty-five Rangers, the first legally recognized, were authorized to guard the frontier. Walter Prescott Webb said, "Though his duties have varied from decade to decade, the Ranger has been throughout essentially a fighting man."

Carry Nation on a visit to Houston. (Houston Metropolitan Research Center, Houston Library)

# OCTOBER 18

### 1914

In the long and glorious tradition of great Texas Aggie football players, few stand taller than Joe Routt. Born October 18, 1914, in Chappell Hill, he went to A&M to study animal husbandry, but Aggie coach Homer Norton hoped the six-footer would spend some time on the gridiron at Kyle field.

Routt spent time there all right, from 1933 to 1938, and as a junior became the first Aggie to be named a Consensus All-American Football Player. He played in the College All-star Classic and the East-West Shrine game.

Commissioned a second lieutenant as he graduated, Routt by 1942 was an officer leading an infantry company in Europe. He won a Bronze Star for his bravery, but on December 2, 1944, Capt. Joe Routt was killed in action in Holland. He was just thirty years old.

Joe Routt poses with his girlfriend, Gay Saunders, wearing boots and jacket awarded him after playing in a New Year's Day game. (San Antonio *Light* Collection, Institute of Texan Cultures)

## OCTOBER 19

### 1862

There was a force of secret police in Texas during the Civil War. Its job was to find Northern sympathizers. There were plenty of them, and one large group operated in what was called the Loyal League or the Peace Party.

They sought to reestablish the Union and spy on the Confederacy.

In the fall of 1862 one of them asked a secret service man to join up. He did, and got names and addresses. On October 1, 1862, armed forces carried out raids in Cooke County and rounded up about seventy men. They were brought to Gainesville where, for the next few weeks, they were tried before a citizen's court. Forty-two were charged with conspiracy, insurrection, and other charges and were summarily sentenced to be hanged.

It was twenty years after the war before any accounts of the citizen court or the great Gainesville hanging were made public.

*Note:* This is not a firm date. The hangings took place in October 1862 at different times.

## OCTOBER 20

### 1838

Moses Lapham was a cultured man who was born in Rhode Island, attended Miami University in Ohio, and came to Texas territory to join the surveying crew of Thomas Borden. In 1831 he taught school for a while at San Felipe, but complained of the lack of cultured people in Texas. He went home to Ohio, but for some reason came back to Texas in time to help Deaf Smith's party chop down Vince's Bridge to block the Mexican escape from San Jacinto. He fought in that battle, and turned up as a surveyor for the new town of Houston.

Still complaining that Texas was a cultural desert, Lapham determined to stay and contribute to the pursuit of finer things for the nation of Texas. On October 20, 1838, as he was on a surveying party near San Antonio, Indians attacked and scalped him. Moses Lapham was just thirty.

## OCTOBER 21

### 1917

Ranger was a town of about six hundred people on October 21, 1917; it was best known for being hot and dry. But that afternoon, people near John McCleskey's farm heard a rumble, then saw a deep-green liquid spurt into the sky from that foolish oil well that W. K. Gordon was drilling.

Until October 21, people thought there was no oil in west Texas. On the twenty-second, everybody knew there was, and plenty of it. The town filled up with prospectors. Ten trainloads of people a day poured into Ranger. Some even rented overstuffed chairs as sleeping places. When the streets became so muddy you couldn't cross them, a man offered to carry people across for a fee. Soon women of easy virtue, card sharks, and killers came to town and Ranger became known as "Roaring Ranger."

It was a classic boomtown like the gold towns of the Klondike, except that it yielded in a year twice the wealth of the best years in the gold fields.

**Also on this date**, in the year 1898, Stanley Walker was born in Lampasas. He became a legendary New York City newspaper editor.

## OCTOBER 22

### 1836

On the morning of October 22, 1836, the Congress of the Republic of Texas ruled that the first elected president should be administered the oath of office at four o'clock that afternoon. Sam Houston was in Columbia, waiting. He was escorted to a barnlike building, and stood in front of a crude table covered with a blanket, to take the oath of office. The president of the new republic did not dash immediately into the duties of the day because of "the want of a suitable pen."

## OCTOBER 23

### 1865

As Capt. Mirabeau B. Lamar mustered out of service at the close of the Mexican War, he wrote a letter to Gen. Zachary Taylor urging him to maintain the fort at Laredo on the Rio Grande. Taylor did, and what was Camp Crawford became Fort McIntosh. The soldiers stationed there battled a few Indians and Mexican bandits. Nine years after it was established it was abandoned. When the Civil War started, the Confederates took it over.

On October 23, 1865, Federal troops reoccupied the fort. Fort McIntosh remained active until the end of the Second World War, when it underwent an amazing transformation. Laredo Junior College took it over, and the old barracks became the Science Building and the Liberal Arts Building. The college even turned the old arsenal into the Homemaking Building. At Fort McIntosh at least, swords really were turned into plowshares.

## OCTOBER 24

### 1941

On October 24, 1941, longtime state treasurer Charlie Lockhart submitted his resignation. He had served nearly ten years, and during his tenure Texas claimed to have the "shortest state treasurer in the nation's biggest state."

Charlie Lockhart was a dwarf; he stood just forty-five inches tall. He was succeeded as state treasurer by Jesse James, who was replaced by Warren G. Harding. Like Charlie Lockhart, and unlike their more famous namesakes, they were as honest as the day is long.

## OCTOBER 25

### 1931

Life behind the walls at the state prison in Huntsville was not meant to be anything but dull; but wardens realized that even a prisoner can take just so much without some kind of diversion. Lee Simmons came up with the plan to stage a rodeo within the prison walls. The inmates would be the cowboys. In October 1931 the Texas Prison Rodeo was born. It featured the standard rodeo fare, plus the main event that packs 'em in every Sunday in October: "Hard Money" features forty cowboys trying to remove a tobacco sack filled with money from the horns of a mad Brahman bull.

*Note*: October 25 was the last Sunday in October 1931. It is not recorded on which Sunday the rodeo was first performed.

## OCTOBER 26

### 1862

When word reached the bustling seaport of Indianola that a Federal gunboat had fired on Galveston, the locals weren't concerned. They figured the artillery at Fort Esperanza in Matagorda Bay could control the Yankees and keep the port open for blockade runners.

On October 25, the Federal fleet approached, and before anyone on land knew what was happening, the ships poured withering fire on the fort, and that was that.

On October 26, 1862, the *Westfield* came into port at Indianola under a flag of truce. The Yankee captain explained the city could surrender and allow a water blockade, or the fleet would fire on the city. The city fathers said they would not surrender. The ship pulled out of the port, took aim, and fired. A brief battle followed. As far as the townspeople were concerned, the resistance was just for show, and in the afternoon they surrendered. Texas was under the blockade.

## OCTOBER 27

### 1902

As early as September 1875, the Galveston *News* was saying recent storm flooding and high winds should "teach us the importance of fortifying the beach against the assaults of terrible gulf breakers. . . ." But there was no seawall in 1900 when the great storm hit with its deadly tidal wave (see Sept. 8).

In February 1902, bond sales began for a seawall that was proposed to be at least five miles long, at least ten feet high, and wide enough on the top for a boulevard.

At two o'clock on October 27, 1902, the first piling was driven at the foot of Fifteenth Street to start what the Galveston *Tribune* called "Galveston's great safeguard."

## OCTOBER 28

### 1806

One of the most enigmatic characters in Texas's early history was Juan Seguin. A hun-

After the disaster of 1900, Galveston begins construction of a seawall higher than the surge of that killer storm. (Rosenberg Library, Galveston)

dred years after his death it is difficult to know whether he was a hero or a traitor.

Seguin was born in San Antonio on October 28, 1806, and there was never any question that his sympathies were with Austin and his Texas colonists. He organized resistance to Mexico City, was a courier at the Alamo, and fought at San Jacinto. He served in the Texas Senate, and was elected mayor of San Antonio when he was thirty-five.

But at this point, something went wrong. One rumor is that Seguin was too friendly to Mexico. It may have been prejudice toward a Mexican, albeit a gilt-edged Texas hero, and it may have been fact; but at any rate a disgusted Seguin resigned as mayor in 1842 and moved

to Mexico. The next time he came to Texas he was marching with the Mexican army. (He was later to claim that he had a choice: go to prison or join the army.)

After six years in Mexico, Juan Seguin wrote Sam Houston, asking permission to come home and saying he would face the music. Apparently there wasn't much, for a few years later he was elected to a minor political office in Bexar County. He was subsequently to return to Mexico to join the army again, then came back to Texas, and finally died an old man in Mexico.

One final irony: although Seguin was buried in Mexico, his remains were brought to Seguin, Texas, in 1974, and reinterred there.

Juan Seguin was a hero of the Texas Revolution, but his later career was shrouded in controversy. (Barker Texas History Center)

## OCTOBER 29

### 1929

Black Tuesday! When trading stopped on the afternoon of October 29, 1929, panic had gripped the New York Stock Exchange, the bottom had fallen out of the market, and as more than one writer has suggested, the Roaring Twenties stopped roaring.

We lived in the best place in the world, and it could only get better. In Texas two-thirds of the north Texas grassland had been plowed under so farmers could grow the big cash crop of wheat. Something else happened in 1929 that was not as easily noticed as a sudden stock market crash . . . it stopped raining, and the wind started blowing.

As stock losses piled up in the East, industry all over the country stagnated. Factories shut down, and it was a common sight in Texas to see entire families walking the highway looking for any kind of work. But corn dived to just ten cents a bushel, and farm foreclosures became commonplace, as cotton, *the* cash crop, bottomed out at a nickel a pound in the early thirties.

In truth, Texas was not affected by the crash and the Great Depression that followed nearly so much as its cousins in the industrial states, but no one who lived through those times will ever forget them.

## OCTOBER 30

### 1855

There is nothing more Texan than the cowboy and the longhorn. Of course the cowboy evolved from Mexico, his horse from Spain, his saddle from the Old World, and his cattle from the same place. The real Age of the Cowboy lasted only about thirty years, from the end of the Civil War to the end of the open range.

But today there are still cowboys—not many, but some—and a lot of weekend cowboys and cowgirls. The stereotype of the "pure American" cowboy continued with the birth of Paul Bauer on October 30, 1855. He was born in Yorktown, Texas, where his immigrant parents moved after coming over from Germany. Back in the old country, Paul's father, Frederick, was a master saddle-maker, and he taught the trade to young Paul.

For nearly a hundred years the Bauers made

saddles for Texas Rangers, cattlemen, dignitaries, and even real working cowboys. And today in Yoakum the Tex Tan Leather Company turns out enough saddles to retain the title of the world's largest saddle company.

# OCTOBER 31

## 1863

Tom Ketchum was born on October 31, 1863, in San Saba County. He had a rotten childhood. His father died when Tom was a year old; when he was four the Indians ambushed him; and when he was nine his mother died. Besides that, everybody insisted on calling him "Jack."

Tom and Sam Ketchum were the 1860s equivalent of punks who turn to a life of crime. They robbed post offices and stagecoaches and trains. By this time the popular press was calling Tom "Black Jack," and the name stuck. Brother Sam got blown away in a Colorado train robbery.

It is generally felt now that the Ketchum boys had a much more notorious reputation than they deserved. Many robberies and daring deeds attributed to them were probably pulled off by others.

"Black Jack" was not your brightest robber, because in 1899 he tried to rob a train by himself. He was wounded and captured. On April 26, 1901, they hung him. Just before they dropped the trap door "Black Jack" Ketchum said, "I'll be in hell before you start breakfast. Let her rip!"

"Let her rip!" signaled Black Jack Ketchum, and another outlaw met his fate. (Western History Collections, University of Oklahoma Library)

Rendering of an early oil drilling operation. (Author's collection)

# NOVEMBER

## NOVEMBER 1

### 1832

The man who drilled the first oil well in Texas, Lyne Barret, was born on November 1, 1832, in Virginia. The Barrets moved to Texas and lived around Nacogdoches.

In the deep piney woods there was a place the Indians called "Oil Springs." They had used the ooze that came up there as a medicine. Lyne Barret signed a lease to drill a well there in October 1865. On December 20, he began using a steam-powered auger, and at 106 feet, he hit oil. The well produced ten barrels a day. He sought financing to drill other wells, but the big play was in Pennsylvania, and not many people believed there was much oil in Texas. Barret never drilled another well. He ended his life as a clerk in a store, a man ahead of his time.

### 1912

The syndicate that built the state capitol took three million acres of the Panhandle instead of cash for the job. They spent just over $3.2 million to build the structure, so the land cost them just over a dollar an acre. Those acres became the XIT Ranch. It covered parts of nine counties in the western Panhandle. Well over 150,000 head of cattle roamed the ranch by 1900. Eventually 1,500 miles of fence were built, along with 100 dams and over 300 windmills to provide water for the herds.

By 1901 the owners started to sell off chunks of the great ranch. On November 1, 1912, the last cattle of the XIT were sold. It had been the world's largest ranch, but its entire lifetime spanned less than three decades.

## NOVEMBER 2

### 1949

It was a heady feeling for the new Republic of Texas to receive the French *chargé d'affaires*, the honorable Alphonse Dubois de Saligny. Later, Texans were to learn that he was not the nobleman he pretended to be. It was also a bit hard to take when the French diplomat in Texas made it clear he preferred to spend his time in New Orleans.

Push came to shove when Austin pig owner Richard Bullock's animals decided to graze and root on the grounds of the French Legation. A French servant killed a Texas pig. Bullock responded by trying to beat up the servant. Saligny claimed that international law gave protection to diplomats and their households. He broke diplomatic relations with the republic. The incident became known as the "Pig War."

With statehood the French did not have need for a legation in Texas. The building was sold, then fell into disrepair. The legislature moved to save it, and on November 2, 1949, the French Legation building was handed over to the Daughters of the Republic of Texas who are its custodians today.

# NOVEMBER 3

## 1793

Stephen Fuller Austin was born in Virginia on November 3, 1793. His life lasted just forty-three years, but without that life there might not have been a Texas. He was, though reluctant at first, the founder of Anglo-American Texas.

When he was ten years old he was sent to school in Connecticut, and later attended Transylvania University in Kentucky. His career after school included service in a militia, the management of his father's lead mining and smelting business, and a term in the Missouri territorial legislature. A business failure in Missouri took him to Arkansas and finally he followed his father on what he viewed as a less-than-brilliant idea about Texas settlement.

When Moses Austin died in 1821 as he was organizing the beginnings of his Texas colony, the mantle of leadership fell to Stephen. He was not yet twenty-eight. He was about to be plunged into the greatest adventure of his life. It would give him fame, joy, deprivation, and finally death in the next fourteen years, and he would give us Texas.

# NOVEMBER 4

## 1911

What Henry Kissinger was to President Richard Nixon, Edward House was to President Woodrow Wilson.

House was born in Houston in 1858. After attending Cornell University, he came back to Texas and settled in Austin to be near the political center of the state. House loved politics, and ran Gov. Jim Hogg's campaign, and later the campaigns of Charles Culberson and Joseph Sayers. Governor Hogg conferred the honorary title of "Colonel" on House, and to the rest of the world he was forever "Colonel House."

His horizon was to expand greatly with the November 4, 1911, meeting with Woodrow Wilson. They became close friends, and House became Wilson's chief aide and intimate. He was never elected to any official position; he simply was always there, and Wilson took very few steps without seeking the advice of his Texas friend. House was sent to Europe to win acceptance of Wilson's Fourteen Points for peace from France and England. He was an official delegate from the United States to the peace conference. Something happened there to hurt the friendship, and when he left Wilson after the signing of the treaty in 1919, he never saw the President again. When Wilson suffered a debilitating stroke, his wife guarded him in the White House, refusing to let House see him, and Wilson never sent for the colonel.

House came home to Texas to live out his days, though he was frequently sought out by other leaders, and was an early supporter of Franklin Roosevelt for the Presidency. House died quietly in New York in 1938 and is buried in Houston.

# NOVEMBER 5

## 1863

The short, sad administration of Gov. Pendleton Murrah began on November 5, 1863. Murrah was born a bastard in Alabama. He was educated in the East and became a successful lawyer and politician in Marshall. He ran for Congress and lost; then, in 1857, was elected to the Texas legislature.

As the Civil War broke out Murrah tried to become a civilian soldier, but couldn't because of his health. Gov. Francis Lubbock resigned to become a soldier in the Confederate army, and a special election was held to find a replacement. Murrah, a strong state's rights man, beat T. J. Chambers in the election. With the war on, there was no social life in Austin. After he was sworn into office, Murrah and his wife went to the hotel for an inaugural dinner of cornmeal cakes.

During this period, the state was made up of Indians, Federal troops, women and children whose husbands and fathers were away at war, and old men and women, plus the sick and the outlaws. It was an impossible situation for the government.

Finally, the war ended the sixteen-month administration of Pendleton Murrah. He put on a uniform and rode away to Mexico on the night of June 17, 1865. Two months later he died of tuberculosis in Monterrey and was buried in an unmarked grave. (See also Feb. 4.)

## NOVEMBER 6

### 1528

Cabeza de Vaca discovered Texas. He did not mean to, and he spent years wishing he hadn't. De Vaca was a member of the Narváez Expedition from Spain. It was a disaster that would take three hundred lives, and set de Vaca and three men on a wild and improbable adventure.

The expedition arrived in Florida, then floated out through the Gulf, chased by hostile Indians. With boats lost, the expedition took to barges and little rafts. The lack of food and water claimed a fierce toll. Finally the little barge de Vaca was on was hurled by a big wave onto a stretch of sand. It was Galveston

Col. Edward House, a Houstonian by birth, was a close friend and advisor to President Woodrow Wilson. (Barker Texas History Center)

Island; the date was November 6, 1528. He named the island "Malhado," which means "Ill Fortune."

De Vaca's ill fortune was to last for years. He was to wander naked most of the time as a captive of the Indians, then as a medicine man; finally as an escapee, a hunted man. Eventually he met up with other survivors and led them on a painful walk through the southwest deserts and into New Spain. The eight years of de Vaca's sojourn were hailed as the making of a hero—and his story of hearing Indians tell of golden cities was the making of the exploration that was to come; for four years after de Vaca came home, Coronado went out looking for those golden cities.

statesman Henry Clay. The cow was perfect for the Americas. It adjusted to any climate, and grew fat leisurely grazing on the lush grasslands. In 1882 O. H. Nelson brought the first Hereford bulls to the Panhandle. Soon the "white-faced cows" became the most popular breed in Texas. On November 7, 1889, a dozen breeders met in San Antonio at a bootmaker's shop to organize the Texas Hereford Association.

## NOVEMBER 7

### 1876

Calm came to Mason County on November 7, 1876, as Texas Rangers arrested George Glidden and Johnny Ringo. With those two men in jail the "Hoodoo War" (see also Feb. 18) was over. It had started a year earlier as a blood feud which involved cattle rustling, lynching, shootings, and finally a detachment of Rangers.

The Hoodoos were vigilantes who disguised themselves with masks and boot-black, and rode about at night dealing out their brand of justice, such as liberating the jails of suspected cow thieves and saving the state the time and trouble of a trial before a hanging.

Glidden was the last of the troublemakers to be tried and sent off to prison. Johnny Ringo beat the rap and went on to a kind of dubious fame as a major league gunslinger in Tombstone, Arizona. Early in 1877 the Mason County courthouse burned and all the records of the people involved in the Hoodoo War were lost. That event, and the passage of time, ended the war; though some old-timers in Mason County say the feud still lives.

### 1889

The first Hereford cattle were imported to the United States from England by the great

## NOVEMBER 8

### 1923

Plots were fermenting and bubbling to the surface in Germany in the years after the Armistice. The pot boiled over on November 8, 1923, when a disgruntled World War I general, Erich Ludendorff, and his men tried to pull off the Beer Hall Putsch. A Ludendorff underling, Adolph Hitler, got nine months in prison for his trouble, and wrote *Mein Kampf*.

The day of the putsch changed the life of a young man from Yoakum, Texas, named Hubert Knickerbocker. He had dabbled in journalism, and taught it briefly at Southern Methodist University, but decided his life would be better spent in psychiatry. He went to Munich, Germany, to study psychiatry, but when he witnessed the putsch, he realized he was meant to write.

As the correspondent for the International News Service, he spent ten years in Berlin and Moscow. His work on articles about the Russian economy won the Texan the Pulitzer Prize for journalism in 1931. His book *Will War Come to Europe?* was written after he was thrown out of Germany in 1933 for writing articles critical of Hitler. He covered the war in Europe, then came home in 1940 to lobby for America's entry into the fray.

After the war, Knickerbocker continued his

Hereford cattle were first brought to Texas in 1882 and rapidly became the most popular breed in the state. (Barker Texas History Center)

worldwide journalism, and died in a plane crash in India in 1949.

# NOVEMBER 9

### 1903

John Nance Garner was born in a log cabin in Red River County, Texas. He was to grow up to become the most powerful man in national politics the state had produced. His political career began when he lost a race for city attorney in Clarksville. He moved to Uvalde

and won an election as county judge, then to the state legislature and finally to Washington as the congressman from the newly created Fifteenth District.

On November 9, 1903, John Nance Garner walked into the congressional chambers for the first time. His rise in Congress was meteoric. Six years later Garner was the Democratic party whip. A few years later he was the party leader, and in 1931 he was elected Speaker of the House. A year later Franklin Roosevelt picked Garner to be his running mate, and in March 1933 Garner became Vice-President. He was later to say that he had "given up the second most important job in government for one that didn't amount to a hill of beans."

The Roosevelt-Garner ticket won a second term in '37, but all was not sweetness and light between the two men. Roosevelt was becoming too liberal for the man they were now calling "Cactus Jack." Garner opposed Roosevelt's try for a third term, and was replaced on the ticket. He came home to Uvalde in 1941 and vowed never to cross the Potomac again. He never did.

The succeeding years were to see a steady stream of politicians, large and small, making the pilgrimage to Uvalde to talk with the aging politician, and generally to be photographed with him.

On Garner's ninetieth birthday, Harry Truman, Lyndon Johnson, and a crowd of state politicians came to present the old Vice-President with a birthday cake made into a replica of his birthplace. Just short of his ninety-ninth birthday, John Nance Garner's heart stopped beating. He was buried in Uvalde.

Former Vice-President John Nance Garner with President Harry Truman and Gov. Beauford Jester. (Barker Texas History Center)

## NOVEMBER 10

### 1914

Ever since the steamship *Laura* came up Buffalo Bayou, Houston leaders had talked of a ship channel. It was a consuming passion. At one point a detractor wrote in a Dallas paper that "Houston wouldn't need to dig a channel if the folks down there could suck as hard as they could blow!"

There were detractors everywhere, especially in Galveston. The island people figured no ship would go on up a channel when it could stop in their city.

Farsighted men persisted and by the summer of 1914, dredging was completed to a twenty-five-foot depth from the Gulf to the turning basin. On November 10, President Woodrow Wilson pressed a button in the White House that fired a mortar at the turning basin to officially open the Houston Ship Channel.

**Also on this date**, in the year 1837, ten Rangers and fifty Indians died in a battle in Archer County.

## NOVEMBER 11

### 1918

Nearly 200,000 Texans served in the army or navy during the great crusade that was the First World War. Five thousand of them died. The American expeditionary force taught us about places like Château-Thierry, Belleau Wood, Saint-Mihiel, and the Meuse-Argonne.

The sweetest news came from the forest of Compiègne, where the historic struggle came to an end with the signing of a peace treaty in a railway car. At the eleventh hour, on the eleventh day of the eleventh month, Hartley Edwards of Denison blew taps, and the war was over.

## NOVEMBER 12

### 1883

As the winter of 1883 settled in on Texas, cattlemen finally admitted the inevitable: wire—especially barbed wire—had changed the west forever. There was bloodshed and death because of wire; wire that kept cattle either in or out. The free access to the lush grass was gone, and fence-builders or fence-cutters would have to rule the day.

On November 12, 1883, a special meeting of cowmen was called in Gainesville. Col. Tom Ball of Huntsville spoke and urged cowmen to change the way they did business; to run fewer cattle, and better cattle, so they could adapt to fenced ranges.

From that meeting came a call for the legislature to pass laws to protect property rights—whether they be farmer's or cowman's. It called on the state to build roads, and to put gates in the fences to allow the roads through.

It all sounds so simple now. The truth is that that declaration was proof the world of the Texas cowman was forever changed, and the brief and spectacular era of the cowboy was over.

## NOVEMBER 13

### 1863

In August 1863 the mutilated body of a horse trader named John Savage was found floating in the Aransas River near San Patricio. A few days later an old Mexican woman,

Chipita Rodríguez, was arrested and charged with the crime. The state alleged that Chipita had hacked the horse trader to bits to steal his gold. She maintained her innocence. In a speedy, somewhat questionable trial, the jury found Chipita guilty, and a judge sentenced her to be hanged by the neck until dead.

On a misty Friday, the thirteenth of November, the hangman helped her onto a wagon and sat her on her coffin for a ride to a hanging tree. The execution was carried out. Chipita Rodríguez became the first, and—so far—the only woman ever legally hanged in Texas.

## NOVEMBER 14

### 1851

About fourteen or so miles north of Abilene stands a marker for Fort Phantom Hill. The fort was established on November 14, 1851, as one of the links in the chain of forts from the Red River to the Rio Grande. It offered just about as bad a life as army life could; too hot in the summer, too cold in the winter, with drinking water hauled in and supplies that occasionally arrived on wagon trains. It was lonely, and the monotony caused a great number of desertions. Occasionally the men went out to chase Indians or escort a wagon train.

The original name was simply "Post on Clear Fork of the Brazos." The name "Fort Phantom Hill" came from more than one soldier who gazed out at the nothingness that surrounded him and thought he saw a ghostly Indian. Three years after it opened it was mercifully closed.

## NOVEMBER 15

### 1836

Lorenzo de Zavala's life took some strange turns before he ended up at San Jacinto. De Zavala was born in the Yucatán and grew up to be an ardent liberal. He was imprisoned for his political beliefs, got out, and, in Mexico's mercurial political world, rose to the top and was elected governor of the state of Mexico. He became the treasury minister, and later decided to try to make money with an empresario contract to settle parts of Texas.

In 1833 de Zavala was serving as Mexico's minister to France when he decided the "Napoleon of the West," as Santa Anna liked to call himself, could not be trusted. De Zavala resigned, and left the splendor of Paris to go to Texas where he bought land on Buffalo Bayou, across from where the San Jacinto River flows in. The people of Harrisburg sent him to Washington-on-the-Brazos to sign the Declaration of Independence. Before he left to come home, the convention elected him vice-president of the Republic of Texas. Zavala's health was failing, and after the revolution ended, as peace finally was within his reach, he died on November 15, 1836.

Lorenzo de Zavala had spent just over a year in the place that claims him now as one of its true heroes.

## NOVEMBER 16

### 1961

Tennesseans who became Texans shaped the new state. Sam Rayburn was Tennessee-born and Texas-raised, and he helped shape the world.

When Sam was five his family left Tennessee and moved to Fannin County, Texas. Young Sam taught school for a while before he went into politics. He rose through the legislature in Austin to become Speaker of the Texas House, then resigned to become the congressman from the Fourth District of Texas. He stayed in Congress for forty-eight years, twenty-one of those years as the Speaker of the House.

Lyndon Johnson, who was a Rayburn protege, said the Speaker was never really understood. Johnson said, "What Texans considered liberal was, to the Washington establishment, conservative." He insisted that his mentor always called the vote the way he saw it—and voted for whatever was best.

Certainly it cannot be questioned that Rayburn's voice, and his management of congressional programs, changed America. He was the most powerful man in Washington, save the President. FDR almost chose him as his vice-presidential running mate in 1944, but turned to Harry Truman at the last minute.

Sixteen years later, Rayburn was furious at Johnson for even considering being John Kennedy's running mate, saying that "being Vice-President was not worth a bowl of warm spit." Rayburn finally consented to Johnson's accepting the offer because he thought Kennedy would lose, and the national exposure would be good for Johnson's 1964 try for the Presidency, which Rayburn was already planning.

Sam Rayburn was seventy-nine when he died on November 16, 1961. At his death he was eulogized as one of the greatest men America had produced. (See also Jan. 6.)

## NOVEMBER 17

### 1882

The legislature of the state of Texas directed that a university of the first class be estab-

lished. The location was left to a vote of the people. Austin, Tyler, and Waco seriously sought the new University of Texas. Waco lobbied that it was "free from the distractions and corrupting influences of a political capital," but the vote went to Austin nonetheless.

Just about a year later, on November 17, 1882, the cornerstone for the first building— "Old Main"—was laid. A speaker said it was the culmination of the dreams of the heroes of San Jacinto.

## NOVEMBER 18

### 1947

The initial advertising budget for the Alley Theatre in Houston was $2.14. A feisty young woman from Yoakum named Nina Vance bought 214 penny postcards and sent them out to folks saying a new theater was opening on November 18, 1947, in a rented dance studio on Main Street. The first play was *A Sound of Hunting*.

A few people passed through the narrow alleyway to get into the theater, and to take part in history. The Alley was to become Houston's resident professional theater. Margo Jones had opened her repertory theater in Dallas a few months earlier. Together Jones and Vance did more to bring good theater to Texas than anyone else. (See also June 3.)

## NOVEMBER 19

### 1854

When Sam Houston married Margaret Lea (see Apr. 11), his friends figured it would never work, given his love for the drink and her devotion to the Baptist church. When people asked her why she married him, she usually said it was because he had won her heart, and then she would add, "I will devote my life to reforming him." Sam promised never to let her hear of his being out on a spree again. That was 1840.

Fourteen years later Margaret Lea Houston experienced her proudest moment as an evangelistic reformer. Preacher Rufus Burleson led Sam to the baptizin' hole on Rocky Creek behind the Independence Baptist Church. When Houston came up out of the water the minister said, "Your sins are washed away." Later the general was to say he hoped so: "But if they were all washed away, Lord help the fish down below." That was November 19, 1854.

# NOVEMBER 20

## 1908

Before Howard Robard Hughes became an oil driller in Texas he was a lawyer, a miner, and at one point studied to get into a military school. For six years, Hughes tried his hand at drilling oil wells. Sometimes he hit; sometimes he did not. More often than not he saw his wells fail because drilling bits kept breaking up when they hit a layer of hard rock.

Hughes went home to visit his parents in Iowa—and there he dreamed up a rock bit: a cone-shaped revolving cutter with steel teeth that rolled and ground the rock. (There is another version of the story: that John S. Wynn came up with the idea and that Hughes bought it from him for $6,000 and improved it.)

On November 20, 1908, Hughes applied for a patent for the Hughes Rock Bit. The bit revolutionized the oil industry. Men could now find oil where they had never been able to find it before. The strata of rock that protected the oil pool were no longer hopelessly impenetrable.

# NOVEMBER 21

## 1869

The man who presided over the constitutional convention in neighboring Oklahoma was a Texan. William Henry Murray was born in Toadsuck, Texas, on November 21, 1869.

After getting a teaching certificate at College Hill Institute in Springtown, he made a couple of attempts to get into Texas politics, but failed. He moved to Indian Territory where he began farming and lecturing on the merits of growing alfalfa. Murray prospered and was called to preside over the constitutional convention when Indian Territory became the state of Oklahoma.

He served in the legislature and in Congress before he was elected governor, running on the platform of the common man, including, among other ideas, the distribution of free seed to farmers. He adopted the nickname "Alfalfa Bill" and walked and hitchhiked to many political gatherings. While governor, he became involved in the famous Red River bridge controversy with Texas (see July 27).

# NOVEMBER 22

## 1963

The thousand days of the presidency of John F. Kennedy ended on November 22, 1963, on the streets of Dallas. As President Kennedy was riding in a motorcade with his wife and Governor and Mrs. John Connally, he was shot. Lee Harvey Oswald fired the shots from the upper floors of the Texas School Book Depository. Kennedy was hit in the head and probably killed instantly. Governor Connally was seriously wounded.

That same day, Vice-President Lyndon Johnson was rushed to the presidential plane, and when it was determined that Kennedy was dead, Federal Judge Sarah Hughes was called to administer the oath of office, making Johnson the thirty-sixth President of the United States.

## NOVEMBER 23

### 1915

The University of Texas and Texas A&M have played each other in football games since 1894. Those games have settled into a late-

November ritual that stirs blood, be it orange or maroon. The 1915 game gave rise to legend and history, and not so much for the game as for what happened afterward. The Aggies were rolling with a 5-wins, 1-loss record heading into the big game with the Longhorns. Texas was 6-1, having lost only to Oklahoma, and only by a single point. The wooden grandstand at Kyle Field was jammed that November afternoon as the Aggies took the measure of the Horns, 13–0.

In their exuberance after the game, some Aggies whose names are now lost to history made their way to Austin and imprinted the score on the big Longhorn steer then serving as mascot of the University of Texas. The old steer looked slightly embarrassed the next morning with a giant "13–0" branded from stem to stern on his side. The Texas boys were furious, but ingenious. They turned the 13 into a "B," the hyphen into an "E," added a

The original Bevo, with the infamous score emblazoned on his side, 1915. (Texas A&M University)

"V," and left the "O." Thus was B E V O born—and thanks to the Aggies, Texas got a permanent name for its mascot.

*Note*: November 23 is an approximate date.

**Also on this date**, in the year 1853, James Henderson became governor and served just twenty-eight days.

# NOVEMBER 24

### 1874

On November 24, 1874, something happened in far-off Dallas, Illinois, that was to change Texas and the West. J. F. Glidden re-

ceived a patent for a process that would twist strands of wire with small spikes in it. He called it barbed wire.

Henry Sanborn brought it to Texas and sold the first ten reels of it in Gainesville. Another ace salesman, John Gates, put on a demonstration in San Antonio that gained a great deal of attention. He built a pen out of barbed wire on San Antonio's military plaza and filled it with the meanest cattle he could find. Gates, who later became known as "Bet-a-Million," bet the locals a hundred dollars that the barbed-wire fence would hold the cattle. The wire held, even though a fencepost broke. Gates advertised the wire as "light as air, as strong as whiskey and as cheap as dirt." Before long, barbed wire was everywhere, and the vast open ranges of Texas disappeared.

Barbed wire: "Light as air, strong as whiskey, and cheap as dirt." (Barker Texas History Center)

### 1868

We call it "ragtime" music because the old-timers played the music in ragged time, without regard for standard rhythmic patterns. The man who made ragtime popular was born in Texarkana on November 24, 1868. He grew up in northeast Texas playing the banjo and the piano.

As a young man he moved to St. Louis and began to write his music: "Maple Leaf Rag," "The Ragtime Dance," "Swipesy Cake Walk," and "The Entertainer." The songs were published and played, but Scott Joplin saw few rewards. White entertainers used his songs to become popular and rich. His attempts at opera were scorned, although years after his death, *Treemonisha* was performed all over the world, to critical acclaim.

Joplin was a lonely, bitter man when he died at the age of fifty-three. His music was to become the rhythm of an era. It was the true beginning of jazz and rock-and-roll.

Scott Joplin was a master of ragtime music. (Larry Melton/Institute of Texan Cultures)

## NOVEMBER 25

### 1850

Texas is big, but it was a lot bigger before the Compromise of 1850. The United States offered Texas ten million dollars for the land north of the thirty-second parallel and west of the 103rd meridian. There was some opposition in the state to the bill, but a referendum was held and Texas decided to take the money.

On November 25, 1850, Gov. P. Hansborough Bell signed the bill and Texas gave up its claim to the region that included the states of Colorado and Wyoming, and set a firm boundary with New Mexico.

**Also on this date**, in the year 1835, the Texas navy was created.

## NOVEMBER 26

### 1864

The legendary Indian fighter Colonel "Kit" Carson's last fight came at the ruins of an old trading post called Adobe Walls on November 26, 1864. While most Indian battles were fights that involved relatively few people, this battle involved thousands.

Colonel Carson took the First Cavalry from New Mexico to raid the winter home of the Plains Indians somewhere south of the Canadian River. Carson had about four hundred men. On the night of November 25, scouts rode into camp to tell Carson the Indians—Comanches and Kiowas—were camped near

Adobe Walls. The next morning Carson attacked a Kiowa village and destroyed it. But some Indians escaped and spread the alarm. By the time Carson's cavalry got to Adobe Walls, several thousand Indians had massed for an attack on the U.S. soldiers.

As the Indians attacked, Carson ordered into action two mountain howitzers he had pulled from New Mexico. The first exploding cannon stopped the Indians; the next shot temporarily put them in full retreat.

Kit Carson was brave, but he was not foolish. He realized the odds favored the Indians and ordered his men to fight their way out of Adobe Walls and head back home for New Mexico. The battle for the rest of the day was a battle for the white men's survival, the occasional blast from the cannon making it possible for them to get away.

Carson lost two men; the Indians suffered sixty casualties. Only one Indian village was destroyed, but Carson's message came through loud and clear: there was no place for the Indian to feel safe; the pony soldiers would come after them on reprisal raids. The pattern was holding; even when the Indians won, they lost. (See also June 27.)

## NOVEMBER 27

### 1944

Macario García was born in Coahuila, Mexico, and came to Texas as a young man. He settled down to live and work near Sugar Land, but the Second World War got in his way. In November 1942 García joined the army despite the fact he was not yet a citizen of the United States.

On November 27, 1944, as an acting squad leader with Company B of the Twenty-second Infantry near Grosshau, Germany, he single-handedly assaulted two enemy machine-gun implacements. Despite painful wounds, he crawled toward the first enemy position and dropped grenades in the implacement. Soon a second machine gun opened up on his men. Again, disregarding his personal safety, he stormed the gun, killed three, and captured four enemy prisoners. Once his men were safe, the sergeant allowed himself to be evacuated for medical treatment.

For his actions that day, Sgt. Macario García was presented the Congressional Medal of Honor by President Harry Truman. It was a great day, but he said later his greatest day was June 25, 1947, when he became a naturalized citizen of the country he fought for.

## NOVEMBER 28

### 1882

There was perhaps no area of segregation in Texas harder to crack than that which existed on the docks at Galveston and Houston. A "screwman" was a specialized longshoreman who used screwjacks to load cotton bales into ships. In 1866, white longshoremen organized a screwman's union—the Benevolent Association. They brought about work reforms on the docks, and made sure no blacks got any of the jobs.

When Norris Wright Cuney (see May 12) started to push for his black "Cotton Jammers" to work on the docks, trouble began to brew. On November 28, 1882, the screwmen called a general holiday to protest the black workers, but there was a shortage of labor, and the shippers began to use the blacks. They organized a separate union, and by the 1920s, when better ways of loading cotton made the screwmen unnecessary, the groups became members of the Longshoremen's Union. The

An artist's rendering of Macario Garcia and the army reserve center in Houston named in his honor. (Author's collection)

black and white unions remained separate, and sometimes equal, until the 1970s.

## NOVEMBER 29

### 1862

John Bankhead Magruder was a West Point man from Virginia. He was caught in that boring routine of one posting after another, following a brief taste of glory in the Mexican War. Then came the War Between the States, which made his career—as an officer for the Confederacy. He left the Federal forces to go home to Virginia, where he won brief recognition for his work at Yorktown in the war's initial battle. But later, in the "Seven Days' Battle," Magruder got a bad rap for indecision and, before he knew it, his star was setting. Texas had a commander, Gen. Paul Hébert, who was not exactly a favorite in the Confederate capital of Montgomery; so Magruder was sent to Texas to take over command—another out-of-favor officer sent to the backwater to

Longshoremen on the Galveston docks separate into white and black flanks for this 1924 photo commemorating a charitable act by J. M. Edel & Co., exporters. (Houston Metropolitan Research Center, Houston Library)

replace one who was sent even deeper into military purgatory.

In November 1862, Marguder took over command of the district of Texas. He was to use the backwater of the war to prove to one and all that he was a good fighting man, for shortly after he arrived he drove the Yankees out, and kept them out of Texas for the duration of the war. (See also Jan. 1.)

*Note*: This is not a firm date.

# NOVEMBER 30

## 1837

Erastus Smith did not want to fight anybody. He came to Texas for his health and settled in San Antonio. His health returned, except for a constant hearing problem, and he married and raised a family.

As the Mexican government became more and more repressive, and Smith's friends talked of war, the man they called "Deaf" remained neutral. He refused to take sides until that fateful day when the Mexican troops refused to let him enter San Antonio to visit his wife and children. "Deaf" Smith became a man possessed, and from that day on he was a scout or fighter at one revolutionary battle after the other. He was on his way to the Alamo when word came that it had fallen. Smith rode to find Sam Houston's army, and at San Jacinto he cut down Vince's Bridge to make retreat impossible for Santa Anna's army.

"Deaf" Smith died on November 30, 1837, only a year after he became a hero in the revolution he tried to avoid.

A 1915 scene in Houston looking north on Main Street from Preston Avenue. (Houston Metropolitan Research Center, Houston Library)

# ► DECEMBER ◄

## DECEMBER 1

### 1956

In the 1950s nobody in the world could run faster than Bobby Morrow of San Benito. In high school he ran the hundred-yard dash faster than anyone ever had—9.6 seconds. And at Abilene Christian College he ran the hundred in 9.1, but had a wind at his back, so the world record was not allowed. The 1956 Olympics were held in Melbourne, Australia, and Bobby Morrow was expected to be the star of the American team. He was.

His first event was the 100 meters. He won it going away. Three days later he won the 200 meters. On December 1, 1956, the American 400-meter relay team, anchored by Morrow, won in world-record time. Bobby Morrow had become the first man to win three gold medals in track and field in the Olympics since Jesse Owens won four of them at Berlin in 1936.

**Also on this date**, in the year 1913, Broadway star Mary Martin was born in Weatherford.

## DECEMBER 2

### 1832

On December 2, 1832, Sam Houston came to Texas for the first time. He was thirty-nine years old, running from several lifetimes, and

Bobby Morrow shows off one of the three gold medals he won in the 1956 Olympics. (Texas Sports Hall of Fame)

heading out of the United States as an emissary of his friend, President Andrew Jackson. He was coming off his deepest depression, his greatest hurt, and his longest bout with the bottle.

Biographer Marquis James, in *The Raven*, said Houston rode a horse with no tail, as he left from where Muskogee, Oklahoma, is now. Heading for the old Jonesboro crossing northwest of Clarksville, on the Red River, Houston rode with a drinking buddy, Elias Rector. Houston supposedly told Rector it would be a shame to ride into Texas on a horse with no tail, so Rector gave him his horse. Houston rode the horse into the sand and water that made up the boundary between the United States and Texas. He rode into a new life and a spot in history on a borrowed horse. He had written a relative to say, "I am about to enter Texas—my spirits are good and my heart is straight. . . ."

# DECEMBER 3

### 1854

The first permanent Polish colony in the United States was established in Texas. On December 3, 1854, about a hundred families from Upper Silesia arrived at Galveston on the *Weser* out of Bremen.

After they reached the mainland, the Poles began to walk west. It must have been a strange procession—men and women, children both young and old, walking through the coastal plain and into the edge of the hill country. They carried all their worldly possessions, or pushed them in carts, or coaxed teams to pull wagons piled high with all manner of things. They could not speak English. They did not know the land, the whims of a December in Texas, and were naked to the dangers of the

wild country. For twenty days they walked until they came to the junction of the San Antonio and Cibolo rivers, where they founded a community they named for the Virgin Mary. At Panna Maria on Christmas Eve, 1854, they gathered for mass under a huge tree.

A year later seven hundred of their fellow Poles came to join them, and the floodtide of Poles to America was beginning.

# DECEMBER 4

### 1835

Texas's battle for independence from Mexico is filled with daring moments of bravado that seem almost foolhardy. The defiant, "Come and Take It" flag at Gonzales (see Oct. 2), the heroic hopelessness of the Alamo, the final desperate charge at San Jacinto— these were the acts of the right men at the right time in history, and if there were cowards among them we did not hear about them.

Ben Milam was larger than life for a few months in Texas. He had been in the Mexican Army for a while, and had seen various money-making ventures turn sour. Later in 1835 he became an activist for Stephen F. Austin, and was sent with Travis, Bowie, and some other men to scout routes and to look into taking San Antonio from the Mexicans. The little army gathered outside the city, as Milam went scouting further south. When he returned, he found the army had not gone into San Antonio, and indeed was about to give up the project and go home. On the night of December 4, 1835, Milam raised his gun and asked the army: "Who will go with old Ben Milam into the Bexar?" Three hundred men said they would—as soon as Hendrick Arnold arrived. Arnold was a black man, a free Negro from Mississippi who lived in Austin's colony.

He was as widely respected as Milam. In the early morning of the fifth, Arnold returned to lead one group, with Milam leading the other; and the battle for San Antonio was underway.

In the house-to-house fight that followed, Milam was killed, but the Mexicans surrendered. Old Ben Milam's rallying cry kept the revolution alive, and allowed Texans to move into the Alamo garrison to set up a high-water mark in man's quest for freedom.

## DECEMBER 5

### 1803

One of the men who did not wait around to go "into the Bexar with old Ben Milam" (see Dec. 4) was Thomas Jefferson Rusk. Born December 5, 1803, in South Carolina, Rusk came to Texas looking for some men who had stolen money from him. He stayed to make his home in the new land. He was a member of the Nacogdoches Volunteers at San Antonio, but left before Milam came back to lead his heroic charge.

Rusk served as inspector general for the army, later signed the declaration of independence, and fought at the Battle of San Jacinto. For a brief time he was named commander of the army. He served in Congress, fought Indians, turned down a chance to run for president of Texas, and was finally named chief justice of the supreme court of the Republic of Texas.

With statehood, Rusk and Houston were elected to become the state's first senators. Rusk's stock continued to rise in Washington, and he was mentioned as a possible presidential candidate. That was 1856—but it was a very bad year for Thomas Jefferson Rusk. His beloved wife, Mary, died in Nacogdoches, and a year later a grieving Rusk committed suicide.

Thomas J. Rusk served Texas as a general, legislator, cabinet officer and U.S. senator. (Houston Metropolitan Research Center, Houston Library)

## DECEMBER 6

### 1949

Huddie Ledbetter was born the son of a tenant farmer in Louisiana. In 1895, when Huddie was ten, the family moved to Texas and settled around Boulder.

A dirt-poor black kid had little or no chance to make anything of himself in those days, but Huddie was lucky enough to pick up a six-string guitar, and before long it was his ticket out. He was soon playing in dives in Dallas and Fort Worth, picking a twelve-string guitar and singing the blues.

Next to singing and playing, Ledbetter liked women and booze. Sometime in 1918 he was convicted of murder, got out of the Texas prison in 1925, and a few years later tried to kill somebody else. His song "The Midnight Special" warns that "if you ever go to Houston, better not fool around, Sheriff Benford will arrest you, and you're Sugar Land bound . . . on the Midnight Special. . . ." Huddie knew Sheriff "T" Benford well, and he was familiar with the sites around the prison farm near Sugar Land.

His singing attracted Texas's famous folklorist John Lomax (see Sept. 23), and it was Lomax who convinced authorities to let Ledbelly, as he was now known, out of prison so he could perform. He was to become a major star on Eastern concert stages and especially the college circuit. He lived to be sixty-four, and died on December 6, 1949. Every few years a new generation of singers comes up with a Ledbelly song that was an east Texas work ditty, or a thing made up to pass the day in jail; and Huddie lives again.

1898

Texas is a state that absolutely dotes on football. Football players are kings. The legislature even passed a resolution saying that University of Texas running back Earl Campbell was a genuine Texas hero.

The very first All-American football player born in Texas was Ben Boynton, who was born in Waco on December 6, 1898. Ben was a star at Waco High in 1913, 1914, and 1915.

At Williams College he quarterbacked the team to an unbeaten season and was named to the International News Service All-American team. When the ball was more round than egg-shaped, you could drop kick it for field goals, and Ben Boynton did that better than anyone. He once ran a kick back 110 yards for a touchdown, and no one will ever break that record.

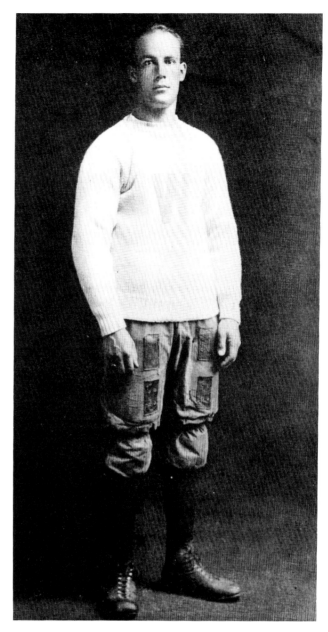

Ben Boynton at Williams College, Massachusetts. He was the first All-American football player born in Texas. (Texas Sports Hall of Fame)

After college, Boynton played in those wild pro games that finally gave way to the National Football League. In a day when the game was played with little or no pads, for little or no money, Ben Boynton played for one pro team on Saturday and a different one on Sunday.

In 1962 Benjamin Lee Boynton was named to the College Football Hall of Fame.

## DECEMBER 7

### 1941

It was a day that would live in infamy—December 7, 1941. The Japanese attacked Pearl Harbor and America was at war. It was a war that was to have a profound effect on Texas. We produced about five percent of the country's population, but sent away seven percent of our men and boys to fight.

The state had a profound effect on the war effort. The Supreme Allied Commander was a Texan; so was the commander of the Pacific Fleet; and the most decorated man from both army and navy came from Texas.

Texas became a prime training ground for the young men who would fly the planes, man the ships, and slug it out on the ground. Great plants rose to build the matériel of war. As the struggle went on, Texas was to become a prime site for prisoner-of-war camps.

At least 22,000 Texas men who went away to fight the war died in it.

## DECEMBER 8

### 1872

Edna Ferber once described Galveston's humidity as being like "a clammy hand held over your face." "But," she said, "the city has a ghostly charm."

Much of that charm lies in its architecture—and the first professional architect in Galveston was a man who left an impressive legacy. Nicholas Clayton was born in Ireland and came to Galveston on December 8, 1872, when he was twenty-three.

Young Clayton came to supervise construction of the Tremont Hotel, and for the next twenty-five years he changed the look of the Island City. He designed St. Mary's Infirmary, Harmony Hall, the Galveston Pavilion, much of the Strand, the Grand Beach Hotel, and the magnificent Bishop's Palace, among other buildings.

He was a quiet, reclusive man who did not marry until he was fifty, and who died quietly in 1916. The paper gave him a brief obituary, nothing more. Clayton had given Galveston much of her charm.

## DECEMBER 9

### 1844

Dr. Anson Jones drifted into Texas after a series of misadventures and bad business moves left him a beaten man. As for so many others who came here running from themselves, or somebody, the change agreed with Jones and he prospered. Following the revolution he was an active politician who took credit for Texas's admission into the Union. (Houston took similar credit.)

After Houston's terms as president of the Republic, he backed Jones, and the doctor won over Edward Burleson. On December 9, 1844, Anson Jones took the oath of office to become the last president of the republic. Just over a year later, as Texas became a state, Anson Jones was to say the benediction for the republic. (See also Jan. 9, Feb. 19.)

## DECEMBER 10

### 1854

Richard King was a riverboat captain who really was the king of Brownsville and the lower Rio Grande. He controlled the riverboat trade and was buying land for ranches when one day, as he was docking his boat, he nearly collided with a houseboat. The captain is said to have unleashed a string of words that might make a sailor blush. A young woman appeared on the deck of the houseboat and gave Captain King a tongue-lashing. She was Henrietta Chamberlain, daughter of a missionary who had come to Texas to save the lost.

Before long, the captain and the missionary's daughter became good friends; then, very good friends. On December 10, 1854, Richard King married Henrietta Chamberlain. Together they built the greatest ranching empire in America. Henrietta was a partner with King in the business, registering brands, keeping up with the stock, and rearing children.

When King died he left Henrietta a half-million acres of land, and a half-million dollars in debts. She turned to Robert Kleberg, a young lawyer who was courting her daughter Alice, and tapped him to manage the ranch. That was in 1885. From that day to the day she died, forty years later, Henrietta Chamberlain King and Robert Kleberg ran the King Ranch.

At her death the ranch covered nearly a million acres of land, where nearly a hundred thousand cattle grazed in a sea of grass that covered a sea of oil. (See also March 29.)

An early aerial view of the King Ranch headquarters. (Barker Texas History Center)

## DECEMBER 11

1879

If it hadn't been for Amon Carter, there would not be a Fort Worth as we know it today. The young man who came to town when he was still in his twenties stayed to make Fort Worth a great city.

Amon Carter was born in Crafton, Texas, on December 11, 1879. He came to Fort Worth first as an advertising man for the Fort Worth *Star* newspaper. Three years later he bought the paper. As the city grew, so did Carter's empire. He opened the city's first radio station; was the youngest president of its Chamber of Commerce; and convinced oil service companies and drillers to make Fort Worth home. His oil investments made him rich. He loved aviation, and owned American Airlines. He brought aircraft industries to Fort Worth, and when he died he left the city much of his wealth, and his priceless collection of Western art.

## DECEMBER 12

1872

Who is a Texan? What is a Texan? To millions of youngsters in the late 1800s, "Texas Jack" was what Texas was all about. The only problem is that Texas Jack was from Virginia. John Burwell Omohundro, Jr., was born in Virginia ten years after Texas won her independence. As a teenager he came to Texas and became a cowboy. He drove cattle and served as a scout and a buffalo hunter.

In December 1872, Buffalo Bill Cody heard about John Omohundro and brought him to Chicago to star in one of Cody's Wild West

In the 1870s, the world viewed Texans as being like J. B. "Texas Jack" Omohundro. (Western History Collections, University of Oklahoma Library)

shows. Soon he was the hero of dime novels, and popular magazines serialized stories about Texas Jack. Most of them were pure fiction.

Texas Jack wrote an article for a popular magazine in 1877. In it he talked of the cowboy's noble qualities, of the dangers of stampedes, and of the importance of singing to the herd at night to keep the animals calm. To millions, that is what a cowboy was—and thus, that was a Texan.

On June 28, 1880, Omohundro died of pneumonia in Colorado. He was not yet thirty-five years old.

*Note*: December 12 is an approximate date.

### 1866

Fort Clark was built on Las Moras Creek in Kinney County in the early 1850s. Hardly a day went by without Indians attacking it, or soldiers riding out to fight the Indians or search for Mexican raiders. The fort was so busy that it took four years for anyone to find time enough to build a post headquarters.

When the Civil War came, the post was abandoned; but on December 12, 1866, Federal soldiers came back. Over the next eighty years of its life the fort was to be the home of most cavalry regiments, as well as infantry and cavalry divisions that stretch all the way to World War II.

With the end of the war, time ran out for Fort Clark. In 1946 it was again abandoned—and eventually became a private ranch.

# DECEMBER 13

### 1931

One of the great oil and gas fields of Texas blew in on December 13, 1931. George Strake drilled a well that flowed with 15 million cubic feet of gas. He followed that with another huge well. Soon wells were shooting oil and gas up through the Piney Woods around Conroe. The Conroe Field was the first of a dozen fields developed in Montgomery County.

Strake, a devout Roman Catholic, gave much of his wealth to the church.

# DECEMBER 14

### 1861

In the early months of the War Between the States, Confederate hopes pushed past mere survival and into the realms of Manifest Destiny. So it was that Henry Hopkins Sibley and his brigade of Texas volunteers rode into Fort Bliss on December 14, 1861, and made preparations for an invasion of the Southwest.

Secessionist sentiment could be scared up in California and in the territories of New Mexico and Arizona, but it was not sufficient to give Sibley and his little band of Texans the edge over the larger force of Federal troops. Even so, Sibley's men enjoyed victory at Valverde in February 1862 and pushed on toward Albuquerque.

The Federals destroyed the supplies in both that city and Santa Fe, depriving the Confederates of much-needed food. In March another battle was fought, at Glorieta, and though Sibley claimed victory, he had had enough. He began a nightmarish retreat in which he was forced to abandon all his wagons and most of his ammunition. In some stretches the men hacked through dense underbrush with their bowie knives and subsisted on substandard rations, if any. When the remnants of the army reached Fort Bliss in May 1862, the dream of a Confederacy that spanned the continent was dead.

# DECEMBER 15

### 1881

The driving of the golden spike in Utah in 1869 united east and west and formed a transcontinental railroad, but there was an immediate cry in Congress for a southern route.

In that same year, the Southern Pacific started east with a line from California. The Texas and Pacific started in east Texas heading west for California. By November 1881 the Southern Pacific had reached the outskirts of Sierra Blanca in Hudspeth County. The Texas and Pacific was ten miles away. Finally, Jay Gould of Texas and Pacific struck a deal with C. P. Huntington of the Southern Pacific, and on December 15, 1881, the lines were joined at Sierra Blanca. America now had its second transcontinental railroad.

American newspapers carried the story in banner headlines, making the little insurrection look like a full-fledged war. In truth the Indians and the Austin colonists didn't think twice about Edwards's deal and joined Mexico in turning on the "Republic of Fredonia." By January 1827 the rebellion was over, and Edwards and his men were driven out of Texas.

From the misbegotten adventure came a clash of cultures that did not escape the notice of political leaders in Washington and Mexico City. Within ten years newspapers were carrying headlines that screamed the story of the true revolution.

## DECEMBER 16

### 1826

The Republic of Fredonia lasted just over a month, but its dramatic birth and death were an early warning sign of what was to come in Texas.

When a Kentucky businessman named Haden Edwards came to settle a colony near Nacogdoches in 1825, he had a clear deal with the Mexicans, but it seemed everyone else did, too. Some of the colonists arrived in Texas only to find the Mexican government was saying "yes" with one hand and "no" with the other. Haden Edwards's brother Benjamin organized two hundred men and whipped up a flag that said "Independence, Liberty, and Justice." They marched on a square building in Nacogdoches called the "Old Stone Fort," and claimed it as the capitol of the "Republic of Fredonia." It was December 16, 1826. Edwards wanted to divide Texas into Anglo and Indian sections; he hoped his actions would bring much-needed help from Austin's colonies and from all the Texas Indians, to unite against Mexico.

## DECEMBER 17

### 1861

It was a short war for Benjamin Franklin Terry, the man who gave his name to one of Texas's most famous fighting forces. Terry was born in Kentucky, and moved to Texas as a boy. He grew up and married in Fort Bend County.

Life was routine for Ben Terry until people started talking secession; and he found himself talking loudest. His Fort Bend neighbors sent him to the secession convention, and waved goodbye as he backed up his words with deeds and rode off to Virginia to fight the Yankees at First Manassas. He came back to Texas to organize what he called "some shirt-tail Rangers." A thousand of them rode out to fight the war in the fall of 1861.

On December 17, 1861, as Ben Terry led a charge against the Union troops near Woodsonville, he was shot and killed. The Eighth Texas Cavalry fought out the war as "Terry's Texas Rangers." (See also Sept. 9.)

## DECEMBER 18

### 1865

In April 1864 a resolution was introduced in Congress to abolish slavery. It failed. After the war, the Reconstruction Amendment, the thirteenth, appeared again. On December 18, 1865, it was ratified.

The amendment said, "Neither slavery nor involuntary servitude, except for punishment of a crime, shall exist within the United States, or any place subject to their jurisdiction."

For many years, traders had brought slaves to markets in Houston, Galveston, and Austin. The slaves generally sold for from $300 to $2,000, depending on age and sex. There were 443 slaves in Austin's colony by 1825, and about 5,000 slaves by the time of the republic. When the Civil War came there were 182,566 slaves in Texas. One out of every four white families owned a slave.

The freedom that the Thirteenth Amendment brought was a freedom in poverty and ignorance and cruel prejudice, but it was not slavery.

## DECEMBER 19

### 1959

In the Mount Pleasant Cemetery in Franklin you can find the gravestone of Walter Williams. He served with Company C, Fifth Regiment, Hood's Brigade, from May 1864 to the end of the war. His military career was not spectacular, but Walter Williams turned out to be the last surviving Civil War veteran.

In 1956 when the last surviving Yankee died, Williams was given a citation saying he had finally won the war for the South. President Dwight Eisenhower made him an honorary general.

On December 19, 1959, Williams died at the age of 117. They laid him out in a Confederate general's uniform, gave him an honor guard, and paraded his funeral procession through downtown Houston. He was buried to the strains of "Dixie" and the "Yellow Rose of Texas."

**Also on this date**, in the year 1859, Mirabeau B. Lamar died.

Texan Walter Williams, the last surviving soldier of the American Civil War. (Texas Collection, Baylor University)

## DECEMBER 20

### 1877

Just so you don't harbor the mistaken belief that being an Old West bad guy paid well, you should know that on December 20, 1877, Sam Bass robbed the Fort Worth-Cleburne Stage. His total take was $11.25.

## DECEMBER 21

### 1821

Jane Long was born on a plantation in Maryland. She made the mistake of falling in love with a dreamer, and thus shared a few of his nightmares. There is no question that Jane Wilkinson loved Dr. James Long. She fell for him the first time she saw him. He was a dashing lieutenant, the hero of the Battle of New Orleans; she was sixteen.

She was seventeen when they married, eighteen when the first child came, and less than twenty-five when she started following him all over Texas and Louisiana as he fought to free Texas from Spanish rule (see June 8).

The doctor left Jane with her maid and baby at Bolivar Point on Galveston Island, when he went out on another adventure. It was an awful winter, with not much food; and life in a tent was a long way from a Maryland plantation.

On December 21, 1821, Jane Long gave birth to a baby girl, Mary James, who is generally credited with being the first Anglo baby born in Texas. The child did not live long; Dr. Long was shot in the back; and Jane lived on to be the Grand Old Lady of the Republic of Texas. (See also July 23.)

**Also on this date**, in the year 1882, Edith Wilmans was born; she was the first woman ever elected to the Texas House of Representatives (1922).

## DECEMBER 22

### 1912

Claudia Alta Taylor was born in Karnack, Texas, on December 22, 1912. A nurse who cared for her said the baby looked as "pretty as a lady bird." She has been "Lady Bird" all her life. After she graduated from the University of Texas she met a "man in a hurry," as she described Lyndon Johnson. Their marriage lasted for thirty-eight years. She had gone from dreams of being a teacher, or maybe a journalist, to being the First Lady of the land.

## DECEMBER 23

### 1820

Moses Austin was a persistent man with a dream. His dream was to bring colonists to Texas. At every turn the idea seemed doomed, until finally on December 23, 1820, he got in to see Gov. Antonio de Martinez in San Antonio. He laid out his plan to bring three hundred families to Texas. Three weeks later the Mexican government approved the plan, and Austin secured a grant to start a trickle of Anglos into Texas. Before long the trickle was to become a flood that engulfed the Mexicans. (See also Nov. 3.)

## DECEMBER 24

1905

Howard Robard Hughes II was born on Christmas Eve, 1905. Hughes was not yet twenty when his father died and left him the tool company, worth about $700,000. Young Howard was not content to stay in Houston and run the family business. He was flying his airplane around, breaking records; he was in Hollywood making movies. He was the handsome young man with a different starlet on his arm every time you picked up the paper.

His eccentricity is, unfortunately, how history will probably remember him. His battle to control airlines, then hotels; his penchant for secrecy; his death on a private jet streaking to Houston's medical center; his alleged wills; and his life as a recluse—all made headlines. The fact is Hughes took a small inheritance and turned it into one of the world's great fortunes.

## DECEMBER 25

Christmas in Frontier Texas

In all but west Texas one could find a suitable Christmas tree. German, Czech, and Polish families decorated them with candles and homemade decorations of miniature dolls, boats, and handcarved birds. Near the seacoast, shells were painted red and green and hung on the trees. The children were left candy and cookies, and if the budget allowed, some kind of store-bought toys.

Life was never easy in frontier Texas, so Christmas was a great celebration. Wild game was killed and cooked; the best pies and cakes were stored up. At formal churches and under brush arbors, or on a lonely stretch of land in the middle of the great rolling sea of grass or sand, the old story of the birth in the stable was repeated, and prayers went up for the promise of Peace on Earth.

## DECEMBER 26

1874

Joe McComb, a native of Alabama, was a cowboy for a while, and later a surveyor. His fame came, however, because of his prowess as a hunter. On December 26, 1874, Joe McComb and two assistants set out from Fort Griffin to start the first commercial buffalo hunt in Texas. In that first season he killed two thousand buffaloes. The hides sold for $1.50 to $2. The carcasses of the proud buffaloes rotted in the sun.

## DECEMBER 27

1836

Stephen F. Austin was a Renaissance man who became a zealot where Texas was concerned. He even told a friend shortly before his death that the prosperity of Texas had assumed the character of a religion for him.

When Houston, the newcomer, beat him in the race for the presidency, and beat him badly, Austin did not sulk and feel his years of nurturing the colony, the fights, and the victory had been wasted. As the secretary of state, he plunged into his duties with the same kind of fervor that had filled his being.

His quarters were in a half-open, two-room clapboard shack that lacked windows and was heated by a fireplace. Christmas Eve of 1836 was a cold, bitter night. With the dawn of Christmas Day, Austin was suffering from pneumonia. On December 27, 1836, he roused from a fevered sleep to say, "Texas is recognized. Did you see it in the paper?"

Texas had not been recognized. Like much of what he worked for it would come after he was gone. Sam Houston wrote, "The Father of Texas is no more. The Pioneer of the Wilderness has departed."

## DECEMBER 28

### 1843

William Barret Travis was a married man when he came to Texas (see Aug. 9). He spent only a few years here, but wrote in his diary that he had made love to fifty-six women. He finally fell in love with Rebecca Cummings of Mill Creek. The fact that he was still married and that he suffered bouts of what he called "venéreo malo" kept him from making Rebecca his second wife. They courted and she reported they were engaged. Nothing came of the courtship because politics and the war got in the way. Travis's famous letter to Rebecca, written a few days before the Alamo fell, reached her after his death.

Six years later, on December 28, 1843, Rebecca married David Portis, an Austin County lawyer.

## DECEMBER 29

### 1845

On December 29, 1845, President James Polk signed the act that made Texas the twenty-eighth state in the Union. One of the terms of the annexation was that Texas retained the right to divide into four states. It will never happen. There could never be agreement over who gets the Alamo, the Cowboys, the Lone Star, and who will get to keep the name.

## DECEMBER 30

### 1896

The coach who brought glory to Texas A&M football, Homer Norton, was born in Alabama on December 30, 1896. His coaching at Centenary College in Shreveport caught the fancy of some former Aggies who wanted to see the maroon and white shine on the gridiron.

In 1934 Norton came to College Station. Five years later the Aggies went through the season without losing a game, and won the Sugar Bowl. The next year they lost only one game. In 1941 and '42 the Aggies played in the Cotton Bowl; in '44 they went to Miami to play in the Orange Bowl.

When he retired in 1947, Homer Norton's record at A&M was 82 wins, 52 losses, and 9 ties, with 3 Southwest Conference championships.

## DECEMBER 31

### 1842

Once upon a time, Houston was the capital of Texas. In the spring of 1842, however, Austin was the capital, and when the Mexican army showed up in San Antonio, President Sam Houston ordered the Texas Congress to meet in Houston in case Austin was overrun. Houston then ordered the archives moved out of Austin and sent some Rangers to get them. The locals in Austin thought this was a scheme of the president's to move the capital back to the town named for him.

The word spread, and hundreds of people gathered to protest. They even had a field cannon loaded with grapeshot. In the confusion, Mrs. Angelina Belle Eberly fired off the cannon. The Rangers gathered up what they could carry of the republic's papers and set out for Houston—it was New Year's Eve, 1842.

The next day the Austin vigilantes caught up with the Rangers and demanded they surrender the archives. President Houston's orders to the Rangers included the warning that bloodshed should be avoided at all cost. The Rangers handed over the republic's papers, and they were lovingly returned to Austin. The Archives War was over.

Texas A&M football coach Homer Norton. (Texas A&M University)

Angelina Eberley made sure the archives stayed in Austin. (Texas State Archives)

# TIME LINE

*The following is a chronological arrangement of events described in this book and includes additional significant dates.*

| | | |
|---|---|---|
| **1528** | November 6 | Cabeza de Vaca is shipwrecked near Galveston. He begins an incredible journey that marks the white man's first exploration of Texas. |
| **1540** | April 22 | The Coronado Expedition sets out for Texas in search of the seven cities of Cibola. |
| **1541** | May 23 | Coronado gives thanks for having found friendly Indians in the Palo Duro Canyon; Texas has a Thanksgiving 79 years before the Pilgrims. |
| **1554** | September 22 | Fourteen years after setting out for Texas, Coronado dies. He is one of the first white men to explore Texas, and leader of one of 20 Spanish explorations of the area. |
| **1687** | March 20 | La Salle, a French explorer, lands in Texas instead of finding the mouth of the Mississippi. |
| **1690** | May 24 | The Mission San Francisco de los Tejas is founded in east Texas. |
| **1693** | May 3 | Don Gregorio de Salinas Varona leads an expedition into Texas, and reports that the land is unsuitable for settlement; a year later Spain abandons the Texas frontier. |
| **1716** | June 24 | To celebrate the feast of St. John, soldiers of the Ramón expedition stage the first horse race in Texas. |
| | July 2 | The Spanish build a presidio west of the Neches River. It marks the beginning of continuous settlement in the province of Texas. |
| **1718** | May 1 | The Mission San Antonio de Valero (the Alamo) is founded. |
| **1731** | March 5 | The Mission San Francisco de la Espada is established at San Antonio. |
| | March 9 | Canary Islanders arrive in San Antonio to start a new life, and leave a grand imprint on Texas. |
| **1766** | September 4 | The first recorded hurricane strikes the Texas coast near Galveston. |

| 1786 | August 17 | David Crockett is born in Tennessee. |
| 1793 | March 2 | Sam Houston is born in Virginia. |
| | November 3 | Stephen F. Austin is born in Virginia. |
| 1797 | July 17 | Philip Nolan receives a passport to go to Mexican Texas. |
| 1798 | July 23 | "Mother of Texas" Jane Wilkinson Long is born in Maryland. |
| | August 16 | Mirabeau B. Lamar is born in Georgia. |
| 1806 | October 28 | Juan Seguin is born in Mexican Texas. |
| 1807 | February 20 | James Butler Bonham is born in South Carolina. |
| 1809 | August 9 | William Barret Travis is born in South Carolina. |
| 1818 | September 12 | A hurricane wrecks the fleet of pirate Jean Lafitte in Galveston. |
| 1819 | January 25 | Anna Raguet is born in Pennsylvania. She becomes Sam Houston's first great love in Texas. |
| | June 8 | The Long Expedition crosses the Sabine to declare a "government" in Texas. |
| 1820 | December 23 | Moses Austin seeks permission to colonize a part of Mexican Texas. |
| 1821 | January 17 | The Mexican government gives Austin permission to settle 300 families in Texas. |
| | May 4 | Jean Lafitte abandons Galveston. |
| | June 10 | Moses Austin dies in Missouri before he can start his Texas colonization plan. |
| | October 13 | Jacob Brodbeck is born in Wurttemberg, Germany. Later, as a Texan, he invents an airplane 40 years before the Wright Brothers. |
| | December 21 | Jane Long gives birth to the first Anglo child born in Texas, a girl named Mary James. |
| 1822 | January 24 | Jared E. Groce arrives on the banks of the Brazos to set up a home. Among his belongings is a supply of cottonseed—the first in Texas. |
| 1824 | July 10 | Richard King, founder of the King Ranch, is born in New York. |
| 1826 | December 16 | The Fredonian Rebellion begins in Nacogdoches. |

| 1829 | January 27 | The Matagorda Colony is founded. |
|---|---|---|
| 1830 | April 6 | Mexico enacts a law to stop American immigration to Texas. It is a prime seed that leads to the revolution six years later. |
| | September 30 | Jim Bowie becomes a Mexican citizen. |
| 1832 | June 11 | Lucy Pickens—"Lady Lucy, Queen of the Confederacy"—is born in Tennessee. |
| | June 13 | The Turtle Bayou Resolutions, documents leading to the revolution of 1836, are adopted. |
| | June 26 | The Battle of Velasco results in the first bloodshed of the revolution. |
| | November 1 | Lyne Barret is born. He is the first to hit oil in Texas. |
| | December 2 | Sam Houston first sets foot on Texas soil, at the Jonesboro Crossing on the Red River. |
| 1833 | April 1 | Santa Anna is inaugurated president of Mexico. |
| | July 8 | Stephen Austin reaches Mexico City with a plan to separate Texas from the state of Coahuila. |
| 1834 | January 3 | Austin is arrested for trying to start a revolution against Mexico. |
| 1835 | May 17 | A.B. Dodson marries Sarah Bradley. She later gives him a flag—a red, white and blue banner with a lone star—for his army company. |
| | June 30 | Mexicans put down an uprising of colonists at Anahuac. |
| | October 2 | The first shots of the revolution are fired at Gonzales. |
| | October 7 | Greenberry Logan, a free Negro, joins the Texas army and later fights in the battle at Concepción and is wounded in the siege of the Bexar. |
| | October 10 | Gail Borden Jr. begins publishing the *Telegraph and Texas Register.* |
| | November 25 | The Texas navy is created. |
| | December 4 | Ben Milam and his men storm the Bexar to drive out the Mexican army. |
| 1836 | February 8 | David Crockett and some of his "Tennessee boys" arrive at the Alamo. |
| | February 11 | Col. James Neill leaves the Alamo; Travis takes command. |

| February 29 | William Oury is sent out of the Alamo with a plea for help from General Houston. (Oury dies in bed 50 years later.) |
| March 1 | Thirty-two men from Gonzales fight their way into the Alamo. No other volunteers come. |
| March 2 | The Texas Declaration of Independence is adopted at Washington-on-the-Brazos. |
| March 3 | Moses Rose chooses to leave the Alamo rather than stay and fight. |
| March 4 | Sam Houston is elected commander-in-chief of the Texas army. |
| March 5 | Charles Goodnight, trail driver, is born in Illinois. |
| March 6 | The Alamo falls. |
| March 10 | Sam Carson arrives late to sign the Declaration of Independence. A week later he loses by six votes becoming the president of Texas. |
| March 11 | Sam Houston assumes command of the army at Gonzales. |
| March 13 | Gonzales is burned as the Runaway Scrape begins. |
| March 19 | James Walker Fannin and his men lose the Battle of Coleto Creek. |
| March 27 | The Texas prisoners from Coleto Creek are massacred at Goliad. |
| March 29 | San Felipe is burned to prevent its falling into the hands of the Mexican army. |
| April 15 | Sam Houston turns his army toward San Jacinto. |
| April 19 | Houston appeals for help to fight the war. |
| April 21 | The Texans beat the Mexican army at San Jacinto. |
| May 14 | Santa Anna and President David Burnet sign the Treaty of Velasco. |
| May 19 | Nine-year-old Cynthia Ann Parker is captured by Indians; it will be 24 years before her rescue. |
| June 3 | Land-based Texas Rangers capture Mexican ships, earning the nickname "Horse Marines." |
| August 26 | The Allen Brothers buy the site for "Houston." |

| | | |
|---|---|---|
| | October 22 | Sam Houston is inaugurated president of the republic. |
| | November 15 | Texas patriot Lorenzo de Zavalla dies. |
| | December 27 | Stephen F. Austin dies. |
| **1837** | January 26 | The steamship *Laura* successfully navigates the Buffalo Bayou but misses the new city of Houston, due to dense vegetation. |
| | April 26 | John J. Audubon comes to Texas to study bird-life and to paint birds for his famous work. |
| | October 10 | Lt. A.H. Miles, who captured Santa Anna at San Jacinto, is killed by Indians. |
| | November 10 | Ten Rangers and fifty Indians die in the Battle of Stone Houses in Archer County. |
| **1838** | October 20 | Moses Lapham, who helped destroy Vince's Bridge at San Jacinto to cut off Mexican escape, is killed by Indians. |
| **1839** | January 16 | The Texas senate votes to buy captured Mexican ships from the French to start a new navy. |
| | January 25 | The Republic of Texas adopts its new flag. |
| | July 16 | Chief Bowles of the Cherokee is killed at the Battle of the Neches. |
| | August 29 | The Colt-Walker pistol is patented. |
| **1840** | March 19 | Peace talks between the Comanches and the Texas government turn into a fight at the Council House in San Antonio. |
| | May 9 | Sam Houston marries Margaret Lea. |
| | June 24 | Col. Henry Karnes calls for a volunteer army to fight Indians, Mexicans and lawless elements on the frontier. |
| | August 12 | The Battle of Plumb Creek near Lockhart sees the white man defeat the Comanche, pushing the Indians farther to the west. |
| **1842** | February 11 | The crew of the *San Antonio* stages the republic's first, and only, mutiny. |
| | March 2 | Robert Potter, signer of the Texas Declaration of Independence, is murdered in the Regulator-Moderator War. |

| | | |
|---|---|---|
| | April 20 | Germans form a society to aid German immigration to Texas. |
| | September 18 | Forty-two people are massacred by Indians at the Battle of Salado Creek. |
| | December 31 | The Archives War: Austin citizens keep the state's papers from being moved to Houston. |
| **1843** | March 25 | The prisoners of the Mier Expedition draw white and black beans from a pot; the 17 who draw black beans are executed by the Mexicans. |
| | December 28 | Rebecca Cummings, who is engaged to William Travis when he goes away to the Alamo fight, marries another man, David Portis. |
| **1844** | August 15 | President Houston calls out the militia to put down the Regulator-Moderator War. |
| | September 3 | Henri de Castro founds Castroville. |
| | December 9 | Anson Jones takes the oath of office as the last president of the Republic of Texas. |
| **1845** | February 1 | Baylor University is founded. |
| | March 14 | Prince Carl of Solms-Braunfels purchases the land that will become New Braunfels. |
| | December 29 | Texas enters the union as the 28th state. |
| **1846** | February 19 | The Republic of Texas is officially declared at an end. |
| | April 25 | A border skirmish near Brownsville marks the beginning of the U.S. war with Mexico. |
| | May 8 | The Battle of Palo Alto, the first major fight of the Mexican War, results in a U.S. victory. |
| | May 9 | Gen. Zachary Taylor defeats the Mexicans at Resaca de la Palma. |
| | May 12 | Norris Cuney, one of the most prominent black men in Texas, is born a slave in Waller County. |
| | September 21 | Ranger Capt. Robert Gillespie dies leading a charge on the Bishop's Palace in Monterrey during the Mexican War. |
| **1847** | January 19 | Nuns of the Ursuline order arrive in Texas. |
| | April 18 | Gen. Winfield Scott and Santa Anna battle at Sierra |

Gorda. The American victors capture Santa Anna's wooden leg.

**1848**   February 2   The Treaty of Guadalupe Hidalgo is signed, ending the Mexican-American War.

February 5   Belle Starr, the Texas bandit queen, is born in Missouri.

**1849**   June 6   Fort Worth is founded.

August 11   Gov. George Wood sends three companies of Rangers to Corpus Christi to guard settlers from Goliad to the Rio Grande against Indian attacks.

October 1   William Sansom becomes the first prisoner at the Huntsville state prison.

**1850**   February 10   Texas's first railroad, the Buffalo Bayou, Brazos and Colorado, is chartered.

November 25   Texas accepts the Compromise of 1850, and gets $10 million in exchange for giving up a claim that stretches all the way to California.

**1851**   November 14   Fort Phantom Hill is established in Jones County to protect the settlers.

**1852**   December 24   The *General Sherman* goes into service as the first locomotive in Texas.

**1853**   November 23   James Henderson becomes governor and serves just 28 days.

**1854**   January 11   Fort Bliss is established to protect El Paso from the Indians.

November 19   Sam Houston is baptized in a creek near Independence.

December 3   One hundred Polish families arrive in Galveston, an event marking the start of major Polish immigration to Texas.

December 10   Richard King marries Henrietta Chamberlain; together they make the King Ranch great.

**1855**   February 7   Charles Siringo, cowboy writer, is born near Matagorda.

October 30   Prize saddle-maker Paul Bauer, the son of German immigrants, is born in Yorktown, Texas.

**1856**   April 29   The first camels arrive in Texas for use by the army in the West.

**1857**   March 3   Congress authorizes the Butterfield Mail and Stage Line.

|  |  |  |
|---|---|---|
|  | July 9 | The first mail leaves San Antonio for San Diego, marking the start of the first successful transcontinental mail route. |
| 1858 | January 9 | Anson Jones, last president of the Republic of Texas, shoots himself. |
| 1859 | February 1 | The Menger Hotel opens in San Antonio. |
|  | June 5 | Herman Lehmann is born in Loyal Valley. He is later captured by Apaches and adopted by them. |
|  | July 13 | An arrest in Brownsville starts the Cortina Wars. |
|  | August 3 | The Comanches are moved out of Texas and into Indian Territory. |
|  | December 19 | Mirabeau B. Lamar dies. He served as vice-president and president of the republic and is called the Father of Texas Education. |
| 1860 | March 12 | Columbus "Dad" Joiner, who finds the East Texas Oil Field, is born in Alabama. |
|  | May 7 | Julius Real, who stages the legislative Whiskey Rebellion of 1911 to keep Texas wet, is born in the hill country. |
|  | June 28 | Southern Democrats nominate John C. Breckinridge of Kentucky for President. |
|  | August 12 | The first child born in the Governor's Mansion is Temple Houston. |
| 1861 | January 21 | Gov. Sam Houston submits the secession resolution to the legislature. |
|  | February 1 | The ordinance of secession passes. |
|  | February 13 | Robert E. Lee leaves Fort Mason on his way back to Virginia, to lead the South in the Civil War. |
|  | February 16 | Local secessionists in San Antonio force Gen. David Twiggs to surrender all U.S. equipment. |
|  | April 13 | Fort Sumter is fired upon; the Civil War begins. |
|  | May 29 | Henry Robinson, famed Indian fighter, is killed near Uvalde. |
|  | August 3 | The *U.S.S. South Carolina* fires on Galveston. |
|  | September 9 | Col. Benjamin Terry organizes his "Texas Rangers." |
|  | December 14 | H.H. Sibley takes command of the "Army of New |

|  |  | Mexico" at Fort Bliss and prepares for his ill-fated attempt to conquer the Southwest for the Confederacy. |
|---|---|---|
|  | December 17 | Col. Ben Terry is killed leading a Rebel charge against the Union in Kentucky. |
| 1862 | March 7 | John Bell Hood assumes command of the "Texas Brigade." |
|  | April 6 | Albert Sidney Johnston is killed in battle at Shiloh, Tennessee. |
|  | May 5 | Cinco de Mayo; the Mexicans rout the French at Puebla. |
|  | August 10 | Vengeful Confederates attack German-American loyalists on the banks of the Nueces; 40 die. |
|  | September 11 | William Sydney Porter ("O. Henry"), who lives and writes for a time in Texas, is born in North Carolina. |
|  | October | The Great Gainesville Hanging. Nineteen men thought to be Union sympathizers are strung up on various days throughout the month in the aftermath of an incident known as the Peace Party Conspiracy. |
|  | October 26 | Federal gunboats blockade Pass Cavallo and take Indianola. |
|  | November 29 | John Bankhead Magruder arrives in Texas to take command of the Confederate forces. |
| 1863 | January 1 | The Confederates win the Battle of Galveston. |
|  | July 1 | Hood's Texas Brigade joins in the fighting at Gettysburg. |
|  | July 26 | Sam Houston dies at his home in Huntsville. |
|  | September 7 | Federal gunboats arrive off the bar at Sabine Pass where Dick Dowling and his men are waiting. |
|  | October 31 | Notorious outlaw "Black Jack" Ketchum is born in San Saba County. |
|  | November 5 | Pendleton Murrah becomes governor when Francis Lubbock resigns the office to fight the Yanks. |
|  | November 13 | Chipita Rodriguez, the only woman ever legally hanged in Texas, meets her Maker. |
| 1864 | April 8 | Confederate forces blunt Union attempts to invade Texas, at the Battle of Mansfield. |

| | | |
|---|---|---|
| | May 6 | Texans rally behind Gen. Robert E. Lee in the Wilderness Campaign. |
| | June 25 | "Rip" Ford's Confederates win one at Las Rucias. A year later he wins the last battle of the Civil War—*after* the war ends. |
| | November 26 | Kit Carson and his men defeat a band of Kiowas and Comanches in a battle at Adobe Walls. |
| **1865** | January 8 | Indians win a battle at Dove Creek. |
| | June 11 | Bandits try to rob the state treasury in Austin. |
| | June 19 | Maj. Gen. Gordon Granger arrives in Galveston with word that slavery has been abolished. |
| | August 8 | George Armstrong Custer leaves for a tour of duty in Texas. |
| | October 23 | Federal forces reoccupy Fort McIntosh at Laredo. |
| | December 18 | The Thirteenth Amendment to the U.S. Constitution is ratified; slavery is abolished. |
| **1867** | June 22 | This is the worst single day of a yellow fever epidemic that sweeps coastal Texas in 1867. |
| | September 23 | John A. Lomax, the Texas collector of folk music, is born in Mississippi. On the same day, William Marsh Rice is murdered in New York. His will sets up Rice University in Houston. |
| | September 25 | Oliver Loving, the dean of Texas trail drivers, dies after an attack by Indians. |
| **1868** | March 4 | Jesse Chisholm, famous trailblazer, dies of food poisoning in Oklahoma. |
| | November 24 | Scott Joplin, of ragtime music fame, is born in Texarkana. |
| **1869** | September 17 | Roy Aldrich, who serves longer as a Texas Ranger than any other man, is born in Illinois. |
| | October 16 | A.D. Topperwein is born in Boerne. He is in the Texas Sports Hall of Fame as the greatest trick shooter of his day. |
| | November 21 | William Henry "Alfalfa Bill" Murray, who later becomes governor of Oklahoma, is born in Toadsuck, Texas. |

| 1870 | January 8 | Edmund Davis becomes the first Republican governor of Texas. |
| | July 12 | The Sixth Cavalry engages the Kiowas in the battle of the Little Wichita. |
| 1871 | January 2 | Boxing promoter "Tex" Rickard is born in Kansas City. |
| | April 17 | Texas A&M is created. |
| | May 18 | Satanta, Big Tree, and their warriors massacre seven men from a wagon train at Salt Creek. |
| | August 31 | Gov. Jim Ferguson, who is the "Pa" of "Ma and Pa Ferguson" fame, is born in Bell County. |
| 1872 | February 29 | Henry Lindsley is born. He becomes mayor of Dallas and the first national commander of the American Legion. |
| | April 20 | An Indian battle at Howard's Well leads to the government's cancellation of hunting permits for Indians. |
| | December 8 | Architect Nicholas Clayton comes to Galveston and builds it into a city of beautiful homes. |
| | December 12 | John "Texas Jack" Omohundro goes to Chicago to star with Buffalo Bill in the Wild West Show. |
| 1873 | September 16 | R.L. More is born in Decatur. He amasses the world's largest private collection of bird eggs in his lifetime. |
| 1874 | January 11 | Gail Borden dies. He had published newspapers during the Texas Revolution, surveyed the wilderness, and condensed milk. |
| | January 17 | Carpetbagger rule in Texas ends with the election of a Democratic government. |
| | April 5 | Houston business tycoon Jesse Jones is born in Tennessee. |
| | May 2 | John B. Jones is commissioned major in the Texas Rangers' Frontier Battalion. |
| | June 27 | The Indians lose the second battle of Adobe Walls. |
| | August 30 | The first fight of the Red River Indian War takes place in Palo Duro Canyon. |
| | September 12 | The battle of "Buffalo Waller" begins in Hemphill County; six men hold off over 100 Indians for three days. |

| | | |
|---|---|---|
| | September 14 | The Sixth Cavalry arrives just in time to scare off Indians attacking Lyman's wagon train. |
| | September 28 | Gen. Ranald MacKenzie led his men in one of the last major Indian battles in Texas, at Palo Duro Canyon. |
| | November 24 | J.F. Glidden patents barbed wire. |
| | December 26 | Joe McComb stages the first commercial buffalo hunt in Texas. |
| 1875 | January 23 | Molly Armstrong, the first woman optometrist in Texas, is born in Bell County. |
| | June 13 | "Ma" Ferguson is born in Bell County. She later becomes first lady once and governor twice. |
| | June 14 | Jefferson Davis is invited to serve as the first president of Texas A&M, but he declines. |
| | September 16 | A hurricane destroys the city of Indianola. |
| 1876 | February 15 | The Texas Constitution is adopted. |
| | June 22 | Santa Anna dies of old age in Mexico City. |
| | September 27 | Former Civil War Gen. Braxton Bragg drops dead as he crosses a street in Galveston. |
| | October 4 | Texas A&M opens with 40 students and a faculty of six men. |
| | November 7 | Mason County's "Hoodoo War" ends with the arrest of two men. |
| 1877 | February 16 | The first train to San Antonio arrives. |
| | June 18 | Charles Goodnight and John Adair form the "J.A." Ranch, the first in the Panhandle. |
| | December 20 | Sam Bass robs the Fort Worth-Cleburne stage. |
| 1878 | March 31 | World Heavyweight Champion Jack Johnson is born in Galveston. |
| | July 21 | Sam Bass is killed by Texas Rangers at Round Rock on his 27th birthday. |
| | October 11 | Bill Longley, killer of at least 32 people, is hanged at Giddings. |
| 1879 | December 11 | Fort Worth leading citizen Amon Carter is born in Crafton. |

| | | |
|---|---|---|
| **1880** | September 13 | Carlysle Raht, who fights Pancho Villa and later works on the atom bomb, is born in Gainesville. |
| **1881** | March 15 | Abilene is born, with completion of the Texas-Pacific Railroad. |
| | May 31 | Fort Griffin, headquarters for buffalo skinners in Shackelford County, is abandoned. |
| | July 11 | William Buckley is born at Washington-on-the-Brazos. His son James becomes a senator from New York, and his son William Jr. is famous as a writer, magazine editor and television talk show host. |
| | December 15 | America's second transcontinental railroad links up at Sierra Blanca in Hudspeth County. |
| **1882** | January 2 | Jay Gould predicts the "end of Jefferson" after the town refuses to give his railroad right-of-way. |
| | January 6 | Longtime Congressman and Speaker of the House Sam Rayburn is born in Tennessee. |
| | July 25 | Judge Roy Bean opens his first saloon west of the Pecos. |
| | November 17 | The cornerstone is laid for the first building at the University of Texas in Austin. |
| | November 28 | A labor-union-called "holiday" on the Galveston docks protesting black laborers begins a segregation battle that lasts for years. |
| | December 21 | Edith Wilmans is born. She is elected to the Texas House in 1922, the first woman to serve in that capacity. |
| **1883** | March 24 | The first cowboy strike in Texas begins in the Panhandle. |
| | July 4 | The first recorded rodeo in Texas is held at Pecos. |
| | September 15 | The organizational session of the new University of Texas is attended by 221 students. |
| | November 12 | Cattlemen meet in Gainesville to work out an end to the Fence-Cutting War. |
| **1886** | March 21 | A shoot-out at Tascosa leaves four dead. |
| **1888** | March 20 | Gov. Coke Stevenson is born in Mason County. |
| | April 4 | Baseball great Tris Speaker is born in Hubbard. |
| | May 16 | The state capitol is dedicated. |
| | July 2 | The Jaybird-Woodpecker feud starts in Fort Bend County. |

| | | |
|---|---|---|
| | September 26 | Texas historian and man of letters J. Frank Dobie is born in Live Oak County. |
| 1889 | November 7 | The Texas Hereford Association is organized in San Antonio. |
| 1890 | January 30 | Louis Jordan is born in Fredericksburg. He becomes an All-American football player and the first officer killed in World War I. |
| | February 4 | Fletcher Stockdale, acting governor for 34 days in the aftermath of the Civil War, dies in Cuero. |
| | March 11 | Texas governor and U.S. senator W. Lee O'Daniel is born in Ohio. |
| | May 15 | Pulitzer Prize-winning writer Katherine Anne Porter is born at Indian Creek. |
| | September 6 | Gen. Claire Chennault, of World War II "Flying Tigers" fame, is born at Commerce. |
| | October 14 | Thirty-fourth U.S. President, Dwight David Eisenhower, is born in Denison. |
| 1891 | January 13 | Chemist Louis Weisberg, who helps develop the atomic bomb, is born in Waco. |
| | January 20 | James Stephen Hogg becomes the first native-born governor of Texas. |
| 1892 | April 22 | The first class graduates from the University of Texas Medical School in Galveston. |
| | June 28 | The first battleship *Texas* is launched. |
| 1893 | March 23 | SMU chancellor and president Umphrey Lee is born in Indiana. |
| | July 6 | Kearie Lee Berry is born in Denton County. He becomes a great athlete at the University of Texas and a hero of the Bataan Death March of World War II. |
| 1894 | March 16 | Killer John Wesley Hardin is given a full pardon while serving a sentence at the Huntsville State Prison. |
| | June 9 | Oil is discovered in Corsicana. |
| 1895 | February 8 | Hollywood film director King Vidor is born in Galveston. |
| | February 14 | A rare Gulf Coast snowstorm dumps up to 20 inches of snow on the Houston-Galveston area. |
| 1896 | February 21 | Judge Roy Bean stages the Fitzsimmons-Maher heavyweight title fight on a Rio Grande island. |

| March 29 | Robert J. Kleberg Jr., longtime manager of the King Ranch, is born in Corpus Christi. |
| April 27 | Baseball great Rogers Hornsby is born in Runnels County. |
| May 25 | The first meeting of the Daughters of the Confederacy in Texas is held. |
| September 15 | A stunt to wreck two trains near Waco results in the death of two spectators. |
| December 30 | Homer Norton is born in Alabama. He becomes the leading football coach in Texas A&M history. |

**1897** January 15 — John Duval, the last survivor of Fannin's army, dies in Fort Worth.

| February 6 | The Dalton Gang comes to the end of the trail. |
| July 3 | Blues singer Blind Lemon Jefferson is born near Wortham. |

**1898** May 15 — Teddy Roosevelt arrives in San Antonio to train the Rough Riders.

| May 30 | The Rough Riders leave San Antonio to charge up San Juan Hill. |
| September 5 | Emma Seelye, the woman spy of the Confederacy, dies at La Porte. |
| October 21 | Stanley Walker is born in Lampasas. He becomes a legendary New York City newspaper editor. |
| December 6 | Ben Boynton is born in Waco. He becomes the first native Texan to achieve All-American football status. |

**1899** January 7 — Legendary Texas Ranger Bigfoot Wallace dies in Frio County.

| February 12 | The temperature drops to $-23°$ F. in Tulia, the coldest day on record for Texas. |
| June 17–28 | A severe flood on the Brazos kills nearly 300. |
| October 5 | Ned Green drives the first car in Texas. It takes five hours to make the trip from Dallas to Terrell, a 6-mph average. |

**1900** May 26 — The famous Frontier Battalion of the Texas Rangers is dissolved.

|  | September 8 | The Great Galveston Storm destroys half the city and kills thousands. |
|---|---|---|
| **1901** | January 10 | The Lucas Gusher hits at Spindletop; America enters the Oil Age. |
|  | January 14 | Clara Driscoll writes the San Antonio *Express* in a plea to save the Alamo. |
|  | March 7 | The bluebonnet is named the state flower. |
|  | July 5 | John Henry Kirby charters his lumber company. |
| **1902** | October 16 | Carry Nation comes to the University of Texas to drive out the demon rum. |
|  | October 27 | Galveston begins construction of the seawall. |
| **1903** | May 12 | "The Eyes of Texas" is performed for the first time, in a UT minstrel show. |
|  | November 9 | John Nance Garner walks into Congress for the first time. Thirty years later he becomes FDR's vice-president. |
| **1905** | January 7 | The Humble Oil Field is discovered. |
|  | January 12 | Singer and film actor Tex Ritter is born in Panola County. |
|  | August 20 | Jack Teagarden, outstanding trombone player of the Big Band Era, is born in Vernon. |
|  | September 19 | Leon Jaworski is born in Waco. He becomes president of the American Bar Association and the Watergate chief prosecutor. |
|  | December 24 | Howard R. Hughes Jr. is born in Houston. |
| **1906** | May 2 | Henry Bullock is born in North Carolina. He becomes the first black professor of arts and sciences at the University of Texas. |
|  | August 21 | Capt. Bill McDonald of the Rangers quells a race riot in Brownsville. |
| **1907** | June 29 | Sculptress Elisabet Ney dies and is buried at Liendo Plantation. |
|  | July 8 | The town of Post, founded by C.W. Post of "Toasties" fame, becomes the seat of Garza County. |
|  | August 7 | Outstanding Longhorn football coach Blair Cherry is born in Kerens. |

| | September 8 | The world-famous Neiman-Marcus store opens in Dallas. |
|---|---|---|
| | September 29 | Gene Autry is born in Tioga. |
| 1908 | February 7 | Fred Gipson, who writes *Old Yeller* and other children's books, is born in Mason. |
| | March 23 | Movie actress Joan Crawford is born in San Antonio. |
| | August 27 | Lyndon B. Johnson, the 36th U.S. President, is born at Stonewall. |
| | October 5 | Josh Logan, the great Broadway director and producer, is born in Texarkana. |
| | November 20 | Howard R. Hughes Sr. applies for a patent for his rock bit, a drill bit that changes the oil patch. |
| 1909 | May 27 | Major league baseball player and manager Michael "Pinky" Higgins is born in Red Oak. |
| | June 4 | The Lone Star Gas Company files for a charter to become the first gas distributor in Texas. |
| 1910 | February 10 | D.L. McDonald, the father of irrigation on the Texas High Plains, finds water near Hereford. |
| 1911 | January 3 | The Slanton water well comes in, helping to transform semiarid west Texas into a breadbasket for the nation. |
| | April 7 | Sarah Bernhardt plays Galveston in her farewell performance. |
| | May 10 | Lt. George Kelly is the first military pilot to die in a plane crash; it happens in San Antonio. |
| | May 21 | Dictator Porfirio Díaz resigns, bringing temporary calm to revolution-torn Mexico. |
| | July 7 | Alphonso Steele, last survivor of San Jacinto, dies at his grandson's home near Kosse. |
| | November 4 | Col. Edward House of Houston meets Woodrow Wilson and becomes his aide and confidant. |
| 1912 | March 8 | Gov. Preston Smith is born in Corn Hill. |
| | March 15 | Lightnin' Hopkins, of blues music fame, is born in Centerville. |
| | May 18 | The second battleship *Texas* is launched. |
| | August 13 | Golfer Ben Hogan is born in Dublin, Texas. |
| | November 1 | The last cattle of the XIT ranch are sold. |

|      | December 22   | Claudia Alta Taylor, the future Lady Bird Johnson, is born in Karnack. |
|------|---------------|-----------------------------------------------------------------------|
| 1913 | January 21    | Thomas Munson, who helps the French save their wine industry, dies in Denison. |
|      | February 14   | The legislature passes a resolution recognizing Johanna Troutman as the Betsy Ross of Texas. |
|      | September 24  | The *Daily Texan* becomes the first daily college newspaper in the South. |
|      | December 1    | Mary Martin is born in Weatherford. She stars on Broadway in *Peter Pan* and *South Pacific*, and is the mother of "Dallas" star Larry Hagman. |
| 1914 | February 9    | Country and Western singer Ernest Tubb is born in Ellis County. |
|      | October 18    | Joe Routt, the first All-American football player from Texas A&M, is born in Chappell Hill. |
| 1915 | January 30    | Rice and Baylor play basketball in the first competition of the fledgling Southwest Conference. |
|      | May 7         | The sinking of the *Lusitania*: World War I is at hand, and Texas will send thousands away to die in the fighting. |
|      | November 23   | An Aggie prank creates "Bevo," the Texas mascot. |
| 1917 | June 21       | The Humble Oil Company incorporates. |
|      | August 5      | The Simms-Sinclair No. 11 Sweet gushes in and becomes Goose Creek Oil Field's greatest producer. |
|      | August 23     | Seventeen people die in the Camp Logan race riots, when black soldiers clash with Houston police. |
|      | August 25     | Gov. Jim Ferguson resigns after being impeached. |
|      | October 21    | The "Roaring Ranger" Oil Field blows in. |
| 1918 | February 28   | Texas ratifies the Prohibition Amendment. |
| 1920 | January 12    | Civil rights leader James Farmer is born in Marshall. |
| 1922 | March 22      | Oilman James Abercrombie invents the oil well blowout preventer. |
| 1923 | May 28        | The Santa Rita No. 1 gusher brings the University of Texas vast oil fortunes. |
|      | July 30       | Roy Mitchell is strung up in Waco; his is the last legal public hanging in Texas. |

| | November 8 | Hubert Knickerbocker of Yoakum witnesses Hitler's beer hall *putsch* and begins a writing career that leads to the Pulitzer Prize. |
| **1924** | March 14 | Charles Lindbergh starts pilot training at Brooks Field in San Antonio. |
| **1925** | January 20 | Miriam Amanda "Ma" Ferguson becomes the first woman governor in Texas history. |
| **1927** | January 31 | The mockingbird is named the official state bird. |
| | May 20 | Lucky Lindy takes off for Paris. |
| **1928** | June 26 | The Democrats open their national convention in Houston. |
| **1929** | April 17 | The League of United Latin American Citizens (LULAC) is founded in Corpus Christi. |
| | April 28 | The army air force carries out the first mass parachute drop in history, at Brooks Field in San Antonio. |
| | October 15 | Two Rio Grande Valley nurserymen develop the Ruby Red grapefruit. |
| | October 29 | "Black Tuesday". . .The stock market crashes and America is plunged into the Great Depression. |
| **1930** | May 6 | The weather bureau says this is the worst single day for tornadoes in Texas history. |
| | October 3 | The Daisy Bradford well blows in, and the giant East Texas Oil Field is on its way. |
| **1931** | January 5 | Dancer and choreographer Alvin Ailey is born in Rogers. |
| | June 5 | David Browning Jr., olympic diving champion from UT, is born in Boston, Massachusetts. |
| | June 23 | Texan Wiley Post starts his flight around the world. |
| | July 27 | Oklahoma Gov. Bill Murray sends the national guard to seal off the entrance to Texas via the Red River Bridge. |
| | October 25 | The famed Texas prison rodeo is born. |
| | December 13 | George Strake's Conroe Oil Field blows in. |
| **1932** | April 2 | Black rodeo star Bill Pickett dies. |
| **1933** | April 30 | Country and Western star Willie Nelson is born in Abbott. |

| | July 22 | A record-breaking rainstorm hits Freeport. |
|---|---|---|
| | July 28 | W.E. Morris becomes the first Texas farmer to be paid for plowing his cotton crop under. |
| 1934 | January 16 | Clyde Barrow breaks *into* a prison to rescue his friend Raymond Hamilton. |
| | May 23 | Lawmen ambush Bonnie Parker and Clyde Barrow, who die in a hail of gunfire. |
| 1935 | April 14 | During a great dust storm, folk singer and song-writer Woody Guthrie pens "So Long, It's Been Good to Know You." |
| 1936 | August 12 | The temperature hits 120° F. in Seymour—the hottest reading ever recorded in Texas. |
| 1937 | March 18 | A natural gas explosion at New London claims the lives of almost 300 students and teachers. |
| | April 10 | Lyndon Johnson wins his first election. |
| | June 15 | Country and Western singer Waylon Jennings is born in Littlefield. |
| | June 17 | The Kilgore Oil Field is discovered. |
| 1938 | July 19 | Douglas "Wrong Way" Corrigan of Galveston flies "by mistake" to Ireland. |
| | August 22 | Sam Robertson, who fights with Pershing and wins a Medal of Honor in World War I, dies in Brownsville. |
| 1941 | June 2 | Andrew Jackson Houston, Sam's youngest son, is appointed to serve out a term in the U.S. Senate. |
| | August 4 | W. Lee O'Daniel resigns his governor's post to become a senator; Coke Stevenson replaces him. |
| | October 24 | Longtime Texas state treasurer Charlie Lockhart resigns. |
| | December 7 | The bombing of Pearl Harbor plunges the U.S. into World War II. |
| 1942 | April 24 | A war bond quota of more than $18 million is set for Texas. |
| | May 16 | Oveta Culp Hobby is sworn in as head of the WAACS. |
| 1943 | January 19 | Singer Janis Joplin is born in Port Arthur. |
| | June 16 | The national guard is called out to put down a race riot in Beaumont. |

|  |  |
|---|---|
| July 14 | Broadway singer and actor Jules Bledsoe of Waco dies in Hollywood. |
| September 9 | The 36th Division invades Italy. |

**1944** June 6–7 — The Allies invade Normandy.

November 27 — Macario García, a Mexican national who lived in Sugar Land, wins the Medal of Honor for actions in the war in Germany.

**1945** January 26 — Audie Murphy wins the Medal of Honor for his courageous fighting on this day.

May 8 — V.E. Day—the war is over in Europe.

August 6 — A Texan scouts out a clear spot over Hiroshima, and the first atomic bomb is dropped.

August 14 — The Texas "Lost Battalion" is liberated, after helping POWs build the bridge on the River Kwai.

September 2 — Adm. Chester A. Nimitz of Fredericksburg accepts the Japanese surrender to end World War II.

**1947** April 16 — The Texas City Disaster claims hundreds of lives.

June 3 — Margo Jones opens her Dallas Theatre-in-the-Round.

November 18 — The Alley Theatre opens in Houston.

**1948** January 4 — The Alford No. 1 comes in: oil is found in the Permian Basin.

August 28 — Lyndon Johnson wins his senate race by 87 votes, thanks to Box 13 in Jim Wells County.

**1949** March 17 — Glenn McCarthy celebrates the opening of his Shamrock Hotel in Houston with a party for 50,000 guests.

July 11 — Gov. Beauford Jester dies en route to Houston; he is the first governor to die in office.

August 24 — Herman Barnett, a black, becomes a student at the University of Texas Medical Branch in Galveston.

November 2 — The Daughters of the Republic of Texas become custodians of the French Legation.

**1952** June 12 — Henry Cohen, founder of the Galveston Plan to settle European Jews, dies in Houston.

August 14 — The first leg of the Gulf Freeway connecting Houston and Galveston is dedicated.

| 1953 | May 11 | A terrible tornado rips through Waco. |
| | May 22 | President Dwight Eisenhower signs the Tidelands Bill, giving Texas rights to its offshore oil. |
| 1955 | March 29 | Football player Earl Campbell is born in Tyler. |
| 1956 | September 27 | Babe Zaharias, America's greatest woman athlete, dies in Galveston. |
| | December 1 | Runner Bobby Morrow of San Benito wins three gold medals at the Olympics. |
| 1957 | April 2 | Ralph Yarborough is elected to the U.S. Senate. |
| | June 6 | Attorney General Will Wilson raids Galveston to close down gambling. |
| 1958 | April 14 | Texas pianist Van Cliburn wins the International Piano Competition in Moscow. |
| | July 24 | Jack Kilby draws up the idea for the silicon chip at Texas Instruments in Dallas. |
| 1959 | February 3 | West Texas's Buddy Holly dies with other rock music performers in an Iowa plane crash. |
| | December 19 | Walter Williams, last surviving veteran of the Civil War, dies at age 117. |
| 1960 | January 28 | Two Dallas millionaires, Clint Murchison and Bedford Wynne, receive a franchise for an NFL team they name the "Cowboys." |
| 1961 | July 29 | Oscar Fox, cowboy songwriter and hill country native, dies at age 82. |
| | September 10 | Hurricane Carla strikes the upper Texas coast. |
| | November 16 | House Speaker Sam Rayburn dies, and is buried in Bonham. |
| 1962 | April 10 | Major league baseball comes to Texas with the Houston Colt .45s' 11–2 win over the Chicago Cubs. |
| 1963 | January 14 | The border dispute between Mexico and Texas is finally settled with the Treaty of El Chamizal. |
| | June 1 | Texas A&M allows women to enroll; the "Maggie" is born. |
| | November 22 | President John F. Kennedy is assassinated in Dallas. |
| 1964 | July 31 | Country and Western singer Jim Reeves of Carthage is killed in a plane crash. |

| | | |
|---|---|---|
| **1965** | April 9 | The Astrodome opens in Houston. |
| | June 3 | Ed White of San Antonio becomes the first American to walk in space. |
| **1966** | August 1 | Charles Whitman kills 17 people in a shooting spree from the University of Texas Tower. |
| **1967** | September 20 | A giant hurricane named Beulah hits the coast. |
| **1968** | October 6 | The first international exposition in the South, the HemisFair, closes in San Antonio. |
| **1969** | April 3 | Texas-born horse trainer Max Hirsch dies at the age of 88. |
| | July 20 | Apollo 11 lands on the moon. |
| **1971** | January 18 | The Sharpstown Bank stock scandal breaks. |
| **1972** | September 1 | La Raza Unida hold its first national convention. |
| **1973** | January 22 | Texas native George Foreman knocks out Joe Frazier to win the world heavyweight title. |
| | August 2 | The famed Chicken Ranch at La Grange ceases operations. |
| **1974** | July 25 | Congresswoman Barbara Jordan of Houston delivers her famous "We, the People" speech on the U.S. Constitution and impeachment. |
| | August 3 | A prison siege at Huntsville comes to a bloody conclusion. |
| **1975** | May 13 | Bob Wills of the Texas Playboys dies following a stroke. |
| **1983** | August 18 | Alicia, the most expensive hurricane in U.S. history, hits Galveston and Houston. |

# BIBLIOGRAPHY

Abernethy, Francis E. (ed.). *Legendary Ladies of Texas*. Dallas: E-Heart Press, 1981.

Abilene *Reporter News*. *Abilene Remembered: Our Centennial Treasury Book 1881–1981*. Abilene, Texas, 1981.

Ashford, Gerald. *Spanish Texas: Yesterday and Today*. Austin: The Pemberton Press, 1971.

Banks, Jimmy. *Money, Marbles and Chalk: The Wondrous World of Texas Politics*. Austin: Texas Publishing Company, 1971.

Barnstone, Howard. *The Galveston That Was*. New York: MacMillan, 1966.

Barr, Alwyn. *Black Texans: A History of Negroes in Texas, 1528–1971*. Austin: The Pemberton Press, 1973.

Barrett, Neal Jr. *Long Days and Short Nights: A Century of Texas Ranching on the YO, 1880–1980*. Mountain Home: Y-O Press, 1980.

Baylies, Francis. *A Narrative of Major General Wool's Campaign in Mexico*. Albany, New York: Little, 1851.

Benjamin, Gilbert Giddings. *The Germans in Texas: A Study in Immigration*. Austin: Jenkins Publishing Company, 1974.

Best, Hugh. *Debrett's Texas Peerage*. New York: Coward-McCann, Inc., 1983.

Bones, Jim Jr. *Texas West of the Pecos*. College Station: Texas A&M University Press, 1981.

Bowman, Bob. *They Left No Monuments*. Lufkin: Lufkin Printing Company, 1975.

Branda, Eldon S. (ed.). *The Handbook of Texas: A Supplement, Volume III*. Austin: State Historical Association, 1976.

Brooklyn Museum. *Buffalo Bill and the Wild West*. Brooklyn, New York: University of Pittsburg Press, 1981.

Campbell, Harry H. *The Early History of Motley County*. Wichita Falls: Nortex, 1971.

Carrington, Evelyn M. *Women in Early Texas*. Austin: Pemberton Press, 1975.

Clark, James A. and Michel T. Halbouty. *The Last Boom*. New York: Random House, 1972.

Clarke, Mary Whatley. *A Century of Cow Business*. Fort Worth: Texas and Southwest Cattle Raisers Association, 1976.

Conway, James. *The Texans*. New York: Knopf, 1976.

Cox, Mike. *Fred Gipson: Texas Storyteller*. Austin: Shoal Creek Publishing, 1980.

Crawford, Ann Fears, and Crystal Sasse Ragsdale. *Women in Texas*. Burnet: Eakin Press, 1982.

Crews, D'Anne McAdams (ed.). *Huntsville and Walker County, Texas*. Huntsville: Sam Houston State University Press, 1976.

Davis, John L. *San Antonio: A Historical Portrait*. Austin: The Encino Press, 1978.

Driskill, Frank A. and Dede W. Casad. *Chester W. Nimitz, Admiral of the Hills*. Austin: Eakin Press, 1983.

Farrell, Mary D. and Elizabeth Silverthorne. *First Ladies of Texas*. Belton: Stillhouse Hollow Publishers, 1976.

Fehrenbach, T. R. *Comanches*. New York: Knopf, 1974.

———. *Lone Star: A History of Texas and Texans*. New York: MacMillan, 1968.

Fields, F. T. *Texas Sketchbook*. Houston: Humble Oil and Refining Company, 1958.

Fischer, Ernest G. *Robert Potter*. Gretna, Louisiana: Pelican Publishing Company, 1976.

Flanagan, Sue. *Sam Houston's Texas*. Austin: University of Texas Press, 1964.

Frantz, Joe. *Gail Borden, Dairyman to a Nation.* Norman: University of Oklahoma Press, 1951.

Fuermann, George. *Houston: The Once and Future City.* Garden City, New York: Doubleday, 1971.

Gaddy, Jerry J. *Dust to Dust.* Fort Collins, Colorado: The Old Army Press, 1977.

———. *Texas in Revolt.* Fort Collins, Colorado: The Old Army Press, 1973.

Gracy, David B. *Littlefield Lands.* Austin: University of Texas Press, 1968.

Gray, Col. William F. *From Virginia to Texas 1835.* Houston: The Fletcher Young Publishing Company, 1965.

Green, Donald E. *Land of the Underground Rain.* Austin: University of Texas Press, 1973.

Griffin, John Howard. *Land of the High Sky.* Midland: The First National Bank of Midland, 1959.

Henly, Dempsie, *The Big Thicket Story.* Waco: Texian Press, 1967.

Hudson, Wilson M. *Andy Adams: His Life and Writings.* Dallas: Southern Methodist University Press, 1964.

Hurley, Marvin. *Decisive Years For Houston.* Houston: Houston Chamber of Commerce, 1966.

Hurt, Harry III. *Texas Rich.* New York, London: W. W. Norton and Company, 1981.

Hutson, Jan. *The Chicken Ranch.* South Brunswick and New York: A. S. Barnes and Company, 1980.

Hutton, Jim and Jim Henderson. *Houston: A History of a Giant.* Tulsa, Oklahoma: Continental Heritage, Inc., 1976.

Ivey, Rosalie. *A History of Fort Bliss.* Austin: Masters Thesis, University of Texas, 1942.

James, Marquis. *The Raven.* New York: Bobbs-Merrill Company, 1929.

Jaworski, Leon. *Crossroads.* Elgin, Illinois: David C. Cook, 1981.

Johnson, Robert and Clarence Buel (eds.). *Retreat From Gettysburg—Battles and Leaders of the Civil War.* New York: Castle Books, 1956.

———. *The Way to Appomattox—Battles and Leaders of the Civil War.* New York: Castle Books, 1956.

Jordan, Barbara and Shelby Hearon. *Barbara Jordan, A Self-Portrait.* Garden City, New York: Doubleday, 1979.

Josephy, Alvin M. Jr., and the editors of American Heritage. *The American Heritage History of World War I.* New York: American Heritage Publishing Company, 1964.

Keating, Bern. *An Illustrated History of the Texas Rangers.* New York: Rand McNally, 1980.

Klein, Joe. *Woody Guthrie: A Life.* New York: Alfred A. Knopf, 1980.

Knowles, Ruth Sheldon. *The First Pictorial History of the Oil and Gas Industry 1859–1983.* Athens, Ohio: Ohio University Press, 1983.

McCallum, Henry D. and Frances. *The Wire That Fenced the West.* Norman: University of Oklahoma Press, 1956.

McCarthy, John L. *Maverick Town: The Story of Old Tascosa.* Norman: University of Oklahoma Press, 1945.

McDonald, Archie P. *Travis.* Austin: Pemberton Press, 1976.

Maguire, Jack. *Talk of Texas.* Austin: Shoal Creek Publishing, 1973.

Malsch, Brownson. *Indianola.* Austin: Shoal Creek Publishing, 1977.

Members of the Potomac Corral of the Westerners. *Great Western Indian Fights.* Lincoln: University of Nebraska Press, 1960.

Morris, Edmund. *The Rise of Theodore Roosevelt.* New York: Coward, McCann & Geoghegan, Inc., 1979.

Nance, Joseph Milton. *After San Jacinto: The Texas-Mexican Frontier 1836–1841*. Austin: University of Texas Press, 1963.

Nicholson, Patrick J. *Mr. Jim*. Houston: Gulf Publishing, 1983.

Nunn, W. C. *Texas Under the Carpetbaggers*. Austin: University of Texas Press, 1962.

Owens, William A. *Tell Me a Story, Sing Me a Song. . . .* Austin: University of Texas Press, 1983.

Partlow, Miriam. *Liberty, Liberty County, and the Atascosito District*. Austin: Pemberton Press, 1974.

Phares, Ross. *Texas Tradition*. Gretna, Louisiana: Pelican Publishing Company, 1954.

Phillips, William G. *Yarborough of Texas*. Washington, D.C.: Acropolis Books, 1969.

Pool, William C. *A Historical Atlas of Texas*. Austin: The Encino Press, 1975.

Presley, James. *Saga of Wealth: The Rise of the Texas Oilmen*. Austin: Texas Monthly Press, 1983.

Ramsdell, Charles. *San Antonio: A Historical and Pictorial Guide*. Austin: University of Texas Press, 1959.

Ray, Edgar W. *The Grand Huckster*. Memphis, Tennessee: Memphis State University Press, 1980.

Rister, Carl. *Fort Griffin on the Texas Frontier*. Norman: University of Oklahoma Press, 1956.

Rose, Victor M. *Ross' Texas Brigade*. Kennesaw, Georgia: Continental Book Company, 1960.

Rundell, Walter Jr. *Early Texas Oil: A Photographic History, 1866–1936*. College Station: Texas A&M University Press, 1977.

———. *Oil in West Texas and New Mexico: A Pictorial History of the Permian Basin*. College Station: Texas A&M University Press, 1982.

Sann, Paul. *The Lawless Decade*. New York: Bonanza Books, 1957.

Sibley, Marilyn. *Lone Stars and State Gazettes*. College Station: Texas A&M Press, 1983.

———. *George W. Brackenridge*. Austin: University of Texas Press, 1973.

Siegel, Stanley. *Big Men Walked Here!* New York: The Pemberton Press, 1971.

Smith, Justin H. *The War With Mexico*. New York: MacMillan, 1919.

Southwick, Noah. *The Evolution of a State*. Austin: University of Texas Press, 1983.

Syers, William Edward. *Texas: The Beginning 1519–1834*. Waco: Texian Press, 1978.

Taylor, Nathaniel Alston. *Two Thousand Miles in Texas on Horseback*. Dallas: Turner Company, 1936.

Taylor, Virginia H. *The Franco-Texan Land Company*, Austin: University of Texas Press, 1969.

Thomas, Gordon & Max Morgan Witts. *Enola Gay*. New York: Stein and Day Publishers, 1977.

Tinkle, Lon. *The Alamo*. New York: McGraw-Hill, 1958.

Valenti, Jack. *A Very Human President*. New York: W. W. Norton, 1975.

Valley By-Liners. *Gift of the Rio: Story of Texas' Tropical Borderland*. Mission: Border Kingdom Press, 1975.

Vandiver, Frank E. *Their Tattered Flags*. New York: Harper's Magazine Press, 1970.

Vines, Robert A. *Trees, Shrubs and Woody Vines of the Southwest*. Austin: University of Texas Press, 1960.

Warner, C. A. *Texas Oil & Gas Since 1543*. Houston: Gulf Publishing, 1939.

Warren, Robert Penn. *Remember the Alamo!* New York: Random House, 1958.

Wauer, Ronald H. *Naturalist's Big Bend*. College Station: Texas A&M Press, 1973.

Webb, Walter Prescott (ed.). *The Handbook of Texas*, Volumes I and II. Austin: Texas State Historical Association, 1952.

———. *The Texas Rangers*. Austin: University of Texas Press, 1935.

Weems, John Edward. *Dream of Empire*. New York: Simon & Schuster, 1971.

Welch, June R. *Going Great in the Lone Star State*. Waco: Texian Press, 1976.

Whisenhunt, Donald W. *Chronology of Texas History*. Burnet: Eakin Press, 1982.

William, Amelia W. *A Critical Study of the Siege of the Alamo and the Personnel of Its Defenders*. Austin: University of Texas Ph. D. Thesis, 1931.

Willoughby, Larry. *Texas Rhythm, Texas Rhyme*. Austin: Texas Monthly Press, 1984.

Wilson, R. L. *The Colt Heritage: The Official History of Colt Firearms From 1836 to the Present*. New York: Simon & Schuster.

Wisehart, M. K. *Sam Houston, American Giant*. Washington, D.C.: Robert B. Luce, Inc., 1962.

Wittliff, William. *Vaquero: Genesis of the Texas Cowboy*. San Antonio: Institute of Texan Cultures, 1972.

Yelderman, Pauline. *The Jay Birds of Fort Bend County*. Waco: Texian Press, 1979.

Zelade, Richard. *Hill Country*. Austin: Texas Monthly Press, 1983.

A Texas Company filling station, Austin, Texas, 1916. (Texaco)

# Index